# Santal Folk Dance Songs
# Contextualizing Art & Culture

# Santal Folk Dance Songs Contextualizing Art & Culture

Dr. Rajesh Kumar

KALPAZ

First Published, 2020

*Published by*

Kalpaz Publications
C-30, Satyawati Nagar,
Delhi – 110052
Ph.: 011-47034999, 9811692060
www.kalpazpublications.com
E-mail: kalpaz@hotmail.com

*Printed at:* G. Print Process, Delhi

**Cataloging in Publication Data—DK**

Courtesy: D.K. Agencies (P) Ltd. <docinfo@dkagencies.com>

**Kumar, Rajesh,** *Colonel*, **author.**

Santal folk dance songs : contextualizing art & culture / Dr. Rajesh kumar.

pages cm

Includes bibliographical references.

ISBN 9789353240899 (HB)

1. Folk songs, Santali—India—Jharkhand. 2. Folk dancing—India—Jharkhand. 3. Santal (South Asian people)—India—Jharkhand—Folklore. I. Title.

LCC DS432.S2K86 2019 | DDC 793.31954127 23

# Contents

# Acknowledgements

I take this opportunity to express my thanks and gratitude to all those who have directly or indirectly helped me in the completion of this research project. First and foremost I acknowledge the financial support which I received as Research Awardee from the University Grants Commission during the course of my research work for the two academic years 2016-18. Secondly, I would like to express my gratitude and thanks to the Principal, Motilal Nehru College (Evening) for having provided me all sorts of help needed during the course of my research work, the college being the research center for my project work; and my thanks are also due to the non-teaching staff members: Sh. Rajesh Handoo, Administrative officer(Admn), Mr Shailendra, Sr. P.A. to the Principal, Sh. Gulshan Kapoor, S.O.(Accounts), Sh. Rajeev Dutta and particularly Sh. Sharwan Kumar, Administrative Officer(Accounts) for his valuable and timely suggestions and advice he gave me whenever I approached him for the same and other members: Sh. Pramod Kumar, Sh. Daljeet Singh, Sh. Sukhram, Sh. Santnu Mohanty, C.P.Sharma, Sh M.L.Gaur, Sh. Harendra Singh, Sh.Vikas Sharma, Sh. Rajendra Meena, Sh. S.K.Yadav, Sh. Imran Khan,and Mohd. Rashid for their ever readiness to help and support me whenever asked for it. Also, I extend my thanks to library Staff: Sh R,S.Joshi( Librarian), Sh. Pan singh, Smt Sunita, Sh. Baboo Ram and Sh. Ravi Tiwari for their ever readiness to support me and for their beautiful and encouraging conversations they have with me.

I was greatly assisted in the several libraries I visited such as Nehru Memorial Museum and Library, Teen Murti House, New Delhi, Sahitya Akademi Library; Sangeet kala academy and Lalit kala academy Rabindra Bhavan, 35 Ferozeshah Road; National Archives of India, New Delhi; Central Library, North Campus, University of Delhi; Ratan Tata Library ,University of Delhi; South Campus Library, University of Delhi; Jawaharlal Nehru University Library, New Delhi; Indian Social Institute Library, 10 Institutional Area Lodi Road; National Library, Kolkata; JOHAR HRD Centre, Dumka. I thank all the staff members of the aforementioned libraries.

I could not have completed my field work without the help of the following persons who have always remained a source of immense help and support for me. First, John Soren, he is the first person I think of when I think of field work. He was the one who always stood by me throughout the field work taking me to several villages for having real feel of the Santali culture and some important persons having good knowledge for interviews on the Santali culture and the Santali Dance-songs. I recall with deep gratitude the hospitality and generous cooperation extended to me by him and also by his family members, whose house was a second home for me. During the period I lived with them I experienced their warm friendship and their readiness to help me to understand the community. Secondly, Ruby Hembrom, the Santali publisher of Aadivani, who guided me regarding who all I should meet when going to Dumka, who could assist me with solid information on the Santali culture. She was the one who gave me a lot of information about the Santali culture. Thirdly, Rev. Father David Solomon, the Director, JOHAR HRD Centre, Dumka, he allowed me to access the library books anytime I wanted, which was of immense help to me. I recall with deep gratitude the hospitality and generous cooperation he extended to me.

I would like to express my heartfelt thanks to two cultural groups (i) Badoli Santali Cultural Troupe, Dumka, Jharkhand and its members who performed several Dance-Songs on my request : John Soren-Leader; Babita Murmu-Singer; Christina Tudu-Dancer; Preety Novela Soren-Dancer; Sumitra Soren-Dancer; Teresa Soren-Dancer; Lina Sujata Murmu-Dancer; Nisha Hembrom-Dancer; Nimbulal Marandi-Drummer; Hemonto Hembrom-Drummer; Santosh Marandi-Nagara player; Earnest Baskey-Jhaal player. (ii) Bir Bajaal Sanskritik Aakhra Kukurtopa, Dumka, Jharkhand and its Manager, Manuel Soren who arranged the group on my request despite the fact that the members were too busy with their own household works.

I would also like to thank the following persons for having allowed me to interview them to acquire knowledge on different aspects of Santali culture and Santali Dance-songs: Ruby Hembrom, the Santali publisher, Smt.Babita Murmu,a Santali Singer, Fr. David Solomon, Director, (Johar, HRD Centre), Manuel Soren, and Bijay Tudu. Their interviews proved to be of immense help to me.

Some people just walk into your life and become special and even part of your life: Dr Ashwani Kumar —my friend first and colleague later— is such a person who has always been then and there whenever I needed his help, accompanying me almost every day to Nehru Memorial Museum and Library, Teen Murti House, New Delhi and even to Kolkata for field work. I thank him a lot for always being with me.

I would also like to thank, with immense regard, my Maa and Pitaji, my mother-in-law and father-in law, for their prayers, blessings and support; all my brothers: Dinesh bhaiya, Virendra bhaiya, Ravi bhaiya and Navin along with their family members for their care and support. Finally a special thanks to Nibha, my wife, who has always been helpful, encouraging and supportive, and has shown belief in me and my work. I heartily thank her for everything she does for me and for having taken care of the family whenever I have been away for my work. For their sweet love and care, I owe special thanks to my daughter, Navya and son, Renish, both of whom, I do feel, must have missed me a lot during the past two years as due to my research work I could not spend as much time for them as much they would have wanted from me. Very special thanks from the bottom of my heart goes to Renish, my son, who helped me with his technical knowledge of computer, which proved to be of immense help to me.

Last but not the least, I wish to thank Mr Amit Garg, Director of Kalpaz Publications and the hardworking staff of Production Division for their staunch support and assistance, who left no stone unturned in giving this book a reality and without whose help it would not have been possible for the book to be published in the shape it has been produced today.

# Introduction

This book entitled *Santal Folk Dance Songs: Contextualizing Art & Culture* charts a hitherto unexplored epistemological terrain to study Santali Dance-songs of Jharkhand as the primary subject matter and to contextualize how 'the Santali culture' is getting manifested in its art form which is through the 'Santali Dance-songs'. It seems to me that the Santali culture is not only about their dance-songs but it is their dance-songs which display their culture in its multidimensional hues. The reason behind selecting the Santali dance-songs is that they are the most valuable documents on and about the Santal society. In fact, the dance-songs offer a window to peep into the world of the Santals, their lives, customs, traditions religions and philosophy. It has been observed that these dance-songs have escaped the overpowering drive to 'civilize' them, be it in the pre-colonial, colonial times or thereafter and thus exist in their natural forms. This is, however, not to suggest that the Santali dance-songs have remained static in their pristine forms, it is a fact that gradual changes have crept into their forms, but not to the extent to alter their soul and spirit. All these factors make the Santali dance-songs worthy of documentation to understand the Santal cultural reality.

Along with giving you a glimpse of the cultural heritage of the Santals of Jharlhand, the project is an attempt to take you for some time to the world of Santhali dance-songs of Jharkhand and give you a panoramic view of the living traditions of the Santhali dance-forms of Jharkhand. All the dance forms will be worthy of documentation to understand the Tribal cultural reality. The life of a tribal is a musical journey. Tribal dances work as a panacea in the tribal society. In the dense forests their life is not easy and their existential hardship necessitates some cultural medium to find solace in creative activity. These folk dances do not exist just for enjoyment; instead they mitigate the adversities of life experienced by the Tribal. The tribal have a variety of folk songs, sung on almost all occasions in their social life. These dances paint the most vivid picture of the tribal society. While performing, a problem is not only posed but it is also negotiated and a conclusion is usually drawn. Their performance is 'beautiful' in its discursivity because it is aesthetically rich in every sense. The binary of nature and culture seems to blur in the tribal society and it is clearly manifested in their folk dances. The performance space (dense jungles), the body decoration (with the objects acquired from trees, animals and birds), and themes (discourses and dialogues ranging from love to spirituality) of these dances represent their culture as another manifestation of nature itself. It is impossible to imagine either tribal or their folk dances in opposition to nature.

Among the arts, dance is at once the most primitive and the most sophisticated. Dance has so much common with poetry that Plutarch called it 'silent poetry'. Bergson, the philosopher interpreted it in terms of 'grace and rhythm' and held it to be 'a symbol of spiritual life'. Nietzsche saw it 'an image of wisdom'. Dancing helps the tribal forget their poverty and anxiety for the time being. It gives them at the same time a sense of discipline and organization and a feeling for group or community. Scores of philosophers, social thinkers and intellectuals have conceptualized and contemplated music. Jean-Jacques Rousseau, for example, wrote in "A Discourse on the Origin of Inequality": "Whether we inquire into the origin of the arts or observe the first criers, we find that everything in its principle is related to the means of subsistence." For Karl Marks music is "the mirror of reality"; for Friedrich Nietzche, the "expression of truth", a "Dionysian mirror of the world." For Sigmund Freud, it is a "text to be deciphered." And according to Pierre Schaeffer, music speaks from person to person in a language of matter. It can be argued that music explores the whole range of possibilities in a given code, faster than material reality can. It conveys through sound that only later comes to be visible, to be imposed, to dominate. It is not only the echo of an era's aesthetic, but something beyond the everyday which heralds the future.

There is hardly a civilization or culture wherein the awareness of human movement as a vehicle of expression of joy and of sorrow is not evident. Perhaps before man began to speak and to paint, he began to dance. It has been rightly said: "The Tribe that dances never dies" and apparently it goes without saying that the Tribal of India feel much deep within their innermost selves, with the blessings of their holy spirits, that dancing is an art that counteracts all the evil forces of death, keeping them out of reach. Tribal music and dance are an integral part of collective life and reflects their mundane and sacred worlds. Far from the maddening civilized crowds, deep down in the woods and valleys, loud beating of the drums, the melodious sounds of the wind instruments, the monotonous singing, the tinkling sound of the bells, from long distance at dead of the night breaks the silence of the forest, to proclaim joyous and happy moods of the tribals.

These sweet melodies remind the urban societies of the strong solidarity, peace and simplicity that exist among the tribal folk. The Tribal don't dance to entertain an audience but to celebrate life and these celebrative dances are now known as folk dances. If life is a boundless river, every dancer is a wave in it. The wave in its graceful rise and fall does celebrate the flow, but it requires a multitude of waves to celebrate the river. Therefore perhaps the folk dances are mostly performed by a group rather than a solo dancer. While dancing in unison with several other dancers each experiences that he or she has had have been multiplied and the Individual has become Universal.

The Tribal of India have, as per the growth of the civilization, developed various dimensions of socio-cultural life namely, Music, dance, folklore and songs, which have become an integral part of their culture; and each Tribe has maintained its own uniqueness about these aesthetic aspects of life. However, the growth of civilization- in the form of modernization and urbanization- has corrupted the happiness of the tribal by adversely affecting their nature-bonded life; and it is, indeed, very disheartening to note that these Tribal music, folk dances , folklores, etc., are gradually vanishing in front of our post-modernist spectacled eyes and still we are left helpless.

Therefore,this project is aimed at:

Exploring and strengthening the unexplored epistemological terrains of Santali dance-songs of Jharkhand.

Situating the different forms of Santali dances: both existing and those becoming extinct

Discussing newly emerging systems and frameworks of thoughts & ideas bringing changes in these Dance Forms

Formulations of new structures of discourse, systems of multidisciplinary approaches, conceptual mechanisms and strategies to promote and preserve the cultures and traditions of Santali dance-songs of Jharkhand.

## The Santal domain of Discourse

The Santals, mostly to be found in Jharkhand and West Bengal, the largest homogeneous tribe in India, are also found in large numbers in the Indian states of Assam, Meghalaya, Chhatisgarh, Bihar and Odisha. When it comes to studying the literature of the Santal world of existence, P.O.Bodding is certainly a name to conjure with. He was a missionary with a difference. It was he who rescued from oblivion the hidden treasure buried among the Santals in Bengal and Bihar(earlier it was Bihar, it has now been bifurcated into two states of Jharkhand and Bihar) over long centuries. The Dictionary of the Santal language that he compiled is a monument of dedication, scholarship and dogged perseverance. Coming from far off Norway, he lived and mixed with the Santal folk of our country as no foreigner had ever done before him. What is most surprising is that he became an authority on santal language and society and even Santal medicine. Between 1925 and 1940 the fruits of his studies in Santal Medicine and Folklore were published by the Asiatic Society in three instalments that soon went out of print (Bodding, Studies in Santal Medicine and Connected Folklore: Part I, II and III, 2001(Second Reprint)).

Although a great deal of information about the Santal world of meaning is scattered in various books, journals, office reports, and missionary accounts, it seems to me, however, that there are two important books which form the most important source books today for the study of Santal universe of discourse. They are: Firstly, *The Traditions and Institutions of the Santhals, Horkoren Mare Hapramko reak Katha*, originally published from the Santali text by L.O.Skrefsrud in 1887—after the translator's death it was edited by Sten Konow ; later translated with notes and additions and published by P.O.Bodding in 1942— as a guide for the Santals, especially in the customary matters dealt with in the book, and also on account of its ethnological value(Bodding, Traditions and Institutions of the Santals(Horkoren Mare Hapramko Reak Katha), 1942).According to P.O.Bodding(Bodding, Traditions and Institutions of the Santals, 1994(First Indian Reprint)) 'the original work was taken down by Skrefsrud from the mouth of an old guru, named Kolean and according to a statement towards the end of the book the dictation was finished on the 15th of February, 1871'.In the words of P.O.Bodding, "Skrefsrud once told me, that he had hunted everywhere among the Santals to find a man who knew his people and their traditions and customs, and that Kolean without comparison was the best authority he had been able to find. Skrefsrud further told me, that the book contains absolutely nothing of his own, the whole being a faithful record of Kolean's words and language"(Bodding, Traditions and Institutions of the Santals, 1942(First Indian Reprint1994))

The second book which deserves to be mentioned here is *Studies in Santal Medicine and Connected Folklore*, written by P.O.Bodding, a Sacandinavian missionary, and published in three parts by the Asiatic Society of Bengal, forms the most important source book today. P.O.Bodding of the Scandinavian Mission in the Santal Parganas and well known for his works on the life and customs of the Santals, proposed in 1922 to publish a series of monographs entitled *Studies in Santal Medicine and connected*

*Folklore* in the Memoirs of the Royal Asiatic Society of Bengal. This was accepted by the Council and Volume X of the Memoirs was assigned to the Series. Part I of the Series under the title of 'the Santals and Disease' and Part II on 'the Santal Medicine' appeared in 1925 and 1927 respectively. Part III entitled 'the Santals and how they live', however, though the manuscript was received as early as March 1938 but delayed due to the revision of the language of the author(whose mother tongue was not English), could not be published then and was published in 1986.

The research scholars suggest the European missionaries were the first to take active interest in the Santals and to study their language and culture. J.Troisie (Troisi J. , 1976, p. 3) narrates that on September 26, 1867, a man who was to do so much to promote Santali language and culture, namely Lars Olsen Skresrud, a Norwegian missionary belonging to the Lutheran Church, took up residence at Benagaria (which I visited as part of my field work in May 2017) in the district of Santal Parganas where he died and was buried forty years later (I had a chance visit his tomb as well). He immediately took up the study of Santal language and customs, being thoroughly convinced of the need for knowledge of the culture and institutions of the people. In 1873, Skrefsrud published *A Grammar of the Santhal Language*, a work that has had an important influence on all later treaties on the Santal language. He was an excellent linguist and a practical phonetician. In the beginning he used Bengal characters for Santali but later gave them up for the system which he himself introduced and which, with minor modifications, is still being used nowadays. In 1879, he started a Santali Printing Press at Benagaria which has been most influential in lifting the Santali language out of obscurity.

Working on Santali myths and legends, Skrefsrud published *Horkoren Mare Hapramko reak Katha* (The book of ancestors) in Santali in 1887, which is a very good collection of Santal myths and legends. It is important to note here that this book formed the beginning of the corpus of Santali literature. As mentioned in the beginning of this chapter that it was taken from the mouth of Kolean, an old Santal guru, whose narrative was based on oral traditions, handed down verbatism by teacher to disciple, from generation to generation. Moreover, this book has been regarded as authoritative on many of the customs of the Santals. In fact, it is frequently referred to in Indian law courts whenever Santal customs are in dispute. It is of priceless value to the ethnologist and the linguist and it is indispensable to all who seek to know the Santals.

Skrefsrud had a mission in his mind right from the beginning to collect Santal words with the object of ultimately publishing a dictionary of the

Santli language. He could never, however, spare enough time to complete his work. In 1890 he bequeathed his work, which contained a little more than 13,000 words, to a junior colleague who was an outstanding scholar, Rev. Paul Olaf Bodding, also a Norwegian missionary. In the course of more than thirty years which he passed at Mohulpahari (which I had a chance to visit as part of field work) in the Santal Parganas, P.O.Bodding published more than twenty-five works on the Santals, including books, monographs, articles, two grammars and a Dictionary, covering every aspect of Santal life. There is no denying the fact that his greatest work is without doubt the *Santal Dictionary*, published in five volumes over 1932-36, which is a comprehensive encyclopaedia of everything that concerns the Santals. In fact, the author's intention in bringing out this work was, as he himself remarked, to show the Santal—how he thinks, speaks and understands life. Bodding's last literary work, which he completed before he died in 1938, was the translation into English of Skrefsrud's book *Horkoren Mare Hapramko reak Katha*. He also wrote *Materials for a Santali Grammar* in two parts, published over 1923-29, which is still considered to be the best source for an advanced study of the Santali language. For the use of beginners he published *A Santali Grammar for Beginners* in 1929. In Santal Folktales published in Oslo in three volumes, he made available a rich treasure of genuine Santal folktales. He also furnished the Ethnographical Museum at Oslo with probably the richest collection of Santal implements that can be found anywhere. The Asiatic Society of Bengal published a number of his articles and also a series of two monographs on *Studies in Santal Medicine and Connected Folklore* and a monograph entitled *How the Santals live* which has been included as partIII of *Studies in Santal Medicine and Connected Folklore*. These are, undoubtedly, invaluable contributions to the scientific study of the literature of the Santals.

There is no denying the fact that the contributions of these two missionaries to the knowledge of Santal language, literature and culture are monumental. It is, however, not possible to mention the names of all the missionaries of various nationalities who were also engaged in the cultural upliftment of the Santals. Mention, however, must be made of C.H.Bompas whose book, *Folklore of the Santal Parganas* is a model of folklore research. Mr Andrew Campbell, a Scottish missionary who for the greater part of his life was stationed at Pokhuria in the Manbhum district, edited his *Santali-English Dictionary* in 1899 which was later supplemented by an *English-Santali Dictionary*. This was the second dictionary after Rev. E.L.Puxley's, published in1868. Campbell also wrote quite a number of articles mostly on Santal folklore. The Rev. W.J.Culshaw's book *Tribal*

*Heritage*, and his articles have greatly helped in promoting a better understanding of Santal religious beliefs and practices. Rev. Johannes Gausdal's book, *The Santal Khuts*, is an ethnographical masterpiece on Santal sub-septs. He also published a number of articles on the same subject.

The fact that besides the Christian missionaries there have been quite a number of colonial officers who contributed invaluable material on the Santals cannot be denied. Sir John Shore's article "On some Extraordinary Facts, Customs and Practices of the Hindus," published in *Asiatic Researches*, 1795, contains the earliest mention of the Santals where they are designated as 'Soontars'. Scholars are of the view that the first account of the Santals of the Rajmahal Hills occurs in Montgomery Martin's book *Eastern India* compiled fromFrancis Buchanan's Journal kept during the survey of the district of Bhagalpur, 1810-11. H.C.Sutherland obtained information about the early history of the Santals through investigations into the land tenures of the Paharias of the Rajmahal Hills and from Captain Walter S.Sherwill's notes taken during his tour of the Rajmahal Hills and published by the Asiatic Society of Bengal. E.G.Man, Assistant Commissioner of the Santal Pargans came with another early account of the Santals through his book *Sonthalia and the Sonthals.The Little World of an Indian Officer,* the autobiography of R. Carstairs, who served as Deputy Commissioner and as Settlement Officer, contains a very good description of the land and its people, the formation of the new district, the Census of 1881 and the government of the district. It is on the basis of the nuber of years he served as Deputy Commissioner of the Santal Parganas and later as the person entrusted with the codification of Santal law, that W.G.Archer wrote not less than eighteen articles and four books on the Santals.

With regard to the Santals' early life, there are other sources of knowledge which include the various government district gazetteers, Census reports and handbooks and the three settlement reports H.L.L.Allanson, J.A.Craven, J.F.Gantzer, and H. McPherson. L.S.S. O'Malley, H.H.Risley, J.H.Hutton, W. Hunter and Col. Dalton have left us very good accounts of the Santals, their land, customs and habits. R.C.Dutt in 1882 through his article "Aboriginal Elements in the Population of Bengal" gave a very fascinating account of the Santals but it was really with the work of Sarat Chandra Roy that the Indian anthropologists started taking interest in the tribes of the Chotanagpur plateau-the districts of Ranchi, Hazaribagh, Dhanbad, Singhbhum, Palamu and those of the Santal Parganas. With Sarat Chandra Roy, anthropological researches in this area witnessed the beginning of a golden and constructive period. Indian anthropologists, sociologists and ethnologists have by now published quite a number of studies on the Santals.

## I

It is pertinent to mention here that dancing and singing hold a very important role in almost all the festive occasions for the Santals and it would not be wrong to assert that a social feature of Santal dancing and singing is their social character. From the time a girl can toddle, she joins the line of dancers, while little boys ape the antics of the drummers (Troisi, 1978, p. 124). The Santals have a large number of different dances according to the special seasons and festivals. According to Mukherjea, 'These dances…are a part and parcel of the tribal religious life' (Mukherjea, 1962, p. 365) Bodding (Bodding, 1993(First published in India)) mentions thirty-one types of dances, most of which are performed by men and women together though some are reserved for either of the sexes. For example, 'the *lagre* is the most common of the Santal dances and may be danced at any time, though preferably during moonlight. *Don* is usually danced during marriage festivals. *Jatur* is performed during the *Sohrae* and the *Baha* festivals. *Danta* is also danced during the *Sohrae*. Women generally do not join in this dance. On the other hand, only women dance the *Baha* dance which, as the name implies, is performed during the *Baha* festival. During the *Karam* festival, the Annual Hunt and *Bitlaha*, the menfolk perform special dances' (Troisi, 1978, p. 124).

J.Troisi comments that drumming plays a very important part during dancing since the rhythm and style of the latter depends much on the way in which the drums are played. The Santals essentially use two types of drums during their dancing—the tamak or kettle drum which is made of iron and is shaped like a big bowl nd covered with buffalo or bullock hide, and the tumdak or dancing drum made of burnt clay and conical in shape, the narrow end being covered with goat's skin and the broad end with bullock, buffalo or goat's hide. The tumdak which is played with the hands sets the rhythm while the tamak, played with small sticks, echoes and adds to the rhythm (Troisi, 1978, p. 124) Dancing is often connected with singing. Raha (Raha, 1967) rightly observes, 'when any new event is marked by the Santals they at once give it a poetic expression and sing spontaneously on their way to or during any festival'. As the Santals have different dances for different festive occasions, so also they have elaborate song cycles for various festivals. According to Bhattacharya (Bhattacharya, 1962) the Santals have more than twenty different tunes though most of the songs are ancestral. It is also part of the vitality of

Santals to compose songs on the spur of the moment and undoubtedly these songs reflect certain feelings, emotions and sentiments of the Santals (Troisi, 1978, p. 125).

What we infer from the discussion of Santali dance-songs is an absolute blurring of the nature/culture dichotomy. It does not mean that binaries don't exist in Santali society but as far as our current debate is concerned, the nature/culture binary seems irrelevant. Instead of a binary what is apparent in Santali dance-songs is a harmonious confluence of nature and culture. Dance-songs of Santals must be viewed as an extension of nature itself because Santal culture constitutes a celebration of nature. Their dance-songs are basically narratives of their daily lives and their communion with nature. They work to inculcate immense respect and love for nature in the future generations. The dance-songs are a means of socialization, used to spread material and spiritual values in the tribal society. Thus, the nature/culture binary also emerges as metanarrative which excludes such societies from its discourse.

The primary subject matter of the Santali dance-songs can also be problematized from an aesthetic point of view and it is found that the debate of art for art's sake and art for society' sake is non-existent. The santals, their appearance, decoration and properties used in the dance-songs depict them as enchanted with the idea of beauty but a separation of their notion of beauty from its social utility is unimaginable. In fact, they epitomize the ancient Indian concept of aucitya(utility) as the defining characteristic of their idea of beauty. Their social occasions, festivals and lyrics are profound with indications that beauty is functional in its essence. Their dance-songs are an important medium of socialization but at the same time it is impregnate with emotions. They beautify themselves for a purpose and their art forms whether performed for others/self-have utility of expressing their emotions or of socializing and binding the society together. It is difficult to discern whether the Santali dance-songs are art forms for their own sake (as their performance is not guided by any external forces say for example, the market , it is performed naturally by them and for themselves) or for the society (as their performances have social function and significance).

The adverse impacts of rural/urban or folk/classical binaries are visible in a negligence of 'folk' culture in India. There is a tendency to conceptualize folk as a matter of antiquity by the people engaged in humanities. There is no denying the fact that the santals and their culture are now exposed to the forces of modernism, urbanization, development like never before. Recent compilations of the Santali dance-songs used for this study also show that the Santals have embraced urban culture to some extent. New themes and issues are being incorporated in their performing arts because of the ever-evolving nature of their culture

## II

The Santali dance-songs are enumerable in number but lack adequate documentation. W.G.Archer has published printed collections of Santal songs in the Bibliography of his book *The Hill of Flutes* (Archer, 1974). The chief collection of Santal songs is *Hor Seren* and *Don Seren*, which was published jointly by Gopal Gamaliel Soren and W.G.Archer in 1943. Hor Seren comprises 1676 songs which are sung at festivals or dances, Don Seren 1824 which are sung at weddings. A further 129 cultivation songs are included in the second volume. The majority of these songs are ancestral but it is part of the vitality of Santal poetry that new songs are sometimes made up on the spur of of the moment. There is no special class of poet, singer or bard, and the songs are accordingly communal in origin and inspiration. Songs connected with the induction ceremony of Caco Chatiar and with the ritual of Karam are given in Stephen H.Murmu's *Karam ar Caco Chatiar* (published 1945). Local person Nanak Soren has published a good collection of songs on several festivals: (Soren N., Jawae Dhuti Seren) (Soren N., Maran Din Seren) (Soren N. , Sohrae Porob ar Sohrae Seren) (Soren N., Jeevet Karam Seren, 1999) (Soren N. , Sohrai Seren, 1999) Narayan Soren has also published a song book (Soren N. ) A complete list of works and publications relating to the Santali dance-songs is available in Chapter two. My present research work will be very helpful for documentation and it will remain a unique research work in the sense that it is for the first time we will be having a work dealing with dance-songs of almost nine important festivals namely (i) LAGRE SEREN, (ii) PATA SEREN, (iii) DONG SEREN, (iv) SOHRAE SEREN, (v) DAHAR SEREN, (vi) BAHA SEREN, (vii) KARAM SEREN, (viii) DASAE SEREN, and (ix) BIR SEREN. I have done some field work collecting and capturing some video recordings of few Santali dance-songs and a pen drive containing these videos is appended to this project work for documentation and research purpose.

The chapterization of this research work is presented as follows:

Chapter One: "A Discourse on the notion of Performing Art and Culture"

Chapter Two: "A Worldview of the Santal Traditions and Folk Dances"

Chapter Three: "Social Dancing I: Considering Contextualization"

Chapter Four: "Social Dancing II: Considering Contextualization"

Chapter Five: "Modern/Postmodern Impact on Santali dance-songs"

Having gone through the reading sources, theoretical reading texts in particular, of my research, my first chapter is essentially a theoretical Chapter entitled "A Discourse on the notion of Performing Art and Culture" which was required also by virtue of the fact that my Project title proposed to deal with contextualizing art and culture. On the basis of theoretical engagement with Santali dance-songs, it is proposed that there emerges a dialectics between theory and culture. Culture works as a thesis for which theory proves to be antithesis and as the result of the negotiation between the two emerges synthesis of a particular cultural reality which is time and space specific, but it turns into a thesis once again. What makes this dialectics peculiar is the role played by agency in it. In other dialectic frameworks derived from Hegel's model, agency is the key in creating an antithesis which is true for theory as 'a set of ideas or tools to explain something'. But this is partially true for 'culture as a process' because its dynamism lies in its relative independence from agency. The subject or agency is crucial in generation, alteration and maintenance of culture but it is relatively independent as well.

The second chapter entitled "A Worldview of the Santal Traditions and Folk Dances" essentially gives us a glimpse of cultural heritage and living traditions of folk dances of the Santals, offering a window to peep into the world of the Santal people, their lives, customs, traditions, philosophy, the growth of the Santali the language, literature and culture and the a list of books published in respect of Santali culture and Santali dance-songs

In Chapter Three entitled "Social Dancing I: Considering Contextualization", a cursory examination and an outline of the Santali dance-songs has been done so as to apprise the readers of the various types of Santali dance-songs as mapped and depicted through the writings of various research scholars. This chapter includes a compilation of four kinds of Santali dance-songs: (i) LAGRE SEREN, (ii) PATA SEREN, (iii) DONG SEREN, (iv) SOHRAE SEREN, and (v) DAHAR SEREN giving us detailed characteristics and contextualization of the songs.

The major concern of Chapter four entitled "Social Dancing II: Considering Contextualization" is to essentially deal with other five varieties of the Santali dance-songs: (vi) BAHA SEREN, (vii) KARAM SEREN,

(viii) DASAE SEREN, and (ix) BIR SEREN. Essential characteristics, definitions and occasions of these dance-songs have been explained along with their social contextualization.

Chapter Five: "Modern/Postmodern Impact on Santali dance-songs" attempts to reveal the adverse impact of modernism/post-modernism in the form of changes taking place in Santali dance-songs. Given the transition taking place in the Santal community, it has been argued that the Santal community is caught up between two worlds of existence: the world of supernatural and the world of the matter-of-fact rational, that is to say, on the one hand they have their mythological past of glorious traditions and on the other hand they have the present modern/postmodern world dominant with cybernetic and hypertextual world of entities. Technology has played its role in encouraging the process of obsoleting of these dance-songs. Stereos, CDs, mobile phones have brought in new waves of music from the outer world to the Santals which are easily available, thereby reducing the aura and charm of the Santali dance-songs. However, it is not that the Santals have stopped performing or loving their music and dance but the decreasing interest of the youth in the traditional forms of music and dance is something to be worried about.

**Conclusion** essentially includes the findings based on the research, which helps us to understand how, in the era of globalization, the organizing processes of cultural practices, cultural resistance, and thereby cultural changes are taking place in the Santal community as seen through the lens of Culture-centered approach by looking at various Santali Dance-songs as they challenge the master narratives of development articulated in the modernist framework. This project engages with possibilities for dialoguing with alternative narratives resulting from the contextualization of numerous Santali dance-songs in the form of Santali subaltern narratives with respect to cultural practices and development that challenge meta-narratives produced by powerful hegemonic discourses.

# Chapter one

# A Discourse on the notion of Performing Art and Culture

The notion that Art transcends the social, the political and the everyday functional dimensionalities has been under attack in a concerted development of work across a number of disciplines. These disciplines include the relatively new areas of cultural studies, film studies, feminist studies, the sociology of arts, the social history of art, and minority voices within multiplicity of literatures. And in all the interdisciplinary activity around these developments, the domain of music has interestingly been strangely absent. It is as though music claims a particular exemption from the sociological critique of culture, retaining its special quality as transcendent and autonomous (Leppert, Richard and McClary Susan, 1987). These changes, especially evident in studies of literature, film, and visual art, in turn have led to a systematic investigation of the implicit assumptions underlying critical methods including prominently the assumption that art constitutes an autonomous sphere, separate and insulated from the outside social world.

'Art' is a historically specific fact, produced in particular and contingent circumstances. The division between 'high art' and both 'popular art' and the so called 'lesser arts' (decorative arts and crafts) is based on social, rather than aesthetic, distinctions. 'Culture', however, is a social product, and the study of culture and the arts must accordingly be sociologically informed. Here it is possible to indicate some of the social processes which have been involved in the production of art. The social and economic factors relevant to the understanding of art include: contemporary forms of patronage; dominant institutions of cultural production and distribution (workshops, academies, art schools, publishers, broadcasting companies, and so on- each of which has its own social history and specific social relations); the relationship of the state to cultural production (censorship, control of certain institutions, funding); the sociology of cultural producers(background, class, gender); and the nature and constitution of consumers(literacy rates, availability of cheap materials as a result of improvements in printing, reproduction and other technological developments, social divisions among audiences/viewers/readers) (Leppert, Richard and McClary Susan, 1987).The history of any art is a history of the interplay of these many factors.

The term 'performance' encompasses a wide range of cultural events, such as various theatrical performances and performing arts, the performance of oral texts, various kinds of political, religious and social rituals, and, eventually, any speech event. The inclusion of so many different events under a single concept of 'performance' is the result of a changing methodological approach in the social sciences (Bruckner, Heidrun.et al., 2007). The 'performance approach' has been developed by various social scientists further since Milton Singer (Singer, 1972) made a statement about religious and cultural performance as 'the elementary constituents of the culture and the ultimate units of observations'. On the one hand some performance theorists such as Victor Turner (Turner, 1982) and Richard Schechner (Schechner, 1985) take theatrical performances on stage and the theatrical potential of social life as their starting point, others, such as Bauman and Briggs (Bauman, Richard and Charles L. Briggs, 1990), on the other hand, apply the term performance in a linguistic sense to any speech event whether artful and elaborated or just everyday verbal interaction. Both the theatrical and the linguistic approaches opened up new perspectives for the interpretation of culture. Not only Cultural performances, such as rituals, ceremonies, carnivals and dramas, but also performances in the linguistic sense, so-called speech events, can be seen as interpretations of social life by actors themselves and are then exhibited to the participants as well as to outsiders. However, it is not as easy for the outsider to read a public performance just like a text as, for instance, Geertz (Geertz, 1972) suggested.

Bauman and Briggs argue that the most crucial aspect in the performance approach, the shift from the study of texts 'to the analysis of the emergence of texts in contexts, leads to another problem (Bauman, Richard and Charles L. Briggs, 1990, p. 66). There are a lot of questions arising out of this situation such as: who is going to define 'context', what should be included, what should be excluded? It is true that an objective description of context is not possible. Moreover, contexts cannot be defined by observing and describing the natural environment of a performance. They rather 'emerge in negotiations between participants in social interactions'. They further argue that this insight results in different perspectives which have to be taken into account by the observer rather than defining an 'objective' context. Bauman and Briggs demand that to avoid reifying 'context' by describing everything that surrounds a set of utterances, which seem adequate for selection by the analyst, language or rather speech should not only be seen in its referential or indexical function, but any use of language should be interpreted as 'social action' in which 'things are done with words' (Austin, 1962).

Talking about how experience and meaning and performance are three important pillars in music performance , Martin Clayton, Byron Duec, and Laura Leante argue that firstly, *Performance* characterizes music as the moment of production—of sound, meaning or consequential action—rather than as model, idea or product. It directs our attention to people producing, experiencing and making meaning from organized sound: people with bodies as well as minds, with a concrete existence in time and space, whose musical behavior is shaped by innate tendencies(such as that towards rhythmic coordination, or entrainment) , as well as by individual, environmental and social factors. (Martin Clayton, Byron Dueck, and Laura Leante, 2013, p. 1); secondly, *Experience* takes our attention away from the ideal and towards the phenomenal: what people actually do, and what they feel, while engaging in music, and thirdly, *Meaning* could be understood in a larger perspective in terms of concepts whose meanings are tied to physical experiences of musical performance, exploring how discourse shapes musical experiences, what performers try to invest in performances and what they think others ought to get out of them.

They further argue that Performance refers first and foremost to the collective acts central to: public concerts, ritual observances, musical collaborations and so on. In focusing on performance, we privilege actual instances of music making, sometimes in ways that highlight distances between the ideal and what in fact happens. 'Performance' can also be understood in terms of what is sometimes called performativity (Martin Clayton, Byron Dueck, and Laura Leante, 2013)

A focus on two phenomenal aspects of musical performance i.e., 'gesture' and 'entrainment' imparts coherence and resonance to the study of performance studies. Though embodiment and entrainment are clearly not the only lenses through which to view experience and meaning, but they do seem to be particularly useful at this juncture. One of the reasons for this is pragmatic: a combination of the interdisciplinary exchange of ideas and the rapid development of digital technologies make it far easier both to conceive and implement new research methods in these areas.

It seems to me that the power of art, music and dance to inspire, touch, influence, uplift, heal and transform has long been a source of wonder for human beings. It is needless to say that the close connection of art and music with the supernatural and the magical has for thousands of years invoked associations of power. Ethnomusicologists have, of course, long recognized and documented such power, and even sought to explain it. The emergence of Poststructuralism in the 1960s, followed by Cultural Studies, Critical Theory and Postcolonial Studies in the 1970s and 80s, were immensely important in bringing issues of power to the fore of academic discourse; yet, while writers such as Jacques Derrida, Roland Barthes, Antonio Gramsci, Michael Foucault, Edward Said, and Jean Baudrillard were reshaping the scholarly landscape of the humanities and social sciences., only a handful of ethnomusicologists—most notably those working on Latin America and the Caribbean—were attending to the profound inscribing of power in every aspect of music production, dissemination, representation and reception (Nooshin, 2009).

Commenting on the theories of power Nooshin (Nooshin, 2009) posits that seeking to understand the nature of power has exercised the minds of philosophers and others for millennia. As early as 1515, in his novel *Utopia*(1515), for instance, English statesman and lawyer Thomas More grappled with questions of power within his vision of the ideal state, a vision heavily influenced by the writings of Plato. Later in the nineteenth century, historians, political economists, philosophers and sociologists such as Karl Marx, Friedrich Nietzsche and Max Weber concerned themselves centrally with questions of power, and power has continued to provide a focus of interest for writers from a wide range of disciplinary backgrounds through to the present day. She further maintains that one of the central problematics in discussing power is the term itself, ostensibly singular and monolithic but which belies a plural, fluid and multi-faceted phenomenon. She is wondering:Is power a 'thing'? a force? an idea? a quality? And what are the relationships between different kinds of power, whether political, ideological, social, economic, semiotic, psychological and so on? Political scientists often distinguish five forms of power: 'force, persuasion, authority, coercion and manipulation' (Allison, 1996, p. 398).

The concept of ideology has always been at the center of any discussion of power the reason being that not only does the exercise of power almost invariably include an ideological dimension, but ideology in turn serves to 'legitimate a system of authority' (Ricoeur, 1986, p. 17), and from a Marxist perspective to mask the real state of power relations. In his *Lectures on Ideology and Utopia*, Paul Ricoeur traces the changing discourses around the concept of ideology, from 'ideology as distortion' (Marx) to 'ideology as legitimation' (Weber) and finally to 'ideology as integration' (Geertz) (Ricoeur, 1986, p. 254). In contrast to somewhat pejorative Marxian connotations of ideology, both Weber and later, the anthropologist Clifford Geertz have argued that ideology is not inexorably determined by economic and material factors, nor should it be viewed solely as a distortion of reality, but as an integral, indeed necessary, aspect of the social fabric through which human beings attach meanings to practice in order 'to render otherwise incomprehensible social situations meaningful' (Geertz, 'Ideology as a Cultural System', 1973b, p. 220). Ricoeur also revisits the relationship between ideology and utopia first expounded upon by sociologist Karl Mannheim in his influential text *Ideology and Utopia* (1936), and discusses the implications for our understanding of power: 'the turning point of both is in fact at the same place, that is to say, in the problem of authority. If every ideology tends finally to legitimate a system of authority, does not every utopia, the moment of the other, attempt to come to grips with the problem of power itself?' (Ricoeur, 1986, p. 17). Attempts to theorize ideology have inevitably had to grapple with the philosophical conundrum identified by Mannheim—and dubbed 'Mannheim's Paradox' by Geertz (Geertz, 'Ideology as a Cultural System', 1973b, p. 194)—that there is no ideologically- neutral space within which such theorizing might take place (Ricoeur, 1986, pp. 159-60).

Nooshin (Nooshin, 2009) further suggests that such dimensions of the power 'complex' have much more relevance to music. And the considerations of power and music extend far beyond to encompass the subtle and often less visible working of power as played out in the musical domain, a domain which clearly transcends 'music as sound' to encompass the many non-sounded dimensions of music. These include the physical and gestural, both within music and dance performance, as well as the way in which music is conceptualized and imagined, the discursive formations within which music is embedded and which saturate the spaces around it, tying it to the social fabric; and of course the social fabric itself- the specified social, political, economic and institutional structures through which music is shaped. Bohlman (Bohlman, 2007) asserts, 'Music is always far more than sound, for it ceaselessly strives to be more than itself. It is because music pushes beyond the bounds of the sonic that the aesthetic and the political accrue to it, affording it the multiple conditions of power. The intersection of the aesthetic with the ideological, political and social seems to be the central problematic dimension at the heart of the discussion between music and power. The aesthetic dimension is particularly tricky, since any discussion of music and power has to take account of the fact that experiencing music is above all a pleasurable experience, which can in itself serve a naturalizing agenda by which the aesthetic camouflages the ideological or political by deflecting attention from intended meanings. And yet, even where such meanings are hidden, music's very presence can be a sign of agency. If music's presence is an indicator of agency, then its absence is often taken to represent the opposite. But such absences are rarely absolute and one needs to be attuned to what James C. Scott (Scott, 1990) terms the 'hidden transcripts' which are often absent from the public domain.

## Michel Foucault

Now, let us turn to Michel Foucault whose work has contributed significantly to our understanding of the nature of power and who has influenced the twentieth century ideas on culture like no other scholar of his generation. He owes a place in the history of cultural studies for his approach to the role of the manifest cultural forms, notions and belief systems in the power structure. Of course his historical studies on the process of knowledge formation and its relation to the exercise of power have had an indelible impact on subsequent cultural studies. At the centre of Foucauldian theoretical paradigms has been the quest to grasp the intricacies involved in understanding the subject and subjectivity in contemporary times. His various standpoints on 'subject', 'subjectivity', 'subjectivisation', through 'governmentality', 'corporeality' and 'technologies of the 'self' make his knowledge of ideas obligatory for anybody who is interested in comprehending culture. Foucault's ideas are useful in a number of ways, most obviously his insistence on the all-permeating nature of power. Foucault claims:

> Power relations permeate all levels of social existence and are therefore to be found operating at every site of social life—in the private spheres of the family and sexuality as much as in the public spheres of politics, the economy and the law.... (Foucault, 1977, p. 27).

Foucault's genealogical discussion of government is notably very significant as it provides the ground for an understanding of 'culture', neither as a social universal nor as a particular expression of the individual, but as the object and means of regulation. In Foucauldian framework, culture is understood as both an object and instrument of government deployed in relation to individuals and population. Foucault displayed through scores of examples how these power-relations triggered the formation of various discourses to control the subject for its own benefit. He analysed the social sphere in which cultural practices constantly shaped the understanding and knowledge of the subject. The subject is always bombarded with powerful images and ideas to comply with the normal way of life without questioning and opposing its legitimacy. It is ostensibly discernible that the subject is interpellated, institutionalized and directly or indirectly controlled-self. In other words, the subject is the self that is subjugated by relations of power. Foucault was emphatic on the generation of knowledge systems and its role in the process of subjectivisation or the making of such controlled selves. Foucault maintained that the modern state exercised power not just through coercive means but by preparing 'docile or disciplinary bodies' kept under constant surveillance.

Stuart Hall explains that Foucault shifts our attention away from the grand, overall strategies of power, towards the many, localized circuits, tactics, mechanisms and effects through which power circulates- what Foucault calls the 'meticulous rituals' or the 'microphysics' of power. These power relations 'go right down to the depth of society'. (Hall, 1997b, p. 50). Apperley Alan (Apperley, 1996, p. 187) is of the view that according to Foucault, power is not merely something that individuals, groups or classes exercise, though of course it can be this. Foucault argues that discursive formations are networks of power within which we are all enmeshed. Power is everywhere and everything can be positive as well as negative.

Thus, to infuse power in every social relationsip and every social action provides a useful framework for understanding how music is embedded in relation of power which impact directly on its social meanings. Most of the formulations will be informed by a Foucauldian perspective, central to which is a deconstruction of binary oppositions between the 'powerful' and 'powerless', between action and reaction, domination and resistance. The operations of power are much more ambiguous and slippery than this, as Averill states: 'Power is far from being the property of the powerful; it is a pervasive quality that adheres to every action and interaction. It is sought , undermined, despised, ignored, resisted, and negotiated' (Averill, 1997, p. 1). Furthermore, Foucault disengages power from concepts of directionality, suggesting instead what Stuart Hall describes as the 'circularity of power' (Hall, 'The Spectacle of the"other"', 1997a) or, in Averill's conceptua-lization, 'a spatial, radial vision of the distribution of power in society' (Averill, 1997, p. 9). There are several other aspects of Foucault's work which are of relevance to the current discussion which include the ways in which discursive formations are implicated in power relations, the interlocking of knowledge and power, and questions of power and representation.

In the context of Santali Dance Songs significant point is Foucault's focus on the body as a site of social and political control, which is especially pertinent to music in its performative dimension, particularly in relation to dance. There is no denying the fact that critiques of Foucault's—particularly sociologist Habermas who has questioned the philosophical basis of Foucault's thinking on the relationship between power and critique— have focused on his somewhat totalizing and reductionist view of power, his theories have great applicability to music and dance and the subtle, often hidden, agendas it can be used to serve. Since power has been seen to be relational and all social relations involve power, and music and dance serve as an important forum for playing out social relations, , music may be crucial in helping us to understand and interpret how power is enforced as well as how it is challenged.

## Antonio Gramsci and Louis Pierre Althusser

The scholars of popular music and culture have been influenced by the works of Antonio Gramsci and Louis P.Althusser who have made significant contribution to enhancement of knowledge in terms of the conception of 'ideology' and how power encodes culture and power is encoded within cultural meanings. These thinkers through their concepts of hegemony and interpellation have tried to articulate how popular cultural forms are means of ideological indoctrination; how current regimes of dominant relations and power structures are maintained through the articulation of cultural meaning.

Antonio Gramsci holds a significant position in questioning the role of culture in exerting power. H talked about culture studies as the discipline of the conjectural stressing the importance of historical specificity and introducing the metaphor of hegemony as a conceptual tool to unearth the subtle machinations of the dominant classes in the realm of culture. Many scholars within the framework of musicology have drawn heavily on Gramsci's work. Gramsci's focus on class relations is of limited relevance; however, other 'axes of difference' take on greater significance, although class issues are often subsumed within these. Nonetheless, concepts of cultural and ideological hegemony and consent are absolutely central to some of the discussions around post-colonial nation formation and cultural ownership. We can see that such hegemonies are persistent and become incorporated into new power structures which often endure long after the demise of the hegemonic regime. Some scholars have, however, argued that binaries of hegemony and resistance offer only a crude tool to understanding the complexities of real lives.

The Gramscian concept of hegemony is an answer to the mysterious modes of control present in any society or political system. Basically, Gramsci developed his theory to explain domination and consent. Domination can be seen as a direct intervention through coercive means to control but consent is evasive and precarious to general perception because it uses subtle mechanisms for the same purpose. Moreover, it works through popular images and cultural production to keep the subject unaware of how it generates consensus for the dominant classes. With his expositions on hegemony and the role of intellectuals in the society, Gramsci reflected on the Marxian praxis in a refreshing manner. We find in him a new working class intellectual who engaged with culture in order to subvert it for the masses to create counter hegemony, culture produced by the masses that intends to unmask the real nature of the culture produced by the capitalist forces. Gramsci was of the view that there is major discrepancy in the left wing politics with the way it thinks and acts. He, therefore desired a sychronisation between theory and practice, called praxis, i.e., an amalgamation of practice and thinking, and an attack on hitherto theoretical formulations without acting upon them. Thus, praxis is a tool for the human beings to not just analyse but to change reality.

Gramsci, with his formulation of the concept of 'hegemony', demonstrates that a class is able to maintain its position as a ruling class, insofar as it is able to form and secure alliances with other classes and class fractions in such a way which supports its rule. Thus, Gramscian hegemony is not only about the mobilization of classes and class fractions into unity; it is concerned with the mobilization of both classes and forces in a favourable manner to achieve a state of equilibrium that maintains ruling class positions/dominance. Hegemony therefore is not domination neither is it a physical or repressive force. It works through consensus, by gaining the consent of the people over which leadership is sought. And consensus is weaved through cultural machinations. In other words, Gramsci understands the politics of rule in terms of the balance of forces in society: a class can only rule by building an alliance of classes and forces and it does so by ideologically cementing the divergent classes together.

Turino (Turino, 'The Charango and the Sirena: Music, Magic, and the Power of Love', 1983) (Turino, 'The Urban-Mestizo Charango Tradition in Southern Peru: A Statement of Shifting Identity', 1984)was one of the first to introduce the concept of hegemony into ethnomusicology and to explore the relationship between the aesthetic and the political, as well as the interplay between what he terms the 'hegemonic factor' and the 'identity factor'. While discussing the impact of socio-economic-political factors on the *mestizo* tradition in southern Peru, Turino considers how shifting relationships in the hierarchy of social power between the urban-*mestizo* middle class and the ruling *criollo* elite on the one hand and the indigenous *campesino* peasants on the other, have effected changes in musical style, performance contexts, instrument structure and choice of genre. Turino holds the view that *mestizos* are caught between the 'need for a regional identity and the persistent force of dominant class values' (Turino, 'The Urban-Mestizo Charango Tradition in Southern Peru: A Statement of Shifting Identity', 1984, p. 258), and whilst they 'seek to differentiate themselves from the criollo by the ideological and symbolic identification with campesino culture(identity factor), they nevertheless remain greatly influenced by the cultural and aesthetic values of the dominant group(hegemonic factor). Each of these factors offer the potential for empowerment, whether through the use of indigenous elements as a form of identity politics or, on the other hand, by drawing on the cultural capital associated with dominant *criollo* aesthetics.

Louis Althusser is well known for his position on the question of structural relations, agency and subjectivity as a pivotal problematic in Marxist theory. He broached the idea of the subject being in tension with the relationship of structure, and gradually went on to propose the idea of relative autonomy of the superstructure. Althusser suggests that there is not simply one economic structure and the superstructure but a number of structurally interrelated structures, including the economic, the politico-legal, the scientific and the ideological. He argues that each historical mode of production or each social formation has a structure that is dominant, a structure that over-determines the social relations within that formation. In other words, in each social formation, the economic, politico-legal and ideological structures that constitute the social totality over-determines each other, but only one resides as the structure in dominance. He introduced the concept of relative autonomy by proposing that, although the economic is not always the dominant structure in any given social formation, it however, does always determine in the last instance in the sense that it determines which structure will actually dominate in any given social formation. Althusser in his essay 'Ideology and the Ideological State Apparatuses'(1971), formulates that a social formation needs to reproduce both the productive forces(i.e. technology, knowledge, labour) and the existing relations of production(I,e. the class relations between the bourgeoisie and the working class). He further argues that the state does so through the repressive and ideological state apparatuses.The ideological state apparatuses operate in the domain of culture and propogate the ideologies of the ruling class to maintain their dominance. He believes that ideology works by interpellating individuals and turning them into ideological subjects whose relation to their real conditions of existence(i.e. the relations of power that govern their existence) is imaginary. Cultural studies scholars have looked at the mechanism of 'interpellation' to explain a range of practices such as advertising, film and other media.

Waterman's (Waterman, 1990) text on identity and power in Nigerian *juju* music was the first extended ethnographic study to examine questions of power in musical performance. Set against the backdrop of complex class and colonial relationships in Nigeria, Waterman explores the relationship between music and social order in Nigeria and the ways in which popular music, specifically *juju*, mediates these relationships. Waterman is particularly interested in how *juju* presents an image of a cohesive social order in the context of apparent opportunities for all, but at the same time subtly perpetuates traditional social divisions, hierarchies and hegemonies. Moreover, Waterman prompts us to 'rethink the role of performance in the construction, expression, and legitimization of power relationships in the modern world'.

The concept of power in the realm of ethnomusicological literature was for many years invoked primarily in relation to music's effective power , including its role in religious and other ritual contexts, but also in contexts of postcolonialism or neocolonialism, as well as more or less overtly political uses of music. Literary discourses such as that of Waterman's paved the way for a radical shift in the 1990s as ethnologists developed a more nuanced and theoretically-grounded understanding of the complex and pervasive workings of power, and stated to explore concepts of power and their culturally-constructed nature. In this context the work of Gage Averill, whose work on popular music in Haiti examines 'music's role in enacting and negotiating authority, domination, co-optation, subordination, hegemony, and resistance…popular music, as a discursive terrain, is a site at which power is enacted, acknowledged, accommodated, signified, contested, and resisted (Averill, 1997, pp. xv,xi).We note in his writing that while Averill documents a situation in which music is more openly politicized and where the central discourses of power revolve around 'race' and class to a much greater extent. Averill asserts that music's close link to memory, nostalgia and collective social experience are important factors in its entanglement with power, he says, 'the powerful appeal of music—

its engagement with human emotions—is the reason it serves effectively as an instrument of politics and a medium of power'. There have been many earlier writers who have examined the well connection between political power and music, pointing to the role of music in official displays which serve to legitimate those in positions of authority, their institutions and their discourses. Such displays 'openly affirm and perpetuate an existing power structures' (Shelemay, 2001) through public transcripts and in this way, power and authority are literally 'performed'.. Scott (Scott, 1990) points out that both the 'powerful' and the 'powerless' have such hidden transcripts such that a 'dominant ideology can be encoded within ordinary objects of everyday life. (Lipsitz, 1994, p. 110).

The intensity and immediacy with which music evokes emotion and memory are no doubt important factors, but these in themselves depend on something else. Whether power is something that music is born with, achieves or has thrust upon it, the music power relationship can only be understood in relation to a third, crucial, element: meaning. Much of the discussion revolves around questions of music's social meanings and how such meanings are shaped by power relations. But there is a paradox. While some writers argue that power only accrues to music because of particular associative meanings, music's power arguably lies in its multiple layers of meaning and the often ambiguous nature of its messages. Music serves as the ultimate naturalizing mechanism; and power is nowhere more insidious and pervasive than when it becomes accepted as 'the way things are'. While the naturalizing tendencies of music may support a conservative agenda, its semantic fluidity also allows it to be used in ways which challenge the status Quo and which are often hard to control. Not only does music's semantic ambiguity allow it to simultaneously convey different meanings, to the extent that 'texts and musical messages can themselves contain inner voices, contradicting or subverting the overt messages but such meanings often arise from, and come to represent competing positions of power, particularly in relation to the control of social space.

## A dialectics on the notion of 'culture'

To define an unexplored terrain of a conception is to explore about the nature and scope of the term, to examine about its inherent characteristics that hold its root of fundamental existence and to locate its epistemological emergence. Colin Sparks argues that to define an academic discipline means to explore, in essentials, three features about the subject of study: firstly, the object of study; secondly, the basic assumptions which underpin the method(s) of approach to the object of study; and thirdly, the history of the discipline itself. Of all the definitions that we have—in the course of the academic debate about what cultural studies is— there is of course no single, absolute definition of cultural studies that covers all aspects of its research practice and theoretical orientation, as Colin Sparks (Sparks, 1996) rightly observes:

> It is not possible to draw a sharp line and say that on one side of it we can find the proper province of cultural studies. Neither is it possible to point to a unified theory or methodology which is characteristic to it or of it. A veritable rag-bag of ideas, methods and concerns from literary criticism, sociology, history, media studies, etc., are lumped together under the convenient label of cultural studies.

Michael Payne (Payne, 1996)offers an exceptionally richly theoretically constructed definition of the term 'culture' by telling us that it is a term of limitless application referring to everything that is produced by human beings as distinct from all that is part of nature. He, however, argues that since nature is itself a human abstraction it has a history too meaning that it is part of culture. Claude Lévi-Strauss (Payne, 1996, p. 128) asserts that 'the distinction between culture and nature is an instance of theoretical BRICOLAGE in the sense that the distinction is simultaneously inadequate and indispensable'. North American Anthropologist and literary Critic Mathew Arnold (Payne, 1996, p. 128) holds the view that 'culture' is the finest product of civilization. Clifford Geertz (Geertz, 1973) has a different interpretation about the term and defines culture by way of semiotics as the "webs of significance" spun by human beings. Raymond Williams observes that "culture is one of the two or three most complicated words in the English language" (Williams, Keywords: A Vocabulary of Culture and Society, 1976). Homi Bhabha (Bhabha, 1994) remarks that 'there can be no ethically or epistemologically commensurate subject of culture'. He further maintains that since a transcendent humanity is not based on a particular culture's sense of value then all that is left is what Bhabha calls "culture's archaic undecidability".

Looking within the framework of political lens, John Fiske (Storey J. , 1996) in the essay 'British Cultural Studies and Television' claims that the concept of 'culture' in cultural studies is not either aesthetic or humanist in emphasis, but political in nature. According to him the concept of culture is neither defined in the narrow sense meaning 'high art' nor in an equally narrow sense as a process of aesthetic, intellectual and spiritual development but as a way of life whether of people, a period or a group. Richard Johnson (Storey J. , 1996) in the essay 'What is Cultural Studies Anyway?' looks at all social practices practices of subjective forms from cultural point of view and contends that the text should not be read as an object of study but as a means in cultural studies or raw material from which certain forms may be abstracted 'but the ultimate object of cultural studies is not ... the text, but the social life of subjective forms at each moment of their circulation, including their textual embodiments' (Storey J. , 1996)

The term 'culture' has been subjected to a range of definitions, since the middle of the nineteenth century, that extend from Arnold's all-embracing sense of the possibility of human perfection to Pierre Bourdieu's systems of symbolic violence. Mathew Arnold sees culture as a redemptive pursuit through literary education of the best that human beings had thought of. For Arnold culture plays as a unifying force harmoniously uniting all of human society. T.S. Eliot also transmitted the mission for literary culture which influenced Britain and the United States very significantly. Post-Arnoldian theories have been profoundly influenced by the thoughts of such renowned literary figures as Charles Darwin, Karl Marx, Friedrich Engels, Friedrich Nietzsche and Sigmund Freud. Whereas Charles Darwin developed his own theory of evolution Lewis Henry Morgan in 1877 developed a system of hierarchically classifying cultures according to evolutionary stages. Other early cultural evolutionists included E.B.Tylor who founded the British School of social Anthropology. Marxist Engels also had evolutionary view of culture. In his work *Origin of the Family, Private Property and the State* he looks at the emergence of civilization as not only advancing the existing system of labour but also creating the merchant class. Friedrich Nietzsche sees 'true culture' emerging from a recovery of the 'moral nature' of the classical Greeks. Culture, for Sigmund Freud, provides not only a bulwark against nature but also as such an unrelenting source of opposition to instinct (Payne, 1996).

Drawing a brief historical outline of cultural studies, Simon During (During, 1999) notes that cultural studies developed as an academic discipline in Great Britain in the 1950s out of Leavisism, a form of literary studies named after F.R.Leavis through Hoggart and Williams— both of whom came from working-class families and had worked as teachers in post-compulsory education though in workers' education and had also experienced Leavisism ambivalently—who consciously wrote in the interests of the working class. Simon During further contends that F.R.Leavis, in order to use the educational system to distribute literary knowledge and appreciation more widely, proposed a very restricted canon, rejecting modern experimental works like those of James Joyce or Virginia Wolf and advocating and promoting the works like those of Jane Austen,

Alexander Pope or George Eliot—proponents of 'the great Tradition'—believing that reading the writers of the 'great tradition' worked as a means of developing mature individuals with a concrete and balanced sense of 'life'.

It seems to me that Leavisian thoughts, views, considerations and postulations were far more appealing to the people of 'bourgeoisie' class than those of 'proletariat' class and were disfavoring 'mass culture' given the fact that his thoughts were very much in tune with the so called 'social democratic power bloc' group which dominated post-war Britain, which proved to be profoundly influential when the education system expanded radically through the 1950s and 60s. Simon During is of the view that Hoggart and Williams did not have very happy experiences with Leavisism; they, however, found it to be ambivalent for the following: even as they accepted the fact that the 'the great tradition' canonical texts were richer than the contemporary 'mass culture', they felt that these canonical texts were not appealing to the masses, that they were not in consonance with the communal forms of life, that rather they were biased towards the so called the 'social-democratic power bloc' group, marginalising the traditional industrial working class communities into which both were born, thereby creating a lacuna between 'the social-democratic power bloc' group and the traditional industrial working class. In order to fill that gap Hoggart published his book *The Uses of Literacy* , the first half of which contains a heartfelt evocation of traditional industrial working class communities. He sort of tried to strike a balance by bringing social analysis into alignment with Leavisite literary criticism. Hoggart thought that the celebration of the old high culture could go along with an evocation of the culture of the youth because both were standing apart from contemporary commercial popular culture because of which both were under threat.

As far as traditional British working-class life was concerned, British history reveals that since the early 1920s the British economy had been dominated by unemployment—around one million people were unemployed during the early 1920s. With Britain, however, having a full employment economy—thanks to the British Government economic policy— there was a paradigm shift noticed in the 1950s in the realm of employment policy and huge number of jobs were made available to the people which witnessed a large-scale immigration from the colonies giving us clear indication that the indigenous workers were no longer called upon to take the least desirable jobs. This phenomenon helped the workers to become increasingly affluent thus bringing a fragmentation in the culture that Hoggart described in his book.

With the old working-class communal life getting fragmented, the cultural studies which followed Hoggart's notion of culture as way of life in his book *The Uses of Literary* became increasingly difficult to sustain thereby the attention shifting from locally produced cultural forms such as pub-life, group singing, pigeon-fancying etc. to a culture which Theodor Adorno and Max Horkheimer called the 'culture industry' such as highly developed music, film and broadcasting businesses, calling essentially for a revision of old paradigms. Within the framework of this context cultural studies theorists considered seriously exploring culture's own political function ans offering a critique of the social-democratic power bloc which was drawing power into the state. Culture in the early 1970s now came to be regarded as a form of 'hegemony', Italian Marxist Antonio Gramsci's term to describe relations of domination which are not visible as such. In the same line of thought and in the same spirit culture could also be seen as what Michel Foucault was beginning to think of as a form of 'governmentality', as a means to produce conforming or 'docile' citizens. Another important concept that emerged in cultural studies from out of encounter woth Gramsci and Foucaul was that of 'articulation' which emphasized how hegemony constantly mutates in terms of its elements and contents, that is, it is a process of making alliances and connections, releasing energies rather than presenting a static set of values and knowledges.

Reflecting upon four perspectives on culture, Robert Wuthnow (Wuthnow, 1984) asserts that outside the mainstream of social sciences, over the past few decades, four approaches have been pursued with growing interest and with some success, that these approaches have been primarily oriented toward the realm of meaning, symbolism, language, and discourse, and that each is different and distinct from the so called 'positive' tradition of contemporary social science. All the four approaches have been described as follows: first, phenomenology; the second, cultural anthropology; the third, structuralism; and the fourth, critical theory.

## Coordinates of Cultural and Cultural Theory (Payne, 1996)

Given the fact that cultural studies developed in Britain under the influence of Hoggart and Williams, Michael Payne argues that much of the discourse of the new interdisciplinary field of cultural studies came to be determined by a set of structural concepts such as human subjectivity and consciousness; ideology and hegemony; critique and polysemy, which proved to be the key coordinates of cultural studies. Michael Payne further claims that as the debate has been going on and on concerning these matters many cultural and critical theorists either advocate or find their forms of thoughts clarified in opposition to the following three contentions:

(i) *Subjectivity and consciousness*: Drawing upon the works of Hegel's *Phenomenology of the Mind* and Freud's *The Interpretation of Dreams*, to justify his considerations about these concepts he contends that the determination of recent thinkers such as Lacan, Derrida and Kristeva to refer to human beings as subjects manifests an effort to resist pre-Hegelian and pre-Freudian assumptions of human unity and ego identity. He further claims that subjectivity , however, recalls a sense of subjection and a resistance to unthought assumptions about essential human freedom , and that the subject is never fully autonomous, when born into the entities of language, culture, race, class and gender politics.

(ii) *Ideology and hegemony*: In order to illustrate his point, Michael Payne quotes Marx and Engels and their works namely *A Contribution to the Critique of Political Economy* and *The German Ideology*. Referring to Marx and his "Preface to *A Contribution to the Critique of Political Economy*" where Marx argues that 'it is not the consciousness of men that determines their existence, but their social existence that determines their consciousness', Michael Payne suggests that forms of consciousness constitute ideologies. As for hegemony, following Gramsci's views on it, he seems to make submission that hegemony is complicity in oppression as normal or as necessarily a part of culture by those who are ruled by it as Gramsci claimed in his *Prison Notebooks* that hegemony is woven out of a network of ideologies and is then transmitted by intellectuals in affiliation with the ruling class.

(iii) *Critique and polysemy*: Michael Payne insists that any attempt to know or theorize the process of society must begin with a radical criticism of the dominating forces of ideology in order to disengage consciousness from what keeps it politically unconscious. As example he cites the Frankfurt school of social theorists namely Adorno, Horkheimer, Marcuse and Habermas who performed a critique of ideology (*Ideologiekritik*) in order to understand its processes and to resist its dominance. He maintains that he is not in favour of simply opposing those forces with moralizing criticism but he hold that along with opposing those forces an attempt must be made to discover a new form of knowledge that is distinct from empirical science and is founded in radical criticism aimed at bringing social changes in the society. He shows that many features of *Ideologiekritik* are found in many forms of feminist, postcolonial, and anti-racist criticism. He considers the discipline of semiotics (entities like language and structures or any signifying form in particular) to be polysemous in a couple of senses: firstly, that they mean many things at once and, secondly, that they may say more than they want to say. Citing Derrida's work *Of Grammatology* he demonstrates that for Derrida all texts whether in written language or in other signifying forms provide deconstructive resources for a critique of ideology.

## British Cultural Studies: Raymond Williams

Michael Friedman argues that Raymond Williams' first book, *Culture and Society*, was an attempt to create an intellectual history of the word culture and inevitably, as Williams saw it, the deeply implicated words industry, democracy, class and art. Williams did not attempt to approach this cluster of words as abstractions. Rather he traced the development of their acceptations as they appeared in the writings of social critics from Burke to Orwell, critics who were struggling to apprehend and make sense of the world that was created when capitalism entered the Industrial Revolution. *Culture and Society* ends with a passionate and brilliant plea for the creation of a true socialist community.

According to Raymond Williams, 'the idea of culture, and the word itself in its general modern uses, came into English thinking' during the Industrial Revolution. By tracing English views on culture from that time to the present, he gives 'an account and an interpretation of our responses in thought and feeling to the changes in English society.'

## American New Historicism and Ethnography: Stephen Greenblatt and Clifford Geertz

There is no denying the fact that The New Historicism in America has a considerably wider geographical, historical and theoretical focus than that of British Cultural studies which was comparatively narrow both geographically and historically. The New Historicism of America, however, is much indebted to British Cultural studies for its significant contribution to the development of this movement. As far as the concept of 'New Historicism' is concerned, Stephen Greenblatt, a professor of English at the University of California at Berkeley, in 1982 edited a collection of essays on Renaissance studies entitled *The Forms of Power and the Power of Forms* and in his introduction to that volume, Prof. Greenblatt used the phrase "new historicism" in a way that seemed to many readers a call for a new movement in literary study (Greenblatt, 1982, p. 1). Greenblatt is well known for his another book entitled *Renaissance Self-Fashioning: From More to Shakespeare* which significantly changed the landscape of English Renaissance studies in which he argues that the idea of the self as an artifact is itself is a cultural production of the Renaissance.

Greenblatt was most powerfully influenced by the cultural theories of the American Anthropologist Clifford Geertz whose concept of culture is fundamentally a semiotic one. Geertz's book (Geertz, 1973)*The Interpretation of Cultures* is a landmark study in the field of anthropology which not only provides a retrospective of 15years of his field work but also his most fully presented theories of culture. Geertz argues that cultural theory is rooted in the soil of ordinary daily life and is discovered there when the ethnographer is too much engrossed into his task of 'thick description'. Geertz demonstrates through his work his argument that the essence of complex national societies or great religions cannot be discovered in certain "typical" small towns or localities, whether Jonesville, Easter Island or Montaillou (Geertz, 1973). He held the view that it is not the generality but the variation of cultural forms that is both anthropology's greatest resource and the basis of its besetting theoretical dilemma.

## Critical Theory and Culture: Jürgen Habermas

It appears that no one is more widely read in contemporary cultural and critical theory than Habermas who has now carried on the tradition of critical theory, whose critical writings provide much more comprehensively than his predecessors a powerful critique of modernity that reaches from Hegel and Marx to Nietzsche and Heidegger and on to Foucault and Derrida, which is amply demonstrated by his work *The Philosophical Discourse of Modernity(Der philosophische Diskurs der Moderne: Zwolf Vorlesungen)* (Habermas, The Philosophical Discourse of Modernity, 1985(1987)). The idea of critical theory is rightly associated with a group of German philosophers, including Horkheimer and Adorno, whose founding text for the Frankfurt school namely *Dialectic of Enlightenment (Dialektik der Aufklarung)* was published long before any of the books by Raymond Williams, Clifford Geertz, or Stephen Greenblatt. Robert Wuthnow (Wuthnow, 1984) claims that Habermas, in his work on culture, draws heavily on the assumptions of his predecessors in the Frankfurt school of critical theory. Habermas's own strategy for the analysis of culture stems from a desire to unmask and transcend the blinders built into the structure of modern thought. He advanced his critique of modern culture by building loosely on the work of Adorno and others such as Horkheimer, Lukacs, and Marx, and carried out his agenda simultaneously on two fronts: on the philosophical front, reflecting his early training in philosophy and on Sciological front, reflecting his indebtedness to Marx and a concern with linking the critique of cultural forms to concrete developments in the economic and political realms. Furthermore, his work bears marks of Hegel, Heidegger, the Frankfurt school, and more broadly the phenomenological and hermeneutic traditions, on the philosophical front and on the sociological front, his work has concentrated on developing an approach to culture that can be defended in terms of a general theory on cultural evolution and an appraisal of contemporary economic and political crises.

In Habermas's work on culture, the basic conceptual distinction, has been observed to be existing between 'rational-purposive action' and 'communicative action'. In fact, the problems of great concern to Habermas have been developing a rational theory of communication, and relating this theory of communication to social conditions. The first has involved him in an effort to clarify types of action and knowledge and to find out a way to set the study of culture on an empirical footing and the second has led him to a theory of evolution. In his book (Habermas, Knowledge and Human Interests, 1971), he sharply distinguishes the cultural sciences from the natural sciences arguing that whereas the natural sciences attempt to construct lawlike regularities applicable to all times and places, the cultural sciences focus on knowledge specific to historical situations, and this distinction gives an important clue to his understanding of culture in the development of his theory. Habermas's formulations on the internalization of culture suggest that he conceives of culture as an objective phenomenon external to the individual and asserts the importance of individuals' internalizing culture. What he has emphasized primarily are points of convergence in the literature on child psychology which serve as a basis for his own views of internalization.

Examining Habermas's assumptions on culture and social structure, Robert Wuthnow (Wuthnow, 1984) upholds that Habermas's work on the relation between culture and social structure has been heatedly debated in the literature on culture.On the one hand, theorists have argued that cultural patterns are shaped decisively by the social arrangements in which they are produced; on the other hand, social scientists have been accused of reductionism, of explaining away cultural patterns by attributing them to social arrangements rather than attempting to understand the internal structure of these patterns in their own right. Habermas has been caught up by this debate as well but his perspectives offer important resolution to the controversy. Habermas's theory of culture reflects some of the reductionistic assumptions of the Marxist tradition from which he has borrowed. According to this tradition cultural elements tend to be regarded as mere reflections of the other and more fundamental features of the world.

It has been noticed by Robert Wuthnow and others (Wuthnow, 1984) that a strong evolutionary perspective runs through Habermas's theory of culture and that his theory corresponds in many respects to contemporary theories of social evolution, such as the theories of Robert N.Bellah, Gerhard Lenski, and Edward O. Wilson. Theoretical considerations and formulations of Habermas' theory (Habermas, Communication and the Evolution of Society, 1979) suggest that he identifies four distinct stages of cultural evolution: *Neolithic societies, archaic civilizations, developed civilizations* and *the modern age.*

Habermas's contribution to the discussion of the concept of 'legitimation' has been immense. Legitimation, to him, has been one of the most significant contributions of modern culture. He elaborates extensively in his book *Legitimation Crisis* (Habermas, Legitimation Crisis, 1975) on the problem of legitimation and on what it means to call something 'legitimate' and extended his discussion to include a sophisticated analysis of the economic and political conditions influencing the nature of legitimation problems in advanced capitalist societies. In his view legitimacy implies recognition, and recognition includes an evaluation which imputes justice and propriety to the situation. It must be borne in the mind that Habermas restricts his discussion of legitimacy primarily to the state, arguing that 'multinational corporations or the world market are not capable of legitimation' (Habermas, Communication and the Evolution of Society, 1979, p. 179).

Habermas's formulations about the critique of ideology is distinctive in at least three respects: he has drawn his assumptions on the Marxist and Freudian perspectives, regarding it as a form of false consciousness; he has drawn his attention toward all-pervasive ideologies including science and technology rather than limited ideologies associated with political interest groups ; and finally he goes beyond the description of ideology to suggest alternatives for overcoming ideology. For Habermas, the solution to ideological domination is the cultivation of what he has termed variously as 'the public sphere', 'an ideal speech community' or 'communicative competence': a cultural context in which political decisions can be discussed.

## Culture and Imperialism: Edward Said

*Culture and Imperialism* (Said, Culture and Imperialism, 1993) is an effort to expose a politically tainted euro-centric epistemology. In Said's writings the object of his critical attention has not been simply attempts by the West to subdue the Orient by force or by economic exploitation; rather he argues that the Orient is virtually an invention of those European disciplines that have set out to study it. In his view, Orientalism, therefore, as a form of epistemological imperialism, is not a foreign but "an integral part of European material civilization and culture" (Said, The Question of

Palestine, 1979, p. 1). Said contends very strongly that not only oriental studies but also linguistics, history, criticism, philosophy, religious studies, sociology, anthropology, psychology, political science, economics are all complicitous in the production of orientalism. *Culture and Imperialism* sets out to demonstrate that orientalism is but one manifestation of imperialism and that in their pursuit of empire Europe and America have used their cultural forms, including such ideals as freedom and individualism, as means of conquest and domination. He writes: "neither imperialism nor colonialism is a simple act of accumulation and acquisition. Both are supported and perhaps even impelled by impressive ideological formations that include notions that certain territories and people require and beseech domination, as well as forms of knowledge affiliated with domination" (Said, Culture and Imperialism, 1993, p. 8). He is of the view that Cultural Theory is compromised from its start.

## Some Important Cultural Theorists

### Karl Marx (1818-1883)

Terrell Carver (Carver, 1982) is of the view that the impact of Karl Marx on our intellectual life has been profound. In the arts and sciences his work has influenced almost every discipline from aesthetics to theology, including anthropology, geography, history, linguistics, literary criticism, almost all branches of philosophy, political science and even psychology. The physical sciences have not been immune from Marx's influence. Marx's view is the object of serious debate in almost all disciplines today when they reflect on the social implications of their work. Carver further calls him 'the archetypal nineteenth-century polymath who could contribute to philosophy in the morning, history in the afternoon, and sociology after dinner' (Carver, 1982, p. 1)

Ellis Cashmore (Cashmore, 1999) acknowledges that Marx's writings have formed one of the most influential contributions to the social theory of culture, despite the fact that Marx wrote comparatively little on cultural analysis as such. As a matter of fact, his philosophy and social theory have been used as he starting point of many different schools of Marxist analysis. What is common for the different schools of Marxist is the following: a theoretical framework which claims to be materialist, historical, and which makes the political and cultural class struggle arising from an economic infrastructure central to the analysis. As can be readily observed that in the Marxist tradition there is an inherent tendency to reduce cultural to economic practice , and a number of different means of trying to prevent this have been elaborated in the major schools of Marxism. Crucial to Marxism, however, is the view that modern society is dominated by a capitalist mode of production whose own logic produces the conditions for the rise to power of a bourgeois ruling class. Further, this class reproduces its conditions of existence—the exploitation of an industrial proletariat of wage- earners —through a political state(a legal and armed repressive organization) and through a system of ruling ideas and culture. This new socio-economic system, capitalism, produces in turn the agency, the proletariat, of a new revolution. This revolutionary process is not determined by progressive reason, or cultural evolution, which are super-structural features, but by contradictions arising in the economic, the material basis of modern society (Cashmore, 1999).

Marx radically transformed the way people comprehend reality, and what is very important to note is the fact that it was him and his ideas that brought about a sea change in social sciences, including cultural studies. His ideas have, since his early writings, influenced generations of thinkers who saw socio-politico-cultural realities in an entirely different way and thinkers inspired by him harbingered a new and decisive phase in cultural studies that establish it as an autonomous discipline eventually liberating it from sociology and anthropology. Besides, the development of the concept of culture in the twentieth century owes much to Marx and his ideas and methodology to make him an epoch making thinker.

## Pierre Bourdieu (1930-2002)

Pierre Bourdieu was a prolific writer and significant post-war intellectual whose influence on contemporary thought in the social sciences and humanities has been immense. His key concepts of habitus, field, and symbolic capital continue to shape research and theory in many disciplines. The author of over 25 books, his *Outline of a Theory of Practice* is the best known of his works. Bourdieu's modest origins made him particularly sensitive to issues of power and prestige in France, shaping his research interests, social activism, and defense of the underprivileged. He was a "scholarship boy" who attended lycee in the regional city of Pau and then went on to lycee Louis-le-Grand in Paris, before eventually entering the Ecole Normale Superieure (one of the elite institutions of higher learning in France.)

Given the wide breadth of his writings, and the uneven timing of translations of his work, knowledge of Bourdieu's many contributions is scattered in the United States according to disciplinary interests, and there are relatively few scholars who are familiar with the total oeuvre. His social activism and political position in France are also not well known among his readers outside of France. During the 1990s, Bourdieu became firmly established, along with Derrida and Foucault, as a major French intellectual presence in American academia. He was at this time, already, one of the leading intellectuals in France, widely known and controversial among the public as well as among scholars. His outspoken criticism of the social class structure provoked a range of critics in France.

Bourdieu accused even the most progressive theorists of cultural studies of augmenting the 'universalisation of particularism' project in twentieth century. His intention was very clear to demystify an insidious and latent process in which the Western academia, publications, and intelligentsia were involved in establishing the ideas and behaviours of the western elite intellectuals as 'universal'. He felt that even the most democratic liberatory sounding intellectuals have contributed to this arcane phenomenon which aimed at neglecting and silencing the dissenting voices. He targeted the contemporary commercial publications and monopoly over the medium of knowledge impartation. Bourdieu believed that commodification reduced the realm of ideas and intellectuals to relations of production, and that it diminished any possibility of radical change. He strongly felt that this labyrinth had to be broken in order to free knowledge from the dominant classes controlling the modes of production.

It is important to notice that in two recent books, *Masculine Domination* (2001) and *The Weight of the World* (1999), Bourdieu addressed social problems of sexism and poverty in his own society through trenchant critiques relying upon the concept of symbolic domination. He also wrote books attacking television (1999) and neoliberalism (1999). Bourdieu was increasingly in the French public eye in the years immediately preceding his death as an outspoken critic of globalization. Bourdieu supported the controversial peasant-hero Jose Bove, who led French farmers to attack a McDonald's restaurant. He also supported Algerian causes at home in France and in North Africa. Bourdieu was not comfortable with labels of his work, and avoided easy characterizations in large part by leaving such a huge legacy of work that crosses disciplinary boundaries. He also avoided facile political labels, often alienating members of left-wing groups in France with which he, for the most part, identified. Bourdieu offered criticisms of the centers of power in France, including his own academic colleagues, with the publication of *Homo Academicus* (1988). His contributions to the study of power in modern society have moved social theory in new directions, helping shape arguments about social agency and structure. His premature death came as he continued up until the end to offer a critical voice in human affairs. Despite his powerful position in French academic circles and the extraordinary influence of his work throughout the world, Bourdieu's demeanor in person could be surprisingly understated and modest. Those who were privileged enough to get to know Pierre Bourdieu attest to his warmth and gentle sense of humor.

It is apparently discernible that Bourdieu is showing his greater concern about the independence of the 'intellectual field' in his book *The field of Cultural Production: Essays on Art and Literature* (1993)(Bourdieu P. , The Field of Cultural Production: Essays on Art and Literature, 1993), arguing that the structures of dominance have left very little scope for a true democratic and revolutionary project to take shape. Accordingly, he warns the progressive forces against the most insidious ways through which the dominant classes controlled the thought process. He was of the view that an utmost care and scrutiny was required in passing uninfluenced judgments about the issues at hand because even the most thoughtful of intellectuals could unintentionally become a victim of structural bias. Bourdieu, accordingly, took up the 'structure/agency'dichotomy to see through this problematic and subvert the exploitative and dominating systems of thought as he firmly believed in subverting the entire modes of power from within.

It seems to me that along with *Reproduction* (1977), Bourdieu's best known books are *Outline of a Theory of Practice (1977), Distinction (1984),* and *The Logic of Practice (1990)*. These three books synthesize Bourdieu's sociological and ethnographic re- search and formulate his theoretical approach. His notion of practice seeks to reconcile structuralist and methodological individualist approaches. It draws from concepts of social actors' "common sense" to understand how noticeable patterns emerge from human behavior. As he has written, he wanted to move from the study of "rules to strategies." Nevertheless, Bourdieu retained a limited view of the possibilities for human agency, and focused on the constraints of the habitus and of systems of symbolic domination. Bourdieu made use of these concepts in his writings in the fields of art, literature, and language, among others.

Bourdieu is well known for inventing and popularising the most talked about terms and concepts in cultural studies like *cultural capital, cultural production, symbolic violence* and *habitus*. He critically examined the French Education system in his writings and has demonstrated how the entire system contributed to the overall subjugation of its citizens. He has displayed how the social structures and knowledge impartation systems played crucial roles in generating authenticity for the contemporary ruling classes. The masses were kept under the illusion of a happy go lucky situation with intoxicating ideas like nationalism only to perpetuate their own oppression. He refers to this attack on individual consciousness as *symbolic violence* because it operated surreptitiously through the social and cultural structures. Similarly his idea of *cultural capital* perceived the consumer as one who is pushed into abyss of infinite competition with his fellow beings.He explains how the objects under capitalism are produced and projected as bearers of social status and the consumer is lured to acquire certain strategic position by having them. For Bourdieu economy was typified not simply by differentiation and equivalences, but by distinction. Bourdieu argued that the question of inequality was at the heart of the logic of the cultural. He believed that the inequality of symbolic goods, cultural capital, and the capacity to produce and acquire such cultural capital existed in the realm of culture. He gives an explanation for the way in which taste was a social and not an aessthetic practice and shows how such taste was constitutive of class differentiation executed on the basis of the unequal distribution of cultural capital, as against economic capital or educational capital.

According to Bourdieu 'habitus'the umbrella term under which the inequality of symbolic goods, cultural capital within the frames of several differentiations took place. He demonstrated how the individual as a member of society is constituted through a process of assimilation, which influence his likes and dislikes in a significant way. Accordingly, symbols, totems, emblems and cultural artifacts are not self-sufficient rather they are a product of traditions and social structures. He asserts that it is a reciprocal process in which the indivudual constructs the reality which constructs him/her in return. It is very easy to comprehend this process at the surface level but Bourdieu problematizes it by putting emphasis on the arcane power mechanism that maneuvered the entire proceess in favour of a dominant class. He further claims that the operation of the mechanism is so subtle that the individual feels enthralled by the external manifestation without realising his/her helplessness to either alter or subvert the exploitative structures.

In Bourdieu's theoretical paradigm 'habitus' is a complex concept. Bourdieu's view is that the idea of 'habitus' provides a link between the structuring of social relationships and the culture of a society, that the 'habitus' is a concept that seems to take meaning at a number of different levels. Bourdieu defines the concept 'habitus' as that which 'at every moment structures new experiences in accordance with the structures produced by past experiences , which are modified by the new eexperiences within the limits defined by their power of selection, which brings about a unique integration, dominated by the earliest experiences, of the experiences stastically common to members of the same class' (Bourdieu P. , The Field of Cultural Production: Essays on Art and Literature, 1993, p. 60). It follows from this that habitus is both a structuring and a structured structure and that it referred to the generative structuring structure tht is at the locus of cultural reproduction. It is noteworthy that Bourdieu talked about the economy of culture in terms of the distribution of cultural capital and the different forms of habitus through which distinction and power is produced and reproduced.

'Cultural reproduction' is another concept which was devised by Bourdieu, which he refers to as 'the process by which culture and the political power of the dominant class was maintained from one generation to the next through the education system'. He makes it clear that continued existence of the society and culture of that society both needed transformation in the sense that the continued exstence of the society required more than just physical reproduction and similarly culture of that society needed to be transmitted to the new generation. Bourdieu further in his deliberation linked cultural production to the role of socialization or the process through which individuals internalized the culture of their societies. Cultural reproduction, in Bourdieu's formulation aimed to legitimize the political structures of the time and to ensure their stability. In theorizing the term 'cultural unconscious', Bourdieu's line of reasoning is that 'cultural unconsciousness' stood for the tacit, assumed and unspoken grounds which preconditioned any cultural production.

It seems to me that Bourdieu's overall formulations could be conclusively assessed in two respects. In the first place, and perhaps most importantly,the fact that he deals very extensively with how the structures of social positioning and culture created structures of the psychological perceptions of the world. Secondly, and also equally important in the same connection is the fact that his work has made invaluable contribution in decoding the colourings of culture on the labyrinths of psychological perspectives of the world.

**Jean Baudrillard(1929-2007)**

Baudrillard, in general, has attempted to establish the limits of Marxist theory for analysing critically advanced society and to offer elements of a new social theory which can reveal the deep structure of corporate capitalism and point to its contradictions. In this sense, Baudrillard may be classified in that group of French theorists who can be called post-structuralists, and include most notably Michel Foucault, Gilles Deleuze and Jacques Derrida.

Baudrillard's main theoretical formulation was that simulation has replaced production at the center of our social system, that contemporary culture has gone beyond the classical Marxist use value/exchange value distinction - a distinction still at the heart of Adorno's frozen dialectic of modernism and mass culture - and operates on the basis of sign value writ large. Sign value is, in this case, the case of theory, obviously name value, the name functioning as the signifier/signified unit that attracts the audience. For instance, retrogressive from a theoretical point of view, at least in a Baudrillardian perspective, the referent still would have to appear in person, would have to walk through the doors of the museum and get up in front of his audience to deliver the goods. In the scheme of simulation, of course, the body as referent becomes so much refuse: "The real itself appears as a large useless body."' At best, it could be seen as residue supporting the system's need to simulate the real.

Several groups of social theorists have, in the twentieth century, labored to unlock the Marxist paradigm from the grip of economic reductionism. The Italian Communist, Antonio Gramsci, the theorists of the Frankfurt School, Adorno, Horkheimer and Marcuse, independent critics such as Ernst Bloch, Walter Benjamin and Karl Korsch, Eastern European Communists, Georg Lukacs in Hungary, Adam Schaff in Poland, the Praxis group in Yugoslavia and Karel Kosik in Czechoslavia, and finally the existential, phenomenological and even structuralist Marxists in France and Italy have all argued that the concept of the superstructure must account for the relative autonomy of culture. They have made this argument on both epistemological and historical grounds. In the same line of argument, Baudrillard's earliest full-length studies criticized the functional and utilitarian basis of both classical and Marxist economics by focusing on the nature of the object in consumer culture. Drawing on Mauss's *The Gift* and Bataille's *Notion of Expenditure*, Baudrillard argued that the use-value/exchange-value pairing was inadequate. He further argued that contemporary society involved the acceleration of sign-value, the mechanism of conspicuous consumption; and in addition continued to be influenced by symbolic value, associated with pre-capitalist forms of cultural organization.

Beginning with an inclination towards the Barthian semiology to explain the production of culture through Saussure's theory of linguistic signification, along with his book *The System of Objects*(1996), Baudrillard tried to apply semiotics to culture, viewing the consumption of objects as a process of signification. His view was that the objects were not always consumed for their propagate usability but for an idealistic signification. The idea behind the object is exploited for one's own benefit. It is an appropriation and maneuvering of the 'signified' which defined the nature of all social relations by situating the act and the subject in a web of signifying practices and structures. Like a true semiotician, he located the meaning of consumption of these objects in relation or 'difference' to other signs and cultural practices; abstract or concrete whatever they may be. Further this semantic signification derived its meaning from an overarching code of signification which evaded the imagination of an average consumer. He, therefore, held the view that any possibility of change in the structures of dominance had to begin with the transformation of the codes of signification.

In his early books-*Le Systdme des objets* (1968); *La Societd de consommation* (1970); and *Pour une critique de I'&conomie politique du signe* (1972)-Baudrillard developed his critical semiology within the context of Marxism. Both Roland Barthes and Henri Lefebvre, Baudrillard's teacher, had earlier pioneered the critique of the media. In *Mythologies*, Barthes illuminated the hidden, ideological significations of various communications systems. A cover of *Paris-Match* advertised the solidity of imperialism by showing a black man in a French army uniform. The surface signification was innocuous; but beneath it, at the unconscious level, the reader of *Paris-Match* imbibed the important message of ideological legitimation.

It was Baudrillard who popularized the concept of 'simulcra'. He, at the philosophical level, intended to expose the perception of reality relating it to the age of information technology. He held the view that with the invention of the computer and the internet reality had become 'hyperreal', and that new technologies had accelerated the process of simulation where signs were produced and used to create self-referential systems of reality. He claimed that with the continuous repetition of this practice, the sign gradually became independent of any signified or referent and ultimately acquired the place of the real. He pointed out that this process of simulation or simulacra is not new but has been functional historically, especially, in institutions like religion which produced the image of a supposed existent which replaced the real, by gaining authenticity and validity. He argued that similar kinds of simulation have been operational in the modern state as well, which used it to subjectivise and subjugate its citizens. It is important to notice that in present time the mass production and media relentlessly produce such images and messages which are taken as real.

Baudrillard's latest works, *The illusion of the End*(1992) and *The Perfect Crime*(1995), portray the modern technological age as pathological, 'white-washed' and at the mercy of any object, event or system that is alien or 'other' to its functioning ( Islamic fundamentalism, the Gulf War, Ethnic 'cleansing'). He argues that the technological culture attempts the 'perfect crime' of the reduction of otherness to homogeneity, which according to him is impossible. H contends that otherness and radical alterity will continue to undermine the systems of homogeneity because the strategies, devices and concepts of homogeneity are themselves, ultimately illusory.

To the question of whether there is or can be a single definition of the term 'culture', the answer is , I think, bound to be that there is none. Although the phenomenon we call culture is the focus of cultural anthropology, there are important differences among anthropologists as to just how to define it. There are different views of its role in human behavior, and there is as yet no fully developed theory of culture. Speaking within sociological framework, Archer (Archer, 1988) says that the conceptualization of culture is extraordinary in two respects, displaying the weakest analytical development of any concept in sociology , and playing the most wildly vacillating role within sociological theory: (i) he holds that at the descriptive level, the notion of 'culture' remains inordinately vague instead of having different 'cultural structures' there are endless 'cultural differences'; and (ii) he argues that at the explanatory level the status of culture oscillates between that of a supremely independent variable, the superordinate power in society and, a position of supine dependence on other social institutions. In 'The Myth of Cultural Integration' Archer advances his interpretation that the conventional anthropological approach to culture in essentials contained two distinct strands within the concept: firstly, there was the view that the notion of a cultural pattern characterized an underlying unity and a fundamental coherence, and secondly, there was the view that there was presence of the notion of uniform action, identified with cultural patterns to produce homogeneity (Archer, 1988, p. 4).

To critically examine the conception of the category of 'culture' essentially demands from a research scholar to revisit the distinguished anthropologists A.L.Kroeber and Kluckhohn both of whom, in 1952, published the most comprehensive assessment of culture as a term and an idea, who carefully distinguished definitions proposed by 110 authors according to 52 discrete concepts used in those definitions. Raymond Williams also rightly observes that "culture is one of the two or three most complicated words in the English language" (Williams, Keywords: A Vocabulary of Culture and Society, 1976). In keeping with such assertion he is giving us two reasons: Firstly, he is of the view that the concept of 'culture' has had its intricate historical development in several European languages; and secondly, it is being used along with other important concepts in several other disciplines and systems of thoughts. Registering his frustration that its complexity defied the tasks of analysis, Raymond William said: "I don't know how many times I've wished that I'd never heard the damned word" (Williams, Politics and Letters, 1979, p. 154). Adam Kuper is also having similar view when he argues that the term is so overused that it is better to break it down into components parts and speak of beliefs, ideas, art, and traditions rather than expect to find a set of shared characteristics which brings them together as part of a wider field of culture (Tony Bennett, 2005). In the words of James Clifford culture is "a deeply compromised idea, but one cannot yet do without" (Clifford, The predicament of culture: Twentieth-century ethnography, literature, and art, 1988). It is not surprising that the many recent attempts to define the field of cultural studies seem no less whimsical than futile human efforts since culture is simultaneously such an elusive and all-encompassing idea.That Cultural Studies and New Historicism both mark a 'sociological turn' in literary studies is quite evident enough. This does not necessarily follow the fact that sociological concerns were absent from literary studies. In fact, Sociological concerns were never absent from literary studies but these two trends bring them to the foreground.

Raymond William's *Keywords* is a very fascinating book in which he is giving us detailed etymological analysis of the term 'culture' arguing that the roots 'cultura' and 'colore' are related to 'colonus' and 'colony' and thus linking agriculture and cultivation historically to colonialism. It seems to me that the important moment in William's definition of the term is the figural shift from humanism on into the eighteenth century in which the signification of cultivation is transferred from husbandry to human development. For Raymond Williams it is the the influence of the German word *Kultur* and the French word *Cultur* which affects this shift in English and finally he asserts that the idea of 'culture' used so blithely in the twentieth century, and adopted by cultural studies comes from the anthropological territory (Bowman, 2003).

'Culture' is not an easily defined term as it can have different meanings in different contexts. The concept, however, that lies at the core of cultural studies is very much the concept that is found in Cultural Anthropology. The concept avoids any exclusive concern with 'high' culture which is still found, for example, in the writings of Arnold, Leavis and elite and mass society theories. It holds the view that all human beings live in a world that is created by human beings, and in which they find meaning. Culture is the complex everyday world we all encounter and through which we all move. It begins at the point at which humans surpass whatever is simply given in their natural inheritance. There are essentially two most important general elements of culture: firstly, the ability of human beings to construct and to build; and secondly, the ability to use language or to embrace all forms of sign system (Sedgwick, 1999).

Thus it is evident that there have been numerous difficulties expressed by cultural theorists and critics regarding the value of the vocabulary of culture. The range of contexts, however, in which that vocabulary now figures, has multiplied extraordinarily in recent years. The earlier qualified uses of the terms such as high culture, folk culture, mass culture, and popular culture still remain but have been weakened. The terms such as national culture and regional culture are increasingly becoming too much complicated as the boundary lines to count as national and regional are being contested. Some more extended terms such as Gay culture, lesbian culture, black culture, ethnic cultures, diasporic cultures, and transnational cultures, however, within the extended range of uses relating to forms of differences that operate within nations and across the nations, are now being universally used by the academics all over the world (Tony Bennett, 2005). Tony Bennett argues that the fact that there has been a strong association that has been established between the concept of culture and the notion of life style has generated another range of extensions-"from subcultures and counter-cultures to club cultures, street cultures, and drug cultures. Body culture, consumer culture, prosthetic culture, material culture, sports culture, media culture, and visual culture similarly point to a proliferation of usage" (Tony Bennett, 2005, p. 64). He further suggests that the use of adjectival cultural has grown very rapidly: "We are told we now live in a cultural economy; cultural policies are an increasingly important field of government activity, with cultural diversity, cultural pluralism, and cultural access and participation important policy objectives. Inner cities are constantly being revived through cultural development, cultural regeneration, or cultural animation programs" (Tony Bennett, 2005, p. 64). Moreover, he goes on to say that "Cultural rights are now a significant aspect of contemporary citizenship entitlements, while cultural heritage, cultural property, and cultural landscape are to be preserved and protected. Cultural imperialism, cultural genocide, cultural tourism, cultural materialism, and cultural capital indicate an extended use of the adjectival form in more specialist and academic languages" (Tony Bennett, 2005, p. 64). Tony Bennet yet further maintains that as cultural studies and cultural criticism are presently making their ways ahead, the fields of cultural psychology, cultural history, cultural geography and cultural evolution have progressed as part of the more general cultural turn in the humanities and social sciences. What is important to notice here is he claims that whole fields of knowledge are now described as cultural (Tony Bennett, 2005).

Peter Brooker (Peter, 1999) is of the view that 'Culture' refers to individual style or character, to a stage social group, to a socio-historical moment or a broad epoch. We talk about a cultured left foot, about the culture of football, about film culture, African, American or Scottish culture or the culture of the 1960s or 1980s. He further says that perhaps the most profitable way of studying such a mutable term is along the lines of Raymond Williams' account of its European usage. He further suggests that in its 'most widespread use' culture has referred in the later nineteenth and twentieth centuries to the world of the arts( literature, music, painting, sculpture, theatre, film). In this sense the term has nevertheless been understood and invariably valued in different ways. In traditional perspective it is seen as embodied in a selective canon of works comprising high culture and valued popular artistic forms such as 'low' or 'mass culture'to which some might wish to deny any genuine 'artistic' status. What is important here is the attitude taken towards mass or industrial or, in the twentieth century, advanced consumer society. Social and economic developments of the period have prompted the debates about culture in much more substantial form. The concept of 'culture' has been defined in relation to the historical form of society, traditionally once more in terms which see one as opposed to the other.

In the writings of Mathew Arnold, F.R.Leavis and T.S.Eliot, culture is seen as having been mobilized to serve a liberal or radical conservative ideology. Peter Brooker further argues that a similar defence has also informed the opposition to mass society of Marxists such as Theodor Adorno and others associated with the Frankfurt School of thought. In both traditions the valued culture is that of a minority or an elite, though the authors, artists, genres and individual works may be as different as the Greek classics, the realist novel, and the contemporary avant-garde (Peter, 1999).

It seems to me that perhaps the most influential conception of culture in the academic work, especially in the Humanities and Cultural Studies, has been Raymond Williams' own founding definition of culture as 'a whole way of life of a social group or whole society'. Writing in 1981, Williams (Williams, Culture, 1981) sees a convergence of the idea of culture a 'whole way of life' and its association with intellectual and artistic activity.

According to him what unites these emphases is the idea of culture as a signifying system, 'through which necessarily...a social order is communicated, reproduced, experienced and explored' (Williams, Culture, 1981, p. 13). It should not, however, imply that there is consensual definition of culture in the contemporary period; even that the idea of culture as a 'whole way of life' is universally accepted. In an early response to Williams, the Marxian Historian E.P.Thompson proposed an alternative definition of culture not as a 'whole way of life' but as a 'whole way of struggle' (Thompson, 'Review of The Long Revolution', 1961). Later on the influence of contemporary feminist, poststructuralist, postmodern and postcolonial theory have led many to reiterate the critiques of earlier notions of minority culture in terms now of white, western and male-centered bias. Further, many cultural critics might raise doubts concerning the homogenizing conception of 'the whole' and unified, or desire for this, in the realm of culture as in other fields (Peter, 1999).

A brief review of the history of anthropological thinking about culture shows where cultural anthropology stands in relation to these issues. It seems to me that the cultural anthropologists were using the term 'culture' to refer to two quite different, though not unrelated things: one a *phenomenal order* and the other an *ideational order* (Goodenough, "Rethinking 'Status' and 'Role': Toward a General Model of the Cultural Organization of Social Relationships", 1965).

The Phenomenal order refers to what an observer sees as patterns in the ongoing conduct of affairs—the actual enactment of activities—in a society or community. These patterns are manifested in the recurring regularities of modality and discontinuity that give apparent structure to events and human interactions and, taken together, constitute what is often referred to as a people's "way of life". In fact these patterns differ from one society to the next, and the term "culture" is often used in reference to them. Culture in this sense is the property of a society or group which does not distinguish humans from other social animals meaning that life among ants or bees is also patterned, and social animals may also be said to have culture in this sense of the term (David, 1996). In accordance with this view, social anthropologists such as A.R.Radcliffe-Brown, taking society rather than individual people as the object of study have treated culture as roughly equivalent to what they refer to as social structure. Distinguishing culture in this sense from that of social animals, and seeing the customary practices that characyerize a given society as learned by its members, Alfred L. Kroeber argued that culture belongs to the domain of what he called the "superorganic" and this has an existence governed by principles that are at a higher oerder of phenomena than those operating at the level of individuals (David, 1996).

Being a product of learning, Culture in the ideational sense, by contrast, consisted of what the members of a human group have to know in order to function acceptably as members of that group in the activities in which they engage (Goodenough, Cooperation in Change, 1963). This showed that in this sense culture is not necessarily shared by all the members of the group; but in the process of learning from one another, people attribute what they learn to one another and to the extent that these attributions enable them to accomplish their purposes with one another, creating the illusion of shared understandings and a common culture. This implied that each person's personal view of the world included an understanding of the expectations of various sets of others, and for each person a group's culture consisted of the expectations that he or she attributed to it. It also gave a sense that since no two persons in the group make identical attributions, the group's culture would be made up of the aggregation of its members' attributions (Goodenough, Culture, Language, and Society, 1981).

## Cultural Studies

Andrew Edgar and Peter Sedgwick (Sedgwick, 1999) propose a number of viewpoints with regard to the notion of "cultural studies". They suggest that the term "cultural studies" may be used not only to refer to all aspects of the study of culture and to encompass the diverse ways in which culture is understood and analyzed, for instance , in the various disciplines of sociology, history, ethnography and literary criticism, but also to refer to a distinctive field of academic enquiry. They further postulate that the historical roots of the concept of "cultural studies" can be traced back to the work of Raymond Williams and Richard Hoggart in the late 1950s and early 1960s and to the establishment of the Birmingham Centre for Contemporary Cultural Studies in 1964 with Hoggart and then Stuart Hill becoming its pioneer directors. It was this school of thought which was responsible for initiating multi-disciplinary approach to culture such as both orthodox approaches derived from the social sciences as well as radical approaches suggested by ,for instance, Marxism, feminism and semiotics. Under the directorship of Richard Hoggart and Stuart Hall from 1968-79, the centre developed many subject-matters of cultural studies and played a pivotal role in the development of cultural studies in UK. It was under the directorship of Richard Hoggart that research topics related with the themes of 'lived' culture of different classes were developed and promoted, being influenced by Hoggart's own work in *Uses of Literature* (1957) and later on themes associated with the centrality of the mass media, subcultures, education, race and gender were also taken up the research scholars as their subjects of study. Drawing mostly from sociology, literary criticism and also from history, the centre became interdisciplinary in nature. That the centre approached the mass media as ideological and hegemonic institutions drawing on the intellectual resources of contemporary Europe including both Althusser and Barthes' Structuralism was quite evident. The idea of popular culture was developed and seen as the site of the resistance and negotiation of marginal and disempowered groups within society (Sedgwick, 1999).

In 'The projection of Cultural Studies' Martin McQuillan ,talking about recognizing the becoming-cultural-studies of English, suggests that one can speak of the becoming-cultural-studies of English in humanities in general because the histories of cultural studies are multiple and contradictory in nature such as: " 'English' cultural studies, 'sociological' cultural studies, 'visual' cultural studies, 'media studies' cultural studies, Kulturwissenschaft, and so on" (Martin, 2003, p. 45). He further maintains that Gayatri Spivak speaks about 'Metropolitan cultural studies' in comparison to subaltern cultural studies whereas Hillis Miller comes up with new concept of 'tele-technology cultural studies' proposing that 'culture names the media part of a global consumerist economy'.

For many of us the freezes of post-modernism and post-colonialism have been refreshing. Be that as it may, there is no simple answer to the accusations that anthropology has served as handmaiden to colonial conquest and government, and for the most part was developed within intellectual frameworks distinctly modernist in design. Although most anthropologists working among the colonized have viewed their programme as one to alleviate the weight of colonialism by reducing its mistakes, anthropology- at least to the extent it has considered itself as a social science and not of the arts- has nevertheless inadvertently served colonialism's aim. It has also served the hegemony of modernist programmes of development and ways of thinking. How did this happen?

Cultural studies is not a monolithic body of theories and methods. Stuart Hall (Hall, 1992) makes this very clear:

> Cultural Studies has multiple discourses;it has a number of different histories. It is a whole set of formations; it has its own different conjunctures and moments in the past. It included many different kinds of work. It always was a set of unstable formations. It had many

> trajectories; many people had and have different theoretical positions, all of them in contention (Hall, 1992, p. 278).

Cultural studies has always been an unfolding discourse, responding to changing historical and political conditions and always marked by debate, disagreement and intervention.

John Storey (Storey J., Cultural Studies and the Study of Popular Culture: Theories and Methods, 1996) argues that Culture' in cultural studies is defined politically rather than aesthetically. The object of study in cultural studies is not culture defined in the narrow sense, as the object of aesthetic excellence('high art'); nor culture defined in an equally narrow sense, as a process of aesthetic , intellectual and spiritual development; but culture understood as the texts and practices of everyday life. Cultural studies regards culture as political— in a quite specific sense—as a terrain of conflict and contestation. It is seen as a key site for the production and reproduction of the social relations of everyday life. Perhaps the best-known elaboration of this way of seeing culture comes from Stuart Hall (Storey J. , 1994). He describes popular culture as

> an arena of consent and resistance. It is partly where hegemony arises, and where it is secured. It is not a sphere where socialism, a socialist culture—already fully formed—might be simply 'expressed'. But is one of the places where socialism might be constituted. That is why 'popular culture' matters (Storey J., 1994, p. 446).

Clyde Kluckhohn (Geertz, 1973, pp. 4-5) in his book entitled *Mirror for Man* has defined culture in turn as: (1) "the total way of life of a people"; (2) "the social legacy the individual acquires from his group"; (3) "a way of thinking, feeling, and believing"; (4) "an abstraction from behavior"; (5) "a theory on the part of the anthropologist about the way in which a group of people in fact behave"; (6) a "store-house of pooled learning"; (7) "a set of standardized orientations to recurrent problems"; (8) "learned behavior"; (9) "a mechanism for the normative regulation 0f behavior"; (10) "a set of techniques for adjusting both to the external environment and to other men"; (11) "a precipitate of history".

Pramod K. Nayar (Nayar, 2006) proposes a different formulation according to which Cultural studies is concerned with practices, institutions and modes of classification through which cultural values and norms are instilled in a population. Cultural studies aims at analyzing the forms and representational strategies of social and cultural power through which certain groups dominate other sections of the population and control the dissemination of meanings and values and cultural and interpretive domination often being coterminous with maintaining political and economic power over the dispossessed and the disempowered. Moreover, Cultural studies presents its methodologies and resources to agents of social change—such as several revolutionary movements—and establishes relations with specific cultural institutions and fields of cultural management.

Immanuel Wallerstein (Wallerstein, 2000) argues that culture is a way of summarizing the ways in which groups distinguish themselves from other groups. It represents what is shared within the group, and presumably simultaneously not shared(or not entirely shared) outside it. He further says that on the other hand, culture is also used to signify not the totality of the specificity of one group against another but instead certain characteristics within the group, as opposed to other characteristics within the same group. His contention is that we use culture to refer to the 'higher' arts as opposed to popular or everyday practice. We use culture to signify that which is 'superstructural'as opposed to that which is the 'base'. We use culture to signify that which is 'symbolic' as opposed to that which is 'material'.

Culture, Pramod K. Nayar (Nayar, 2006) informs us, can be defined as ideas, knowledge and modes of doing things. Cultural studies reveals what we assume to be natural and immanent in 'culture' as being rooted in complex negotiatios of power over meanings. During the course of this negotiation, some elements of the cluster are closed off and marginalized. Soon the valorized elements become established as 'true'('high') culture, whilethe other elements are 'lost'. And finally, once this hierarchy of 'high' and 'low' is in place, it becomes 'naturalized'.

'Culture', according to Raymond Williams (Williams, Keywords: A Vocabulary of Culture and Society, 1976), is a very complex word in English Language which includes both material things and symbols. Pramod K.Nayar (Nayar, 2006) argues that the bourgeois class in the modern state has to govern with the actual consent of the governed and for this consent to happen the class becomes an 'educator' as it seeks to raise the mass of the population to a moral-cultural level that suits its own interests (Gramsci, 1971, pp. 258-60). He further is of the view that cultural mechanisms of the arts, religion anf education are the means through which consent is secured and power effected. The state itself divides into political society and the cultural ideological apparatus of civil society and important thing to note here is that the relation between these levels is the arena of Cultural studies. Furthermore, public culture is a component of this civil society, a realm of social meanings and pleasures, the globalized, hybridized spaces where elite/non-elite, urban/non-urban, literary/oral, cosmopolitan/local, metropolitan/folk elements mix messily. Public culture is a space where meanings are contested, distorted and revived in a continuous process. Public culture includes cinema, advertisements, television, celebrity gossip in magazines and newspapers, autobiographies and biographies of public figures ,websites and web-pages of institutions, tourist guides and leaflets, museums, comic strips etc.

Cultural studies is interested in the ways in which culture works its strategies of inclusion and exclusion. It is interested in the process by which power relations between and within groups of human beings organize cultural codes, forms of knowledge and identities located in the realities of race, gender, class and caste. Moreover, an emphasis on discourse and textuality is central to Cultural Studies. Subjects, identities and relationships are constructed out of discourse. Cultural Studies ask questions about the process through which the understanding and reading of cultural texts is effected. Cultural Studies analyses modes of representation in popular/mass culture, while locating both within political economy. It thus pays particular attention to the material conditions of cultural production, such as the printing and publishing industry, the advertisements and forms of media publicity, reviewing and the politics of institutional teaching. It shifts focus from the author as the transcendent authority to social contexts of the production of texts and meanings.

Cultural studies also deals with the question of the 'Other'. It suggests that the dominant class has maintained its power through process of Othering, classifying social groups as philistines, savage and 'uncultured', treating them as objects of knowledge and, therefore, subject to power and control. In addition, Cultural Studies is also interested in the socio-cultural process through which women, the differently abled, the working classes, the non-white races and qeers become 'othered' or marginalized. As an example of the process of power-negotiations within a society, one can look at the marginalization of the Dalitbahujan culture in India. Sanskrit and English both functioned as controlling devices—they established 'national cultures' by ignoring and deliberately silencing other cultural forms and languages. Culture is thus power: who wields it and who controls the narrative-interpretive acts.

Within Indian context, with its own systems of domination, reading culture involves 'interfacing' the intracultural and intercultural. We need to radically contextualize local(folk,tribal, genders pecific, caste-linked) cultures.

Chris Jenks (Jenks, 1993, p. 7) maintains that the idea of 'culture' can be witnessed emerging in the late eighteenth century and on into the nineteenth century as part of, and largely as a reaction to, the massive changes that were occurring in the structure and quality of social life. These changes, at the social, political and personal levels, were both confusing and disorienting; and at least controversial. Such changes, through industrialization and technology, were unprecedented in human experience; they were widely expansionint, horizons were simply consumed; grossly productive, for good and ill; and both understood and legitimated through an ideology of progress. The social structure was politically volatile, being increasingly and visibly divisive. This was a situation brought about through the new forms of ranking and hierarchy that accompanied the proliferating division of labour, through urbanization, and improved system of communications.

He further argues that in one sense the overall aesthetic quality of life, compared with the previously supposed rural idyll, was threatened by the machine-like excesses of industrial society. There was an increasing gap between the creative and the productive, formulated for materialism by Marx as 'alienation', and for the romantic-idealist tradition by Carlyle as a loss of the folk purity of a past era. The machine was viewed as devouring the natural character of humankind, a call to be echoed in the work of the Frankfurt School, Benjamin's 'Age of Mechanical Reproduction', even Marcuse's sense of 'one-dimensionality', and finally the cri de Coeur of Baudrillard's evocation of postmodernism with its horror of simulacra. Whereas we began with 'culture' mediating between 'man' and 'nature', it can now be seen to mediate between 'man' and 'machine'. This provides us with several available 'meanings' of culture.

Chris Jenks (Jenks, 1993, p. 157), answering the question as to what cultural studies means, concludes with a list of almost nine points in the form of attributes deriving from Agger's (B.Agger, 1992) formulation.

1. Cultural studies operates with an expanded concept of culture. It rejects the assumptions behind the 'cultural debate' and thus rejects the high/low culture binary or, indeed, any attempt to re-establish the grounds for any cultural stratification. It adheres more closely to the anthropological view of culture as a totality.
2. Following from the above, cultural studies legitimates, justifies, celebrates and politicizes all aspects of popular culture. It regards popular culture as valuable in its own right and not a 'shadow phenomenon' or simply a vehicle for ideological mystification.

3. The proponents of cultural studies, as representative of their age, recognize the socialization of their own identities through the process of mass media and communication that they seek to understand..
4. Culture is not viewed as stasis, as fixed or as a closed system. Cultural studies regards culture as emergent, as dynamic and as continual renewal . Culture is not a series of artefacts or frozen symbols but rather a process.
5. Cultural studies is predicated upon conflict rather than order. It investigates and anticipates, conflict both at the level of face to face interaction but also, and more significantly, at the level of meaning. Culture cannot be viewed as a unifying principle, a source of shared understanding or a mechanism for legitimating the social bond.
6. Cultural studies is 'democratically' imperialistic. As all aspects of social life are now 'cultured' then no part of social life is excluded from its interests—opera, fashion, gangland violence, pub talk, shopping, horror films and so on… they are no longer colonized, canonized or zoned around a central meaning system.
7. Cultural representations are viewed by cultural studies at all levels- inception, mediation and reception, or production, distribution and consumption.
8. Cultural studies is interdisciplinary, it acknowledges no disciplinary origin, it encourages work on the interface of disciplinary concerns and it acknowledges a shifting and sprightly muse.
9. Cultural studies rejects absolute values- it does what it wants.

Ken Hirschkop and David Shepherd (Hirschkop,Ken and shepherd, David, 1989) are of the view that the idea of a common language and the goal of a democratic society have long been linked. After the establishment of the modern nation-state, it was assumed that access to an arena of public vernacular discourse was equivalent to access to political power, in so far as it allowed one to participate in the deliberative process whereby social values and priorities were determined. The advent of 'mass' forms of politics, general literacy and 'mass' culture should have led to thoroughly democratic societies based on the discourse of an entire nation.

'Culture' has over the past few decades become one of the buzz words of our contemporary times dominating the media, popular discourse and social science. There seems to be at the popular level an ever-increasing interest in the rituals, folkways, dialects, food habits and similar phenomenon which constitute culture in the popular understanding. Instead of promoting the homogenization of cultures, contrary to the predictions of many thinkers, globalization of the economy and media seems only to have increased awareness of differences since understanding a culture and its symbols and meanings is now perceived as a necessary prerequisite for effective corporate promotion. Globalisation has been a cause of the current interest in different cultures. It has certainly made other cultures more easily accessible to us (Joseph, 1998).

Because of the widespread assumption that understanding the guiding principles of a culture can help to explain and predict the attitudes, responses and actions of members of a culture, culture is now often used as a catch-all explanation for a wide range of phenomena. Cultural explanations are seen as an alternative to the economistic explanations which had dominated social science for so long. Widespread recourse to culture as a source of social explanation has unfortunately not been matched by a corresponding deepening of our understanding of the role of culture in society. In much of the discussion in social science, culture has been conceptualized as constituted of world-views, belief systems, aesthetic expressions and other ideational phenomena and as a relatively autonomous social process. Even where it has been conceptualized as the 'whole way of life of a people', the grounding of culture in the material dimensions of social life has not been adequately theorized (Joseph, 1998).

The study of culture in social science has been closely linked to the problem of understanding the 'other'. Anthropologists who followed the colonial expansion of the Western powers believed that the key to understanding other societies lay in understanding their culture. Culture, they held, expressed the specific genius of a community and cultural practices helped to reproduce the community and maintain a stable cultural identity for it. A powerful model of premodern societies gained currency in anthropology which presented these societies as static, organically integrated, and guided by cultural values rather than by rationality. Culture, according to this model, represented the ensemble of ideas and beliefs which helped to reproduce the society over time. It constituted the ethos through which members of the society lived and experienced their lives (Joseph, 1998).

## Postmodern Art and Technoculture

Margot Lovejoy (Thomas Carmichael and Alison Lee, 2000, p. 95) in the article "Transaesthetics" states that living in the postmodern conditions of the interim between one country's end and the beginning of the new; we confront a greatly revised cultural context brought about by major technological advances. Today's crisis in art is far more profound than the one that took place at the beginning of the last century when photography and cinematography shattered existing traditions of representation. Today's universal digital technologies deeply affect new conditions for communication—the way art is produced, disseminated, and valued. They shift totally the very paradigm of cognition and representation under which we have been operating since the Renaissance (Lovejoy, 1997).

It is important to note that fundamental to the understanding of the impact of technology on cultural change is the work of cultural critic Walter Benjamin, who, in his significant 1935 essay "The work of art in the age of mechanical Reproduction"(widely disseminated in translation by the early seventies), brought into a key position for the first time critical awareness of the relationship between art and technology. His assessment creates an important framework for understanding how widespread integrated changes in technological conditions can affect the collective consciousness and trigger important changes in cultural development. Benjamin argues, using photography as a prime example of the relationship between major changes in technological conditions and the formation of culture, that the very invention of photographic processes from 1850 essentially undermined the existing function of art, not only because it could provide visual reportage but also because it it threatened the "aura" and value of the original, the handmade object that relied on the specialized skills of the artist. Benjamin understood that once a camera record images or events unique to a particular time and space, a disruption of privacy takes place. A loss of original magic, spirit, authenticity, or aura occurs. Uniqueness is destroyed.

Benjamin's postulation was that photography was not simply a visual medium but a means of reproduction for making endless copies from a single original, an aspect that Benjamin acknowledged as the major factor affecting art in its relation to the new age of mechanical reproduction. He asserts that the copying processes of photography undermined the marketplace value of the original , threatening the very foundations of the existing art establishment that were based on the aura of "unique works of original genius" created by hand skills of individual "great masters". According to Benjamin , photographic reproduction and the cinema raised social questions about the role of the artist, about the audience for art, and about art as communication rather than art as object, thus bringing into focus the social function of art as opposed to its commodity value. The copying of an artwork increases its currency in the public consciousness. Art that is enlarged , reduced, and printed in different forms such as postcards or billboards and is widely disseminated reaches an expanded audience beyond the confines of art institutions and the gallery system. As a consequence , the cultural sphere is broadened , enriched, and democratized. Paradoxically, this added exposure increases the value of the original. However, when artworks are seen in many different contexts removed from their original time periods and settings, their meanings change. They begin to mean something else and to fragment into new sets of fresh associations.

Benjamin was the first to stud mass culture as a focus of philosophic analysis. In his essay " The Author as Producer", he anticipated the current crisis of identity and the loss of moral authority of the author/artist. His interdisciplinary thinking anticipated the interwoven, layered structuring of associations and observations that has come to be understood as the postmodern. However, it is clear from Benjamin's writings , particularly the "Arcades Project", that while he understood the potentially positive influence of technology on art and culture, he was also aware of the major losses incurred by its advances.

Benjamin's work has influenced contemporary cultural critics and theorists from various sources who have gone beyond him to provide the most illuminating commentary on current representation issues vis-à-vis mass media and major new technological advances in the digital realm: Baudrillar on simulacra, simulation, and hyperreal; Barthes and Foucault on intertextuality and interactivity; and Derrida and the feminist movement on deconstruction. Their contemporary theoretical understanding, furthering those of Benjamin, are useful tools for probing the postmodern and its relationship to technological advance. It is interesting to note that some of these theoretical concepts closely correspond to the structure and functioning of electronic media tools themselves.

There is no denying the fact that Postmodernism is a shift to an essentially broader territory where the suppression of social and cultural influence is no longer possible. The defining moments in the visual arts, when the shift to postmodernism began, was in the late fifties, when architectural forms of representation began to be radically revised away from pure formalist tendencies of "Modernism" and and "International Style" toward the more vernacular. New technological conditions, including electronic communication networks such as television, deeply invaded private space, creating a new kind of cultural infrastructure. Postindustrial capitalism based on electronic technologies under development from the fifties and sixties ushered in a new kind of "information society", a "society of spectacles". Television acted as the crucible for a postmodern consciousness by challenging our concepts of space, simultaneity, and individuality. The very structure of television is postmodern one where equal value is asserted between all the elements. One of the first effects of television on the mind is the "marked mitigation of the distinction between public and private consciousness. A manifestation of this is an increasingly altered sense of ourselves as we become more media dominated; our television becomes our real selves. We lose our private selves in publicity. With the invasion of television into the living rooms, the boundaries between high art and popular culture began to shift when a group of pop- movement artists began to demonstrate the direct connections between art and increasingly technologized consumer society.

Several Avant-garde movements in sixties and seventies moved in opposition to the still-dominant modernist aesthetic toward an expanded dematerialized view of art that refused the object: Earth Art, Fluxus, Performance, Conceptual Art, and work that incorporated the new electronic media tools, especially video and the computer. What is interesting to note here is the fact that the incorporation of of mass culture and photographic reproduction methods into the fine arts by the pop representation, marks the moment of a major crisis for representation. Ironically. Once photography was accepted into the fine arts canon, all the issues denied for so long under the rubric of modernism became the very focus of it, the very means of deconstructing it. The deconstruction of the fine arts canon began through widespread use of tools of critical theory—particularly concerning the issues brought out earlier by Walter Benjamin(concerning aura, identity, the copy and the original, death of the author, originality and genius)— along with poststructuralism, psychoanalysis, and feminist theory. The deconstruction process, particularly by feminists, raised consciousness regarding the marginalization of certain artists not only because of gender but also because of race or class.

In "The Death of the Author", Barthes( (Barthes, "The Death of the Author", 1977) asserts that the author(or artist) is never the source and site of meaning and that meaning is never invented or locked in. A work exists in a "multi-dimensional space in which a variety of writings, none of them original, blend and clash. The text is a tissue of quotations drawn from the innumerable centers of culture" The artist/author is no longer the only container for feelings, impressions, and passions, but he is rather "this immense dictionary from which he draws a writing (image) that can know no halt: life never does more than imitate the book, and the book itself is only a tissue of signs, an imitation that is lost, infinitely deferred." (Barthes, "The Death of the Author", 1977, pp. 146-47) Foucault also wrote about representation in *The Order of Things* and in "What is Author?"

The very pervasiveness of media technologies in modern society creates a new set of questions calling for new theories of the relationship between language, behavior, and belief, and between material reality and its cultural representation. Baudrillard (see (Baudrillard, 1988)speaks about the veritable bombardment of images and signs as causing an inward collapse of meaning where mass media feedback dominates reality. Is there any absolute knowledge when there is no longer an authentic message, when there is only the absolute dominion of information as digitized memory storage banks? The constant melting down of forms causes a kind of "hyperreality", a loss of meaning due to the neutralization of difference and of opposition, that dissolves all claims to universal truth.

Sherrie Levine makes use of 'appropriation' as an important element. Her critique of the market system involves rephotographing and thus appropriating in their entirety the works of other well-known artists (such as Walker Evans, Alexander Rodchenko, and Piet Mondrian) and signing the fabricated copies as her own. Like those of Duchamp and Warhol before her , this outstandingly radical neodadaist body of work Hs created a sensation, forcibly bringing the issue of the copy and the original into focus.Levine's use of other artists' work to question the copy and the original recalls the issues raised by Duchamp when he exhibited in a gallery his readymades—objects not only made by machines but also produced industrially as multiples of an object. Duchamp pointed out that the meaning and value of art is constructed product of the mind and that changing the context of an object could create a new meaning for it and could enable it to be seen in a different perspective.

Barbara Kruger's work essentially offers a further illustration of these major tendencies in art and their relationship to technology. She raises ironic questions about representation in relation to social constructs. She uses the copy and appropriation as the major site for her theoretically based work. Her strategy is to reproduce found images from mechanically produced sources and to add text to them so that they function effectively as an active commentary. This forcefully raises issue about female presence so long excluded by the patriarchy. Her work is confrontational, agitational, and is aimed at destroying a certain order of representation: the glorification of the original that up until now has been all male.

Thus it can be argued that deconstructive strategies opened the way to alternative representations that involve social and cultural issues as a major context in the way ideas can be presented. The feminist movement that evolved as a result of the dramatic social change of the sixties contested the modernist canon with its formalist criticism in ways that profoundly ruptured art's social position and practice. Using the deconstructive strategies concerning the rhetoricity of texts first developed by Paul De Man, in combination with the theories of Walter Benjamin and Roland Barthes, feminist artists unearthed very different views related to history. They questioned the male dominated litany of aesthetic values, of artistic criteria, and of art-historical practices. Suppressed and marginalized for so long by the dominant power structure, they began to interrogate profoundly and to alter the subject matter for art and the way art is practiced and positioned. By introducing into their work feminist content through the use of innovative new materials and techniques, they brought into the field of representation new views of gender, of identity, and of the body as subject matter, and they dismantled, as we have seen, traditional notions of originality and authorship with their fresh outlook they created new forms of mixed media exploration such as the body art of Hannah Wilke, the performance work of Carolee Schneemann, and the video installation of Adrian Piper.

It would not be wrong to state that , culturally, postmodernism is characterized by major change: from the concept of a single Eurocentric cultural stream dominated by white male privilege to one that recognizes diverse identities and voices interacting in a complex web of ideological and behaviorist associations. Eurocentric thought assumed a centered, authoritative voice based on a single worldview, structured through domination and transformation of subjected cultures. This attitude, no doubt, now seems outdated in the face of a globalized, transnational information economy. Even the process of analysis itself is suspect and subject to deconstruction, a factor that has led to uncomfortable "correctness" issues in relation to the overthrow of traditional Western systems of thought, as they have been practiced up to now in intellectual and critical communities to reveal their darker underside.

## Folk Culture and Folk Song

Chitrasen Pasayat (Pasayat, 1998) demonstrates that Folklore is commonly believed to be the oral literature that is handed down to us from generation to generation through oral tradition. It generally incorporates folk songs, folk dances, folk tales, superstitions, myths, etc. The scope of folklore is much wider. It includes material and nonmaterial, verbal and non-verbal cultures. Therefore, an attempt to study folk culture in its true sense should thereof include an analysis of folk speech, folk architecture, folk costumes, the notion of time in Folk society, i.e., folk year, folk religion, folk recreation, folk literature, folk dances, folk play, folk arts etc. The list is inexhaustive, but it does suggest the fact that the area of folk culture embraces into its fold the total way of life and in this sense, folklore is only a part of the folk culture.

John Storey's point of view with regard to the 'folk culture' is that 'in the late eighteenth, throughout the nineteenth, and into the early part of the twentieth century, different groups of intellectuals, working under the different banners of nationalism, Romanticism, folklore, and finally folk song, "invented" the first concept of popular culture. In fact these and debates eventually produced two definitions of popular culture. The first was popular culture as a quasi-mythical rural "folk culture", and the other—and it was very much the "other"—was popular culture as the degraded "mass culture" of the new urban-industrial working class'.

In the late eighteenth and early nineteenth centuries, as "traditional" popular culture, and the "traditional" cultural relations between dominant and subordinate classes, began to collapse under the sweeping impact of industrialization, urbanization, and the emergence of an urban-industrial working class, many European and American intellectuals started to take a special interest in the culture of the "folk" (Burke, 1996).Middle class men and women began to demand stories and songs from the people from whom they had previously demanded only labor and respect. In this way, then, folk culture was very much a category of the learned, constructed by intellectuals, especially collectors, editors, and publishers, and not a concept generated by the people defined as the folk.

John Storey (Storey J. , Inventing Popular Culture: From Folklore to Globalization, 2003) asserts that the collecting of, and the theorizing about, the culture of the folk occurs in two historical periods. The first period.(when the objects of collection and study were "ballads" and "folk tales") began with the publication of Thomas Percy's *Reliques of Ancient English Poetry* in 1765 and ended with Francis James Child's *The English and Scottish Popular Ballads* (the first volume of the first edition was published in 1857, the third edition in 1898). The second period (when the object of collection and study was the "folk song") began with the publication of Carl Engel's *An Introduction to the study of National Music* (1866) and ended with the publication in 1907 of Cecil James Sharp's *Folksong: Some Conclusions.*

The term folk-lore (later folklore) was introduced into the English language in 1846. In a letter to the *Athenaeum*, W.J. Thoms(writing under the alias Ambrose Merton) proposed that what had previously been known as "popular antiquities" would be better described as "Folk-Lore—the Lore of the People". A year later Mary Howitt introduced the term folk song (*Howitt's Journal of Literature and Popular Progress*, April 17, 1847).

The collecting of songs and stories was institutionalized with the formation of the Folk-Lore Society in 1878 (the first International Folk-Lore Congress was held in 1891) and the Folk Song Society in 1898.

John storey(2003) maintains that the "discovery" of folk culture was an integral part of emerging European nationalisms. The role of actual folk—rural workers—was mainly symbolic. From the very influential work of Johann Gottfried Herder in the 1970s to the last major contribution to the debate on folk song, that of Sharp in 1907 (Sharp, 1907), *folk culture is the very embodiment of the nature and character of a nation.* In Herder's work on folk culture the natural and the national blur. The value of *Volkslied* (folk or people's song), is that it is almost an outgrowth of nature: it is the nature in which the culture of the nation can be grown. Herder argued that folk song still possessed what all poetry had once possessed a moral or civilizing function. Folk song thus represented a fundamental challenge to artificial and inauthentic modes of living. As such it suggested the possibility of return to a more "grounded" or "rooted" culture; a return to culture before the Fall into the corrupting conditions of industrialization and urbanization, which for Herder was producing artificiality at the "top" and degradation at the "bottom" of society (Storey J. , Inventing Popular Culture: From Folklore to Globalization, 2003).

John storey(2003) thinks that the collectors of folk culture idealized the past in order to condemn the present. The rural worker—the peasant—was mythologized as a figure of nature, a 'noble savage' walking the country lanes and working without complaint the fields of his or her betters the living evidence of , and a link to a purer and more stable past. The urban-industrial worker, however, was fixed firmly in the present, completely detached from any salvation the past may have been able to offer. Further, proof of fall from grace was for all to see in the urban-industrial worker's unquenchable taste for the corrupt and corrupting songs of the music hall. John Storey(2003) contends that whereas the middle class could be encouraged to connect to a more organic past by embracing folk songs, the working class would have to be forcefully schooled in folk song in the hope of softening their urban and industrial barbarism, especially as it was made manifest in their enjoyment of the songs of music hall. Sir Hubert Parry, in his "Inaugural Address to the Folk Song Society" in 1899 warned his audience that 'there is an enemy at the door of folk music which is driving it out, namely, the common popular(music hall) songs of the day; and this enemy is one of the most repulsive and most insidious". Music hall is presented as symptomatic of the supposedly degraded culture of the urban working class.

Hubert parry (Parry, 1899) shows his concern about the fact that the problem was not just that music hall was so bad but that it "will drive out folk-music if we do not save it. For even in country districts where folk-songs linger, the people think themselves behindhand if they do not know the songs of the seething towns; and as soon as the little urchins of distant villages catch the sound of a music hall tune , away goes the hope of their troubling their heads with the old fashioned folk-songs" (Parry, 1899, p. 2). He states that unlike the music hall produced by "town civilization", English folk music is "among the purest products of the human mind". He was very happy about the founding of the Folk Song Society believing that it was 'a hopeful sign'.

Cecil Sharp (Sharp, 1907, p. 137) pressed for the introduction of folk songs into elementary schools as a means to civilize the masses. 'Folk-songs", according to him had greater 'value as an educational force'. He strongly believed that the "study of folk-song will…stimulate the growth of the feeling of patriotism" (135), bringing us back to questions of nationalism. He insisted that not only are folksongs an educational force, their presence in the education system would change the practice of education for the betterment of the society.

Commenting on 'Imagining the Past to Make the Present' John Storey argues that the idea of folk culture was a romantic fantasy with a view to healing the wounds of the present and safeguarding the future by promoting a memory of a past which had little existence outside the intellectual debates of the late eighteenth, nineteenth, and early twentieth centuries. There existed a lost world of the authentic, a culture before the fall into industrialization, urbanization, and the unavoidable visibility of class relations. There was no denying the fact that folk culture survived in the oral traditions of the folk, people did not understand the treasure they held, and the fact that they were disappearing as a group; it was, therefore, the task of the intellectuals —true inheritors of folk culture—to secure its continuation, with a view to using it to solve the social and cultural problems produced by industrial capitalism (Storey J., Inventing Popular Culture: From Folklore to Globalization, 2003).

According to Robert Redfield (Redfield, The Folk Society and Culture, 1940)differences in concept, problem, and field procedure between anthropology and sociology are in part functions of differences in their usual subject matters: the primitive societies as contrasted with the urbanized societies. Awareness of this fact has been developed by studies made of peasant societies and of primitive peoples changing under urban influence.

There results a conception of an ideal primitive or folk society. The urbanized, peasant, and tribal society may be compared in part in terms provided by Maine, Durkheim, and Tonnies. The concept of "culture," developed by anthropologists, reflects the integrated body of conventional understandings corresponding to a self-sufficient community, as observed in folk life. Other characteristics of anthropological analysis of society, as contrasted with sociological, similarly expressive of the nature of folk society, are the disposition to represent the society and culture in terms of "pattern" or "structure"; the relatively small development of problems of sampling, the emphasis on formalized kinship institutions, and certain emphasis of meaning in such words as "status" and "class." These considerations lead toward recognition of opposing or complementary processes: that by which the ultimate values of a society develop an organization and consistency which gives a group moral solidarity; and the expansion of the technical and economic system with consequent impairment of the moral organization.

It is evident from Redfield's views discussed above that the usage of the term 'folk' is in the juxtaposition to the concept of 'urban', thereby creating binaries and strengthening dichotomies. Talking about the folk society Robert Redfield (Redfield, The Folk Society, 1947) says that 'Understanding of society may be gained through construction of an ideal type of primitive or folk as contrasted with modern urbanized society. Such a society is small, isolated, non-literate, and homogeneous, with a strong sense of group solidarity. The ways of living are conventionalized into that coherent system which we call "a culture." Behavior is traditional, spontaneous, uncritical, and personal; there is no legislation or habit of experiment and reflection for intellectual ends. Kinship, its relationships and institutions, are the type categories of experience and the familial group is the unit of action. The sacred prevails over the secular; the economy is one of status rather than of the market. These and related characterizations may be restated in terms of "folk mentality"

George M.Foster (Foster G. M., 1953) holds anthropologist Redfield responsible for providing such terms as 'folk' and 'urban' societies. In this paper, Foster discusses Redfield's hypothesis and logical assumptions of 'folk culture', suggesting an alternative concept of folk culture and providing a theoretical framework within which a number of culture problems of a general nature may be explored. According to Foster Redfield approached the problem of folk culture both from an empirical and rational or logical point of view. As a skilled field worker trained in the inductive thinking of traditional American anthropology he recognizes that culture theory must be based upon the facts of real life societies. As a theorist whose thinking- as he himself points out- has been markedly influenced by European philosophical sociology, he is interested in relating ethnographic fact to a broader schema of culture. In a descriptive sense he finds folk societies self-sufficient groups homogeneous in race and custom. Their components parts are closely interdependent, personal relationships are face to face. Technology is simple and division of labor is slight. The family plays a large part in societal institutions, the sanctions which govern conduct are predominantly sacred, piety is emphasized, and ritual is highly developed and expresses vividly wishes and fears of the people. Such a society is relatively immobile, change is slow, the ways of life form a single web of interrelated meanings and habits of members tend to correspond to custom. The total list characterizes the hypothetical ideal society. Any particular real society would have most but not necessarily all of the elements. In a theoretical sense he places folk societies in a logical system made up of two ideal polar types represented by urban and non-urban (i.e. 'folk') societies. The ideal folk society is a mental construction (and presumably also the ideal urban society) in that no society precisely corresponds to it primitive, though primitive societies studied by anthropologists approximate it. It is rationally defined "through assembling, in the imagination, the characters which are logically opposite those which are to be found in the modern city..." (Foster G. M., 1953, p. 160).

For Simon Frith (Payne, 1996) "Folk Culture" is a term which only makes conceptual sense by reference to a particular interpretation of "industrial culture". Shiach (Shiach, 1989) argues that the idea of the "folk" was developed in the context of industrialization and can only be understood by reference to the critique of industrial society developed by Romanticism. Folk culture described the culture of preindustrial (premarket, precommodity) communities, and was therefore taken to be organized around a number of characteristics: the oral transmission of songs, tales and history; aesthetic authorization by the tradition; the integration of nature and culture, body and mind; expression through rituals, in the collective deployment of symbols. Shiach maintains that "folk" is not an anthropological term rather it is an ideological construct and it necessarily includes a critique of "modern" societies.

Simon Frith (Payne, 1996) further believes that the idea of folk culture has in fact served a number of different political and cultural ends. As an aspect of nationalist ideology, folk culture is taken to be expressive of the true spirit of a nation, of its underlying beliefs and values, as articulated in specific forms of dress, speech, music, storytelling, cookery, design, etc.

Thus folk music became an essential part of the construction of European national identities in the nineteenth century (and folk songs and dances were a feature of the "national" compositions.

The idea of folk culture was also taken by Marxists in the construction of working-class consciousness ("the folk" it should be noted, describes only serfs and peasants; members of ruling class are, by definition, excluded). On the one hand, "the folk" defined the continuity of proletarian culture; on the other hand, folk culture could be presented as the "pure" form of working-class culture, untouched by the seductions of commerce. Finally, the most common use of the idea of folk culture today is almost certainly as a tourist, a way of signaling what makes a country or locale different. In this sense, "folk culture" now describes ways of singing, dancing, dressing, and indeed of making things, which are artificially preserved by the state as a kind of domesticated exotica(and as the basis of a business in souvenirs) (Payne, 1996).

Robert Redfield (Redfield, 1934)), in the course of ethnological work carried on among Maya of Yucatan on behalf of the Carnegie Institution of Washington, observes two types of society: The one type of society, approached in the village, is a relatively immobile society, culturally homogeneous, in which the ways of life form a single web of interrelated This culture is closely adjusted to its local milieu. The Relationships are personal, and the important institutional controls are familial. The sanctions which control conduct are prevailingly sacred, piety is the force of moral rule. Ritual is highly developed, and expresses vividly the wishes and fears of the people. On the other hand, as one leaves the village and moves through the town to the city, one goes toward a contrasting type of society. This society is much more mobile, and culturally heterogeneous. The ways of life are less closely interrelated; group habits exist more in terms each of itself, and do not to the same degree evoke a body of closely associated and definatory acts and meanings. These ways of life rest upon, but are not of, their natural environment. Relationships are increasingly impersonal, and formal institutions qualify the acts of the individual. The familial organization is much reduced in importance as an instrument of control. Life is secularized; economic advantage and valuation have penetrated the social body; and the individual acts from constraint or convenience rather than from deep moral conviction Religious belief and action are much reduced; the individual can no longer express himself in the comfortable groove of sacred ritual. What is of importantance for us all to note here is the fact that he calls the former type of society as "Culture", and the latter type as "Civilization". He argues that this kind of experience is one of deculturalization, rather than of acculturalization and it may be more acceptable to describe this study as that of the change from folk culture to city culture.

Lord Raglan (Raglan, 1947) says that the cult of folk-music in this country is, of course, due largely to Sharp, and we owe to him the preservation of many beautiful songs dances which would without him have been lost. But our admiration his efforts in the cause of folk-music does not compel us to accept his theories of its origin. In a paper which he read before this Society in 19o8, he said that there were two schools of thought, of which one held that the folk-tune was composed by an individual just like any other tune; that there is distinct line of cleavage between folk-music and art-music; that anonymity of authorship is a mere accident, and that the popular song is popular not in origin but in destination. On the other hand, he continued, are those who affirm that folk-music can be sharply distinguished from art-music, and that the former is generis. He was convinced that the latter view was the correct one, and gave his reasons. The first is that a great deal of English folk-music is cast in a mode that is scales, which in art-music have been obsolete for at least three centuries. He says that before 16oo, skilled musicians were not tune-makers but tune-manipulators, and frequently drew upon the store of folk-tunes for their themes, acknowledging the fact on the title-pages of their compositions.

Lord Raglan (Raglan, 1947) further claims that for Sharp folk-music is sui generis because a great deal of it is in these old modes ; it follows that at least some of it is in the newer art modes, and that on his own showing folk-music is not sui generis. Sharp goes on to say that art-music down to the year I550 was "of course built upon folk-music"; the "of course" is the other way round; the unskilled have always learned from the skilled, and not vice versa. He then tells us that after 1550 new developments revolutionized music, but that the folk continued to make their own way, just as they have preserved their own forms of folk-speech. But making and preserving are two very different things.

## Performing Art: Dance Analysis

Many of the early texts on dance were written by dance instructors, dramaturges and critics. Dance Criticism—the analysis and evaluation of dance works—focused on not only assessing the work of choreographers but also highlighting the aesthetics of a dance form and validating a form of practice. Dance criticism also integrated dance studies into the academy as critics produced writing that addressed the social and cultural significance of dance. While dance critics take viewing and description as their base from which they offer evaluation and interpretation, other dance writers attended to the question of how dance is viewed and described in the first place. One of the most pivotal shifts for dance studies was the expression of semiotics into the analysis and interpretation of choreography. Recourse to structuralist thought allowed dance to establish itself as an autonomous field, demonstrating that dance possessed a legibility that rendered it available to analysis.

Janet Lansdale(writing as (Adshead, 1988), for example proposed such a method for the observation, description, interpretation and evaluation of a dance work. In her early work, Lansdale did not take up a textual metaphor but her attention to the breaking down of a dance into components parallels structuralist studies of language. Her explicit discussion of the process of dance analysis indicates the extent to which an informed viewer can 'read' a dance, interpreting its meanings by understanding its fundamental units.

Poststructuralist texts complicated the analysis of dance by highlighting the constructed nature of knowledge and its intertwinings with the structures of power, challenging the idea of objectivity and encouraging a shift away from scientific models in the humanities. (Foster S., 1986), for instance, drew upon both structuralist and post-structuralist positions. Contesting the ephemerality, naturalness and ineffability of dance, Foster also argued for its legitimacy as an area of academic inquiry. Her text, by mobilizing literary and rhetorical theory in the interest of the analysis of dances, located the interpretation of meaning in the work itself through a consideration of its codes and conventions, while also engaging the cultural and historical construction of those codes, a move that brought dance into dialogue with the more recognized disciplines of English and philosophy.

The legacy of textual analysis in dance studies is bifurcated. For some authors, such as Stephanie Jordan, formal scrutiny and the combination of formalism with semiotics remain primary. For others, attention to form and to the close study of dances provided the background against which further interpretation can be carried out. A significant shift for dance studies was the interpretation of dance studies in political terms, especially , those associated with the politics of identity, such as gender, race, class and sexuality. Gender interpretataions influenced the early phase of' new dance studies' scholarship, either tied to the close reading of a particular dance work (Daly, 1987), to the politics invested in a specific dance form (Meduri, 'Bharat Natyam: What are you?, 1988) Foster 1996b), or to the choreography of masculinity and femininity in particular cultural and historical circumstances (Adaire, 1992), (Burt, 1995), (Franco, 1995), (Banes, 1998)).

The idea of studies of identity later extended to the production of race in dance (Dixon- Gottschild 1996, DeFrantz 2002, 2004a, 2004b, Chatterjee, 2004, Manning 2004). Political readings of dance also included economic and class based interpretations of performance (Martin 1996, Graff 1997, Franco 2002), sexuality and performance (Desmond 2001) and the choreographing of nationalism (Manning 1993, Savigliano 1995). Choreographic analysis served a dual purpose for dance studies by clearly eslablishing a field of investigation as well as by attending to specific works in the interest of interdisciplinary inquiries, especially those focused on the politics of identity. This turn to social, cultural, and political meaning intersects with strategies deployed by artists working in areas that cross dance and performance art.

Lord Raglan (Raglan, 1947) asserts that it is now generally realized that what are now called folk-dances were formerly danced at courts. Folk-dance enthusiasts, however, never cease to assure us that the folk-dance originated on the village green. This is apparently a collective term, so that we are asked to suppose that by some miraculous process "Brighton Camp" sprang up spontaneously on a thousand greens, where, by another miracle, it was given the same name. We know that at courts there were professional dancers, dancing- masters, and composers and organisers of masques and seasonal pageants. To suppose that these experts went to yokels if they wanted a new step for their dances is as absurd as to suppose that professors go to fourth-form boys if they want a new idea for a book

Dance as an epistemology is a diverse cultural matrix where invariably new contemporary dance occurs alongside continuing traditions such as tribal folk, court dances and ritual practices, expressing all aspects of life, tradition and change. Dance is also a 'meeting point' for modernity and post-modernity, history and 'post-history', the present and the future where complex aesthetic and philosophical challenges are negotiated. Moreover, artists keep on addressing these challenges with integrity and subtlety through developing unique performance styles that are constantly evolving (Burridge, Stephanies, and Wang Yunyu, 2012).

The period from the 1980s to the early 2000s was one of intense activity in dance scholarship , characterized by fundamental shifts in the field. The dance work and the artist's biography did no t remain the primary concerns of the Dance writers but they dealt with how dances engage with their social, historical, political and economic contexts. Most publications of the mid to late 1990s speak of the emergence of 'new dance scholarship' framing its major preoccupations, including the overt acknowledgement of the need to translate the moving body to the written word, the consideration of dance as 'text', the relationship of the practice of dance to its theorization, and the interconnections between the dancing body and individual and group identities (Morris, 1996). These concerns positiomed dance studies as an interdisciplinary field as they indicated both the approaches it borrowed from other fields and the ways in which it could inform other disciplines. Scholars, at the Sme time, legitimized the field by claiming its distinctiveness, especially from theatre, music and physical education with which it had been conventionally associated.

Given the development of influence, it is necessary to examine the key investments of this field and aligning them with the socio-political concerns of the time of their emergence(1980s and 1990s) as well as with issues in choreographic production. Moreover, it is better to place new dance studies in a broader context, linking its interests to those of the writings that preceded it.

Janet O'Shea (Alexandra Carter and Janet O'Shea, 2010) suggests that four strands of intellectual activity, each of which predate the emergence of dance studies as a separate arena, laid the ground for the present day field: anthropology, folklore, and ethnography; the writings of expert viewers and dance analysis; philosophy, especially aesthetics and phenomenology; historical studies including biography and dance reconstruction. These categories, according to her, are not exhaustive or watertight; there is some overlap between them. All of these approaches transformed over time to address issues of identity and their articulation in dance, a shift from an authoritative position to a multiplicity of voices, and changing relationships between performance, choreography and writing. In dance studies, as in other fields, English operates as the *lingua franca*. While recent conferences have attempted to challenge the exclusionary effects of this English-language dominance, the exchange still moves primarily in one direction—English-language texts into translation more than non-English texts translated into English.

## Indian Perspective

Dance is at once, amongst the arts, the most primitive and the most sophisticated. In *Traditions of Indian Folk Dance* Kapila Vatsyayan argues:

> There is hardly a civilization or culture wherein the awareness of human movement as a vehicle of expression of joy and of sorrow is not evident.

> Perhaps before man began to speak and to paint, he began to dance (Vatsyayan, 1976).

Tribals or adivasis in India, Padma Vibhushan Pandit Birju Maharaj claims, have been the first settlers of the undistributed forests, mountains, and valleys, wherein they have developed various domains of socio-cultural life. Music, Dance, Folklore and songs, which are an integral part of their culture have also been developed therein. Each tribe has maintained its uniqueness about aesthetics. At the same time many tribes also share certain aspects of dance and music in common. He further maintains that:

> I strongly believe that the theatrical aspect of the traditional dances of India such as Kathak, Kathakali etc., have their roots in folk dance forms. These artists may have borrowed several aspects from tribal dances in the due course of development (Tribhuwan, Robin D. and Preeti R. Tribhuwan, 1999).

It is said: "The Tribe that dances never dies" and apparently it goes without saying that the Tribal of India feel much deep within their innermost selves, with the blessings of their holy spirits, that dancing is an art that counteracts all the evil forces of death, keeping them out of reach. Consequently, the moving claws of Death appear frozen and invisible as they celebrate their lives. It implies the fact that the Tribal don't dance to entertain an audience but to celebrate life and these celebrative dances are now known as folk dances. If life is a boundless river, every dancer is a wave in it. The wave in its graceful rise and fall does celebrate the flow, but it requires a multitude of waves to celebrate the river. Therefore perhaps the folk dances are mostly performed by a group rather than a solo dancer. While dancing in unison with several other dancers each experiences that he or she has had have been multiplied and the Individual has become Universal. What must be borne in the mind here is the fact that in the group dancing "I" is a political term, which is to say, "I" drowns itself in "We". It follows the conceptual understanding that here self "I" belongs to the public "We" and the public find a voice in the self.

The Tribal of India have, as per the growth of the civilization, developed various dimensions of socio-cultural life namely, Music, dance, folklore and songs, which have become an integral part of their culture; and each Tribe has maintained its own uniqueness about these aesthetic aspects of life. Moreover, it would be appropriate to say that the theatrical aspects of the traditional dances of India such as *Kathak, Kathakali*, etc., have found their roots in folk dance forms.

However, the growth of civilization- in the form of modernization and urbanization- has corrupted the happiness of the tribal by adversely affecting their nature-bonded life; and it is, indeed, very disheartening to note that these Tribal music, folk dances , folklores, etc., are gradually vanishing in front of our post-modernist spectacled eyes and still we are left helpless.

Dance for the tribal is not just a form of recreation, rather their entire life and being are interwoven with music and dance and a full appreciation of them is not possible without a knowledge of their life and living. Music and dance are not specialized aspects of tribal life as they are in ours. "The dance," says Curt Sachs, the author of the monumental work, 'History of the Dance', "is the mother of the arts. Music and poetry exist in time; painting and architecture in space. But the dance lives at once in time and space". The Fact that the tribal are poor and economically backward does not deter them from dancing. Even though they may not have any instruments or materials for other arts, merely their rhythmic pattern of movement of the body can itself be a source of joy for them and the whole community. The nature has endowed them with a fine body and music and dance are in their soul becoming the chief instrument of their culture (Sachchidananda, 1965).

The kind of role dance and music play in the socialization of the tribal child is enormously substantial and significant. Children, having been spell bound by the music and dance, sit themselves between their father's knees, their tiny hands striking the cymbals or metal keys or holding the drumsticks, eventually effecting them into absorbing the rhythm and postures of the dance. For every occasion, birthdays and weddings, for purification, feasts, for driving away diseases and demons there is appropriate music and dance. There are, in practice, two ways of participating in dance. People either dance and sing or sit as spectators. It is almost a state of being part from within the feeling rather than action. Once the tribal enter the exotic atmosphere of dance, they remain there being intoxicated by the warmth of the charged atmosphere as if in their familiar landscape. There is no demand for anything from anywhere; it is just there to be enjoyed in a variety of ways.

Sachchidananda in his book *Profiles of Tribal Culture in Bihar* (1965) rightly points out that "an exploration of the hidden springs of music and dance in tribal life is rewarding" (p.47). He argues that the tribals live, move and have their being among the sights and sounds of nature. The murmur of a forest streamlet, the sight of a waterfall, a peacock spreading his multi-coloured feathers, a herd of goats or sheep grazing quietly, a bell tinkling here and there, trees laden with flowers and fruit swell the spring of music. A tribal youth tending cattle in a lonely valley or on a hill top beguiles his solitude with melodies produced by the flute. Wherever they are, the tribal give vent to their emotions of joy or sorrow without any inhibition. Music and dance mark these occasions and through them the tribal express themselves. Their numerous festivals give them repeated opportunities for the display of music and dance for long periods. One interesting characteristic of their festivities is the fact that on these festivals and occasions there is a free flow of the native tribal drink , a kind of home brewed beer prepared from rice , mahua etc. The drink acts as a stimulant and gives them so much energy that even a whole night's dancing does not tire them out. For the time being they forget all their troubles, economic and otherwise. They have no emotional tension, no mental reservations and the only restraints on their behavior are those prescribed by the social code. Dance and song supplement each other. The sweeter the melody, the more vigorous and spirited is the dance. There are no silent dances. The full throated melody and the exquisite footwork are vitally connected.

One unique feature of the tribal society is that the social structure of the tribal promotes song and dance. And that is because there is complete equality between the sexes. Young men and women meet in the dancing ground of their own village and go in a body for visits to other villages where they are honored guests. The dancing ground is not only a place of entertainment or training in song and dance, it is also a rendezvous for courtship. This role of music and dance is fully recognized by society. Gils and boys excel each other in these arts so that they may attract the best partners. Their songs laden with the love theme have a seductive charm. Due to its association with tribal courtship it has even been called an expression of stylized animality. A closer study of the social function of dance in tribal India reveals that it is much more than this. Its roots may be found in love and war, while some of the best dances have sprung from the expression of religious devotion. Dance has so much common with poetry that Plutarch called it 'silent poetry'. Bergson, the philosopher interpreted it in terms of 'grace and rhythm' and held it to be 'a symbol of spiritual life'. Nietzsche saw it 'an image of wisdom'. Dancing helps the tribal forget their poverty and anxiety for the time being. It gives them at the same time a sense of discipline and organization and a feeling for group or community.

## Intertextuality

The notions of trace, absence and flickering presence are central to the construct of intertextuality. Whether the notion of intertextuality as used in literature is the same as that used in dance or music or film and media is something that needs debate. When used in music it seems to be a less open concept, where texts are linked from within to contextual information, as in 'intertextual correspondences'. This is closer to source criticism, where notions of influence continue to be evident. It is a version of intertextuality in which late works illuminate early ones and early works point to meanings in later ones.

The construct of 'intertextuality' is helpful in several senses. Firstly, it is a method of tracing the interrelationships of actual people, hiding behind, and reflected in, the terms 'author', 'text' and 'reader'. Secondly, it can identify and clarify the potentially conflicting sets of genre coding that add other layers to the possible modes of interaction—between the choreographer, the dance and the spectator. Thirdly, intertextuality can reveal both what is present in these texts and what is absent, pointing to the traces that dominate and those that appear to retreat as we construct different readings. Since people interacting and dancing are inevitably embodied, the body itself becomes highly visible, although often through(paradoxically) its absence in critical writing and its metaphoric use elsewhere. Fourthly, intertextuality focuses on the social and cultural representation of embodied human beings, since it looks outside the conditions of dance discourse to its interaction with other discourses.

According to Peter (Peter, 1999) 'Intertertextuality' is a term implying that individual texts are inescapably related to other texts and their meanings are correspondingly provisional and plural according to how these relations are discerned and highlighted. He claims that the term is associated with the 'linguistic turn' to structuralism, and with the insights of Derrida's deconstruction. He further argues that a further brief theorization occurs in an early essay by Julia Kristeva (Kristeva, 1986) who saw in Mikhail Bakhtin's concepts of dialogics and carnival the logic that 'any text is construed as a mosaic of quotations; any text is the absorption and transformation of another (Kristeva, 1986).

Peter (Peter, 1999) further contends that intertextuality implies a method of composition but essentially it has determined a way of reading; one which is neither confined to the supposedly immanent meaning of a given text nor seeks this meaning in an 'external' source. Instead, intertextuality promotes a lateral reading across the surface of different interwoven texts. Roland Barthes asserts in 'The Death of the Author' that 'we know that a text is not a line of words releasing a single 'theological' meaning…but a multi-dimensional space in which a variety of writings, none of them original, blend and clash. The text is a tissue of quotations drawn from the innumerable centres of culture.' (Barthes, The death of the author, 1977, p. 146). He continues on the next page saying that 'in the multiplicity of writing, everything is to be disentangled, nothing deciphered; the structure can be followed, 'run'...at every point and at every level, but there is nothing beneath: the space of writing is to be ranged over, not pierced (Barthes, The death of the author, 1977, p. 147)'.

Elaborating on the differences between a structuralist and poststructuralist models of intertextuality, Peter (Peter, 1999) asserts that the poststructuralist model has been the more influential though there are significant differences between poststructuralist models of intertextuality. Peter points out that in the situation where intertextuality is understood as the very condition of language and the production of meaning, there is in principle no restraint on the writings 'ranged' over and made relevant. He cites, for instance, an example of the version of poststructuralism adopted by the Yale school of literary critics in the United States for having taken this route and charged in English commentary particularly with the production of errant and self-indulgent readings. Further, a more focused and 'centred' intertextual reading will follow the references, echoes and allusions of a given text situating it. There is another reading concerned with a given text, which might detect and foreground marginal, self-contradictory, or repressed textual and ideological meanings. What is important to note here is the fact that an intertextual reading may also join with other approaches such as psychoanalytic, feminist, Marxist or postcolonial approaches.

Stephen Heath (Payne, 1996, p. 258) defines the term 'intertextuality' as 'a term proposed by Julia Kristeva, drawing on Mikhail Bakhtin's notion of dialogism ("the necessary relation of any utterance to other utterances") to indicate a text's construction from texts: a work is not a self-contained, individually authored whole, but the absorption and transformation of other texts, "a mosaic of quotations" (Kristeva, 1986). This is not about influences but of the multifarious and historically variable relations between works as heterogeneous textual productions. Julia Kristeva developed this perception in a generic study of "the text of the novel" as resulting from the combination or transposition of several different SIGN systems (Kristeva, 1986), while Roland Barthes analyzed a single Balzac story as a tissue of "voices", redeploying and recasting fragments from a range of discourses on which it depends for its intelligibility (Barthes, S/Z, 1970 (1975)). It follows, Stephen Heath thinks, that such an approach through intertextuality situates literary structure within social structure as itself textual.

In the context of poststructuralism, Stephen Heath further submits that intertextuality displaces intersubjectivity: the reading of the text is seen not as a subject -to- subject exchange between author-source and reader-receiver, but as performance by author and reader of a multitude of writings that cross and interact on the site of the text. It is important to notice that a text is thus never finished , written once and for all; it exists in the continuing time of its intertextual production, which includes the texts of its future(those that will be brought to its reading)-as intertext it has, in Barthes' words, "no law but the infinitude of its recurrences."

Michael Riffaterre (Riffaterre, 1979 (1983)) defines 'intertextuality' as 'the reader's perception of the relations between a text and all the other texts that have preceded or followed it.' He advocates for two kinds of intertextuality: *aleatory intertextuality* (the reader brings the text into play with his or her familiar texts) and *obligatory intertextuality* (the "hypogram" or core intertext that is a work's matrix, presupposed in its reading). Gerard Genette (Genette, 1982) propounds five types of transtextuality, his overall term for the relations a text may hold with others; with intertextuality limited to the specific relation of copresence, the effective presence of one text in another through quotation, plagiarism, or allusion. Henry Louis Gates (Gates, 1988) presents a particular intertextual historical account of the Afro-American literary tradition as characterized by signifying: texts talking to and from other texts in a self-reflexive process of repetition and revision that seeks to make representational space for "the so called Black Experience" (Payne, 1996, p. 259).

Andrew Edgar and Peter Sedgwick (Sedgwick, 1999) are of the view that the term 'intertextuality' was coined by Julia Kristeva to indicate that a text (such as a novel, poem or historical document) is not a self-contained or autonomous entity, but is produced from other texts. They seem to suggest that the interpretation that a particular reader generates from a text will then depend on the recognion of the relationship of the given text to other texts. They argue that intertextuality may be understood as the thesis that no text exists outside its continuing interpretation and reinterpretation, that there can then never be a definitive reading of a text, for each reading generates a new text, that itself becomes part of the frame within which the original text is interpreted.

## References

A.L. Kroeber and C. Kluckholn. (1952). *Culture:A Critical Review of Concepts and Definitions.* New York: Vantage Books.

Adaire, C. (1992). *Women and Dance:Sylphs and Sirens.* New York: New York University Press.

Adshead, J. (1988). *Dance Analysis: Theory and Practice.* London: Dance Books.

Alexandra Carter and Janet O'Shea. (2010). *The Dance Studies Reader.* New York: Routledge.

Allison, L. (1996). 'Power'. In I. McLean(ed.), *The Concise Oxford Dictionary of Politics* (pp. 396-9). Oxford: Oxford University Press.

Anand, S. (2014). *Annihilation of Caste: The Annotated Critical Edition.* New Delhi: Navayana Publishing Pvt Ltd.

Apperley, A. (1996). 'Foucault Michel'. In I. McLean(ed.), *The Concise Oxford Dictionary of Politics* (p. 187). Oxford: Oxford University Press.

Archer, M. S. (1988). *Culture and Agency: The place of Culture in Social Theory.* Cambridge: Cambridge University Press.

Archer, W. (1943). 'Santal Poetry'. *Man in India*, XXIII, 147-53.

Archer, W. (1944). 'Festival Songs'. *Man in India*, XXIV, 70-74.

Archer, W. (1944). 'More Santal Songs'. *Man in India*, XXIV,141-44.

Archer, W. (1945). 'Santal Rebellion Songs'. *Man in India*, XXV, 207.

Archer, W. (1946). 'Santal Transplantation Songs'. *Man in India*, XXVI, 6-7.

Austin, J. L. (1962). *How to Do Things with Words.* Oxford: Oxford University Press.

Averill, G. (1997). *A Day for the Hunter, Aday for the Prey: Popular Music and Power in Haiti.* Chicago,IL: Chicago University Press.

B.Agger. (1992). *Cultural Studies as Critical Theory.* London: Falmer.

Banes, S. (1998). *Dancing Women:Female Bodies on Stage.* London: Routledge.

Barthes, R. (1970 (1975)). *S/Z.* trans. Richard Millar,Oxford: Blackwell.

Barthes, R. (1972(1957)). *Mythologies.* London: Trans. Annette Lavers, Cape.

Barthes, R. (1972(1964)). *Critical Essays.* Evanston,ILL: Northwestern University Press.

Barthes, R. (1977). "The Death of the Author". In t. Heath, *Image-Music-Text* (pp. 142-48). New York: Hill and Wang.

Barthes, R. (1977). The death of the author. In R. Barthes, *Image-Music-Text.* Ed.Stephen Heath,London: Collins.

Baudrillard, J. (1988). *Selected Writings. Ed.Mark Poster.* Stanford, Calif.: Stanford University Press.

Bauman, Richard and Charles L. Briggs. (1990). Poetics and Performance as Critical Perspectives on Language and Social Life. *Annual Reviews of Anthropology 19*, 59-88.

Bhabha, H. K. (1994). *The Location of Culture.* London: Routledge.

Bhattacharya, S. (1968). *Ethnomusicology and India.* Calcutta: Indian Publications.

Bhowmick, A. C. (1999). Santal Dance. In R. D. Tribhuwan, *Tribal Dances of India* (pp. 303-305). New Delhi: Discovery Publishing House.

Bodding, P. (1916). *The Traditions and Institutions of the Santals.* Second Edition of HORKOREAN MARE HAPRAMKO REAK' KATHA with a foreword by P.O.Bodding.Benagaria: Santal Mission Press.

Bohlman, P. (2007). *The Silence of Music.* British Library/Royal Holloway Lectures in Musicology 2006/7, February/March 2007.

Bompas, C. (1909). *Folklore of the Santal Parganas.* London.

Bourdieu, P. (1993). *The Field of Cultural Production: Essays on Art and Literature.* Trans. Richard Nice. Cambridge: Polity.

Bowman, P. (2003). *Interrogating cultural studies: theory, politics, and practice.* London: Pluto Press.

Brandel, R. (1961). *The Music of Central Africa.* Natherlands: The Hague Martinus Nijhoff.

Browning, B. (1995). *Samba: Resistance inMotion.* Bloomington, IN: Indiana University Press.

Bruckner, Heidrun.et al. (2007). *The Power of Performance: Actors,, Audiences and Observers of Cultural Performances in India.* New Delhi: Manohar Publications.

Burke, P. (1996). *Popular Culture in Early Modern Europe, revised reprint.* Aldershot: Scolar Press.

Burridge, Stephanies, and Wang Yunyu. (2012). *Identity and Diversity: Celebrating Dance in Taiwan.* New Delhi: Routledge.

Burt, R. (1995). *The Male Dancer: Bodies, Spectacle, Sexualities.* London: Routledge.

Carver, T. (1982). *Marx's Social Theory.* Oxford: Oxford University Press.

Cashmore, E. a. (1999). *Dictionary of Cultural Theorists.* London: Arnold.

Castaldi, F. (2006). *Choreographies of African Identities: Negritude, Dance, and the National Ballet of Senegal.* Champaign, IL: University of Illinois Press.

Clifford, J. (1988). *The Predicament of Culture: Twentieth-Century Ethnography, Literature, and Art.* Cambridge, M.A.: Harward University Press.

Clifford, J. (1988). *The predicament of culture:Twentieth-century ethnography, literature, and art.* Cambridge,MA: Harvard University Press.

Coles, A. (2000). *Site Specificity: The Ethnographic Turn.* London: Black Dog Publishing.

Culshaw, W. (1949). *Tribal Heritage: A Study of the Santals.* London: Lutterworth Press.

Culshaw, W. (2004(Indian Edition)). *Tribal Heritage: A Study of the Santals.* New Delhi: Gyan Publishing House.

Daly, A. (1987). 'The Balanchine Woman of hummingbirds and channel swimmers'. In *The Drama Review(TDR)31* (pp. 3-12).

David, L. a. (1996). *Encyclopedia of Cultural anthropology,Vol.1.* New York: Henry Holt Books.

Deshmanjhi, C. (1938). *Chotrae Deshmanjhi reak Katha.* Benagaria.

During, S. (1993). *The Cultural Studies Reader.* London and New York: Routledge.

During, S. (1999). *The Cultural Studies Reader.* New York: Routledge.

Foster, G. M. (1953). What Is Folk Culture? *American Anthropologist*, New Series, Vol. 55, No. 2, Part 1 (Apr. - Jun., 1953),pp. 159-173.

Foster, S. (1986). *Reading Dancing: Bodies and Subjects in Contemporary American Dance.* Berkeley,CA: University of California Press.

Foster, S. (1986). *Reading Dancing: Bodies and Subjects in Contemporary American Dance.* Berkeley,CA: University of California Press.

Foucault, M. (1977). *Discipline and Punish: The Birth of the Prison.* Harmondsworth: Penguin.

Franco, M. (1995). *Dancing Modernism/Performing Oilitics.* Bloomington,IN: Indiana University Press.

Gates, H. L. (1988). *The Signifying Monkey.* Oxford: Oxford University Press.

Geertz, C. (1972). Deep Play: Notes on the Balinese Cockfight. *Daedalus 101*, 159-69.

Geertz, C. (1973). *The Interpretation of Cultures.* New York: Basic Books.

Geertz, C. (1973b). 'Ideology as a Cultural System'. In C. Geertz, *The Interpretation of Cultures* (pp. 193-233). New York: Basic Books.

Genette, G. (1982). *Palimpsestes: la litterature au second degre.* Paris: Seuil.

Goodenough, W. H. (1963). *Cooperation in Change.* New York: Russell Sage Foundation.

Goodenough, W. H. (1965). "Rethinking 'Status' and 'Role': Toward a General Model of the Cultural Organization of Social Relationships". In B. Michael, *The Relevance of Models for Social Anthropology.* London: Tavistock.

Goodenough, W. H. (1981). *Culture, Language, and Society.* Calif: Benjamin-Cummings.

Gramsci, A. (1971). *Selections from the Prison Notebooks.Selected and tr. by Quentin Hoare et.al.* London: Lawrence and Wishart.

Greenblatt, S. (1982). *The Forms of Power and the Power of Forms in the Renaissance.* Norman: University of Oklahoma Press and Pilgrim Books.

Habermas, J. (1971). *Knowledge and Human Interests.* Boston: Beacon.

Habermas, J. (1975). *Legitimation Crisis.* Boston: Beacon.

Habermas, J. (1979). *Communication and the Evolution of Society.* Boston: Beacon.

Habermas, J. (1985(1987)). *The Philosophical Discourse of Modernity.* trans. Frederick Lawrence, Cambridge: Polity Press.

Hall, S. (1992). 'Cultural Studies and its Theoretical Legacies'. In L. E. Grossberg, *Cultural Studies.* London: Routledge.

Hall, S. (1997a). 'The Spectacle of the"other"'. In S. Hall(ed.), *Representation: Cultural Representations and Signifying Practices* (pp. 223-79). London: Sage/ Open University.

Hall, S. (1997b). 'The Work of Representation'. In S. Hall, *Representation: Cultural Representations and Signifying Practices.* London: Sage/Open University.

Herzfeld, M. (1991). 'Silence, Submission, and Subversion:Towards a Poetics of Womanhood'. In P. L. Papataxiarchis(eds), *Contested Identities: Gender and Kinship in Modern Greece* (pp. 79-97). Princeton, NJ: Princeton University Press.

Hirschkop,Ken and shepherd, David. (1989). *Bakhtin and cultural theory.* Manchester and New York: Manchester University Press.

Jenks, C. (1993). *Culture.* London: Routledge.

Joseph, S. (1998). *Interrogating Culture: Critical Perspectives on Contemporary Social Theory.* New Delhi: Sage Publications.

Kristeva, J. (1986). 'Word, dialogue and novel'. In T. Moi, *The Kristeva Reader.* Oxford: Blackwell.

Kunst, J. (1955). *Ethno-Musicology.* Natherlands: The Hague Martinus Nijhoff.

Kurath, G. (1964). *Iroquois Music and Dance.* Washington: Smithsonian Institution Bureau of American Anthology.

L.O.Skrefsrud and Kolean, Haram. (1928(7th edition1968)). *Horkoren Mare Hapramko reak' Katha.* Benagaria: Santal Mission Press.

Leppert, Richard and McClary Susan. (1987). *Music and society: The Politics of Composition, Performance and Reception.* New York: Cambridge University Press.

Lipsitz, G. (1994). *Dangerous Crossroads: Popular Music, , Postmodernism and the Poetics of Place.* London: Verso.

Lomax, A. (1968). *Folk Song Style and Culture.* Washington: American Association for the Advancement of Science.

Lovejoy, M. (1997). *Postmodern Currents: Art and Artists in the Age of Electronic Media. 2nd Ed.* Upper Saddle River, NJ: Prentice Hall.

Man, E. (1867). *Sonthalia and the Santhals.* Calcutta: Geo Wyman & Co.

Martin Clayton, Byron Dueck, and Laura Leante. (2013). *Experience and Meaning in Music Performance.* New York: Oxford University Press.

Martin, M. (2003). The Projection of Cultural Studies. In P. Bowman, *Interrogating Cultural Studies: Theory, Politics and Practice* (pp. 41-55). London: Pluto Press.

McMains, J. (2006). *Glamour Addiction: Inside the American Ballroom Dance Industry.* Middletown,CT: Wesleyan University Press.

Meduri, A. (n.d.).

Meduri, A. (1988). 'Bharat Natyam:What are you? In *Asian Theatre Journal,5,1(Spring)* (pp. 1-22).

Merriam, A. (1967). *Ethnomusicology of Flathead Indians.* New York: Wenner-Gren Foundation for Anthropological Research.

Morris, G. (1996). 'Introduction'. In G. Morris, *Moving Words: Re-writing Dance.* London: Routledge.

Nayar, P. K. (2006). *Reading Culture: theory, praxis, politics.* New Delhi: Sage Publications.

Ness, S. (1992). *Body, Movement and Culture: Kinesthetic and Visual Symbolism in a Philippine Community.* Philadelphia, P.A.: University of Pennsylvania Press.

Nettle, B. (1956). *Music in Primitive Culture.* Cambridge: Harvard University Press.

Nooshin, L. (2009). *Music and the Play of power in the Middle East, North Africa and Central Asia.* England: Ashgat ePublishing Ltd.

Novack, C. (1990). *Sharing the Dance: Contact Improvisation and American Culture.* PhD dissertation: Columbia University.

O'Shea, J. (2010). Roots/Routes of Dance Studies. In A. C. O'Shea, *The Dance Studies Reader* (pp. 1-15). New York: Routledge.

Parry, H. (1899). "Inaugural Address". *Jounal of the Folk Song Society*, 1:1, 1-3.

Pasayat, C. (1998). *Tribe, Caste and Folk Culture.* New Delhi: Rawat Publications.

Payne, M. (1996). *A Dictionary of Cultural and Critical Theory.* Oxford: Blackwell.

Peter, B. (1999). *Cultural theory: a glossary.* London: Arnold Publishers.

Prasad, O. (1987). *Folk Music and Folk Dances of Banaras.* Calcutta: Anthropological Survey of India.

Qureshi, R. B. (2002). *Music and Marx: Ideas, Practice,Politics.* New York: Routledge.

Raglan, L. (1947, Jun). The Origin of Folk-Culture, Vol. 58, No. 2. *Folklore*, pp. 250-260.

Ray, S. (1973). *Music of Eastern India.* Calcutta: Firma K.L.Mukhopadhhaya.

Redfield, R. (1934). Culture Changes in Yucatan. *American Anthropologist, New Series, Vol. 36, No. 1 (Jan. - Mar., 1934)*, 57-69.

Redfield, R. (1940). The Folk Society and Culture. *American Journal of Sociology*, Vol. 45, No. 5 (Mar., 1940), pp 731-742.

Redfield, R. (1947). The Folk Society. *American Journal of Sociology*, Vol. 52, No. 4 (Jan., 1947), pp. 293-308.

Ricoeur, P. (1986). *Lectures on Ideology and Utopia.* ed. Geogre H.Taylor. New York: Columbia University Press.

Riffaterre, M. (1979 (1983)). *Text Production.* trans. Terese Lyons, New York: Columbia University Press.

Sachchidananda. (1965). *Profiles of Tribal Culture in Bihar.* Calcutta: Firma K. L. Mukhopadhyay.

Sachs, C. (1937). *World History of the Dance, trans. Bessie Schonberg.* New York: W.W. Norton.

Said, E. (1979). *The Question of Palestine.* New York: Random House.

Said, E. (1993). *Culture and Imperialism.* New York: Alfred A. Knopf.

Savigliano, M. (1995). *Tango and the Political Economy of Passion.* Boulder,C.O.: Westview Press.

Schechner, R. (1985). *Between Theatre and Anthropology.* Philadelphia: University of Pennsylvania.

Scott, J. C. (1990). *Domination and the Arts of Resistance: Hidden Transcripts.* New Haven,CT: Yale University Press.

Sedgwick, A. E. (1999). *Key Concepts in Cultural Theory.* London: Routledge.

Sharp, C. J. (1907). *English Folk-Song: Some conclusions.* London: Novello.

Shelemay, K. K. (2001). *Soundscapes: Exploring Music ina Changing World.* New York: Norton.

Shiach, M. (1989). *Discourse on Popular Culture.* Cambridge: Polity Press.

Singer, M. (1972). *When a Great Tradition Modernizes: An Anthropological Approach to Indian Civilization.* London: Pall Mall Press.

Sinha, P. (1970). *An Approach to the Study of Indian Music.* Calcutta: Indian Publications.

Slobin, M. (1976). *Music in the Culture of Northern Afghanistan.* Vikingfund Publications in Anthropology No.54.

Sparks, C. (1996). 'The Evolution of Cultural Studies...'. In J. Storey, *What is Cultural Studies?: A Reader* (pp. 14-30). London: Arnold.

Storey, J. (1994). *Cultural Theory and Popular Culture: A Reader.* Hemel Hempstead: Harvester Wheatsheaf.

Storey, J. (1996). *Cultural Studies and the Study of Popular Culture: Theories and Methods.* Edinburgh: Edinburgh University Press.

Storey, J. (1996). *What is Cultural Studies? : A Reader.* London: Arnold.

Storey, J. (2003). *Inventing Popular Culture: From Folklore to Globalization.* UK: Blackwell Publishing.

Thomas Carmichael and Alison Lee. (2000). *Postmodern Times.* Dekalb: Northern Illinos University Press.

Thompson, E. (1961). 'Review of The Long Revolution'. *New Left Review,* 9, 24-33.

Tony Bennett, L. G. (2005). *New Keywords: A Revised Vocabulary of Culture and Society.* UK: Blackwell.

Tribhuwan, Robin D. and Preeti R. Tribhuwan. (1999). *Tribal Dances of India.* New Delhi: Discovery Publishing House.

Troisi, J. (1979). *The Santals: Readings in Santal Life; Volume 1: Religion and Magic.* New Delhi: Indian Social Institute.

Turino, T. (1983). 'The Charango and the Sirena: Music, Magic, and the Power of Love'. *Latin American Music Review*, 4(1),81-119.

Turino, T. (1984). 'The Urban-Mestizo Charango Tradition in Southern Peru: A Statement of Shifting Identity'. *Ethnomusicology*, 28(2), 253-70.

Turner, V. (1982). *From Ritual to Theatre: The Human Seriousness of Play.* New York: Performing Arts Journal Publications.

Vatsyayan, K. (1976). *Traditions of Indian Folk Dance.* New Delhi: Clarion Books.

Wallerstein, I. (2000). Culture as the Ideological Battleground of the Modern World-system. In D. V. Brydon, *Postcolonialism: Critical concepts in literary and cultural studies* (pp. 1824-45). New York: Routledge.

Waterman, C. A. (1990). *Juju: A Social History and Ethnography of an African Popular Music.* Chicago, II.: University of Chicago.

Williams, R. (1976). *Keywords: A Vocabulary of Culture and Society.* London: Fontana.

Williams, R. (1979). *Politics and Letters.* London: Verso.

Williams, R. (1981). *Culture.* London: Collins.

Wilson, J. (1858). *India Three Thousand Years Ago.* Bombay: Smith,Taylor and Co.

Wuthnow, R. J. (1984). *Cultural Analysis: the work of Peter L. Berger, Mary Douglas, Michel Foucault, and Jurgen Habermas.* London: Routledge & Kegan Paul.

## Chapter Two

# A Worldview of the Santal Traditions and Folk Dances

The Santals, mostly to be found in Jharkhand and West Bengal, the largest homogeneous tribe in India, can also be found in large numbers in the Indian states of Assam, Meghalaya, Chhatisgarh, Bihar and Odisha. When it comes to studying the Literature of the Santal world of existence, P.O.Bodding is certainly a name to conjure with. He was a missionary with a difference. It was he who rescued from oblivion the hidden treasure buried among the Santals in Bengal and Bihar(earlier it was Bihar, it has now been bifurcated into two states of Jharkhand and Bihar) over long centuries. The Dictionary of the Santal language that he compiled is a monument of dedication, scholarship and dogged perseverance. Coming from far off Norway, he lived and mixed with the Santal folk of our country as no foreigner had ever done before him. What is most surprising is that he became an authority on santal language and society and even Santal medicine. Between 1925 and 1940 the fruits of his studies in Santal Medicine and Folklore were published by the Asiatic Society in three instalments that soon went out of print (Bodding, Studies in Santal Medicine and Connected Folklore: Part I,II and III, 2001(Second Reprint)).

Although a great deal of information about the Santal world of meaning is scattered in various books, journals, office reports, and missionary accounts, it seems to me, however, that there are two important books which form the most important source books today for the study of Santal universe of discourse. They are: Firstly, *The Traditions and Institutions of the Santhals, Horkoren Mare Hapramko reak Katha*, originally published from the Santali text by L.O.Skrefsrud in 1887—after the translator's death it was edited by Sten Konow ; later translated with notes and additions and published by P.O.Bodding in 1942— as a guide for the Santals, especially in the customary matters dealt with in the book, and also on account of its ethnological value (Bodding, Traditions and Institutions of the Santals(Horkoren Mare Hapramko Reak Katha), 1942).According to P.O.Bodding (Bodding, Traditions and Institutions of the Santals, 1994(First Indian Reprint)) 'the original work was taken down by Skrefsrud from the mouth of an old guru, named Kolean and according to a statement towards the end of the book the dictation was finished on the 15th of February, 1871'.In the words of P.O.Bodding, "Skrefsrud once told me, that he had hunted everywhere among the Santals to find a man who knew his people and their traditions and customs, and that Kolean without comparison was the best authority he had been able to find. Skrefsrud further told me, that the book contains absolutely nothing of his own, the whole being a faithful record of Kolean's words and language" (Bodding, Traditions and Institutions of the Santals, 1942(First Indian Reprint1994))

The second book which deserves to be mentioned here is *Studies in Santal Medicine and Connected Folklore*, written by P.O.Bodding, a Sacandinavian missionary, and published in three parts by the Asiatic Society of Bengal, forms the most important source book today. P.O.Bodding of the Scandinavian Mission in the Santal Parganas and well known for his works on the life and customs of the Santals, proposed in 1922 to publish a series of monographs entitled *Studies in Santal Medicine and connected Folklore* in the Memoirs of the Royal Asiatic Society of Bengal. This was accepted by the Council and Volume X of the Memoirs was assigned to the Series. Part I of the Series under the title of 'the Santals and Disease' and Part II on 'the Santal Medicine' appeared in 1925 and 1927 respectively. Part III entitled 'the Santals and how they live', however, though the manuscript was received as early as March 1938 but delayed due to the revision of the language of the author(whose mother tongue was not English), could not be published then and was published in 1986.

Before coming back once again to the literary development of Santali language and literature let me give you a cursory historical overview of how the foundation of the written literature of Santali discourse took its inception. Joseph Troisi (Troisi J. , 1976) in 'Introduction' narrates that As the Santals did not have any written record of their own, various conjectural theories have been advanced regarding the origins of these pre-Dravidian aboriginals who, according to their traditions, are represented as a race wandering from one country to another. But whatever their original habitat might have been, authentic records show that during the eighteenth century many Santals began settling down in Chotangpur and in the neighbouring districts of Midnapore and Singhbhum. These people , who demonstrated considerable skill in clearing the jungles for cultivation, began to migrate to the Rajmahal Hills on the north-eastern side of the Chotanagpur Plateau.

Regarding the advent of the Santals, R. Carstairs (His name is commemorated by Carstairs town in Deoghar. It is remarkable that there are several localities in Deoghar which commemorate some of the early British administrators like Bompas, William etc. (P.C.R.C.), who served the district as a Deputy Commissioner and the Settlement Officer for several years, has observed in his book *The Little world of an Indian District Officer* as follows:

"The first mention of Santals having entered this area is in the report of Mr. Sutherland, Joint Magistrate of Bhagalpur who was sent about the year 1820 to enquire into the state of the hill tracts. He found that there had begun to filter into the hill tracts men of a new and hitherto unheard race , called 'Santals' or 'Soutars' who were reported to be excellent pioneers. They had first been heard of in this district about the year 1810 and had come from the south-west. As a Bhagalpur man, he could not take much interest in Beerbhoom affairs; and the Santals may have appeared earlier in Beerbhoom. This account of R.Carstairs supplements the information given by Mr. Sutherland mentioned in the old *District Gazeteer of Santal Parganas (1938)*" (O' Malley, District Gazetteer of Santal Parganas, 1938); (Chaudhury, 1965, pp. 852-984)

J.Troisi (Troisi J. , 1976, p. 1) believes that there could be two reasons for this migration. In the first place, towards the end of the eighteenth century, many of the Chotanagpur jungles had been cleared and there was a considerable influx of population from the infertile uplands which could not support them. Secondly, as a result of the introduction of the Permanent Zamindari Settlement by the East India Company in 1793, a new of landlords was created. These landlords began hiring Santal labourers to clear the virgin forests in the Rajmahal Hills area so as to bring more land under cultivation. This area had been the homeland of the Malers, and the Mal Paharias, notorious robbers and cattle lifters, who often raided the villages in the plains. Their villages were andstill are, situated on the hill-tops. Various efforts were made by the British government to win over these tribals and to bring them under control. For a time the situation seemed to be in their hand, but later the same old trouble started again. The government, in 1833, demarcated an area surrounding the Rajmahal hills, including portions of Dumka, Godda, Pakur and Rajmahal sub-divisions. This area came to be known as the Damin-i-koh, which means 'The skirts of the hills'. The idea behind this move was to deaclare this hill tract occupied by tribals the property of the government.

Upon this initiative of the government the Santals were now encouraged to settle down in this area. During the next fifteen years, they moved to this region in such great numbers that the population of the area increased by more than 30per cent. The Damil-i-koh soon became the centre of Santal tribal life. Little did the government think that these same Santals were to become rebellious twenty-two years later. The chief cause of this rebellion, during which many people lost their lives, was the joint exploitation by the Hindu traders and money- lenders (mahajans), and the corruption of the police and court clerks. Consequent upon the Santal rebellion, the district of Santal Parganas was erected by the Act XXXVII of December 22, 1855. This act was, however, largely amended by the Act X of 1857 which slashed down the district to a smaller area. Santal Parganas thus became the homeland of the Santals. Another result of the rebellion was that Christian missionaries took up work among the Santals in this new district

**Origin of Name** (O' Malley, District Gazetteer of Santal Parganas, 1938, pp. 108-119); (Chaudhury, 1965, pp. 852-984)

Regarding the origin of the name Santal, physical characteristics and the general characteristics the old *District Gazetteer of Santal Parganas* (1938)) has mentioned as follows:

"The name Santal, spelt in one way or another (e.g., Sonthal), is an English form adopted from Hindi, which corresponds with the form Saontar used by the Bengali-speaking people. Both names are only applied to the tribe by non-Santals, and the Santals do not use them in speaking about themselves except as a concession to foreigners; then they prefer the form Saontar. Both Santal and Saontar have the same origin according to phonetic law and practice in the different languages. The Santals themselves state that they got this name through foreigners commencing to call them so whilst and because they were living in Saont (Sant, as they pronounce the name of the country), which has been identified with the modern Silda *pargana* in the Midnapore District."

"Mr. W.B. Oldham, C.I.E., is of opinion that the name is an abbreviation of Samantawala. Samanta, he says, is another name given to the Silda pargana, whence the immigrant Santals discovered by Mr. Ward in 1828 deposed that they had come. 'As in Bengal all trans-frontier Pathans, even if Khorasan or Baluch, are called Kabuli, or as in the Santal Parganas all Hindustani money-lenders, even Marwaris, are called Bhojpuria, because the first and most conspicuous of their kind came from Bhojpur in Shahabad, so would so remarkable a people as the Santals on their first appearance in Burdwan and Birbhum be called after the place whence some of them were known to have come'. There are signs of a fairly old Santal settlement in the *pargana*, and round about it a dense population of Santals accounting for over one-third of the inhabitants. There is also a tract called Samantbhum or Santbhum in the Bankura District, which the Santals claim to have colonized, and legend relates that it was held by 12 Samanta brothers, a number which will recall the 12 Santal sects.

"Regarding these theories Mr. Bodding writes—"That Sant and Saont are to be derived from the (originally Sanskrit) word Samanta seems to be very probable. As a matter of fact all the forms (Sant, Saont and Sat) are easily derivable from this according to common Aryan phonetic laws. There is no doubt that the word itself is of Aryan origin. If a translation of the word is sought, the original meaning would be something like 'bordermen', but as they have probably got the name in the way mentioned, the meaning implied by the users of the word would not be that;they are 'Saonters'. "The Santals call themselves simply Har, meaning man, and state that they were formerly called Kharwar. It is only since 1917, that a Santal has learned to tell a stranger what his name and sect is. Prior to that, as a rule, he would simply say *Manjhi*"

"Whatever may have been the original habitat of the race , there is no doubt that within hstoricntimes they were settled in the Chota Nagpur plateau and in the adjoining districts of Midnapore and Singhbhum, and that they began to make their way northwards towards the close of the $18^{th}$ century. The earliest mention of them appears to be contained in an article entitled *'Some Extraordinary Facts, Customs and Practices of the Hindus'* by Lord Teignmouth ( sir John Shore), which was published in the Asiatic Reseraachers of 1795. In this article they were designated 'Soontars' and described as a rude unlettered tribe residing in Ramgur (Ramgarh), the least civilized part of the Company's possessions, who have reduced the detection and trial of persons suspected of witchcraft to a system. The first mention of the Santals in this district occurs in Montgomery Martin's *Eastern India* (compiled from Buchanan Hamilton's manuscripts), which contains two references to them, in one of which their names are spelt 'Saungtar', while in the other a printer's error has converted it to 'Taungtar'... These references, according to Mr. H.McPherson, are interesting as they illustrate three peculiarities of the Santals, *viz.*, their contempt of Hindu prejudices, their superstitious belief in witchcraft, and their communal system, all of which survive in undiminished strength to the present day." (Chaudhury, 1965, p. 859)

"Further information about the Santals at this early time has been obtained by Mr. H. McPherson from the unpublished manuscript of

Buchanan Hamilton, in which it is stated—'The Saungtars are a tribe that has a peculiar language. So far as I could learn, about 500 families are now settled in the wilder parts of the district. This, however, is a late event, and they came last from Birbhum in consequence of the annoyance which they received from its zamindars. The original seat of this tribe, as far as I could learn from them, is Pallamau and Ramgarh…" (Chaudhury, 1965, p. 860)

The extract given above is sufficient to show that by the end of the first decade of the 19th century the Santals had settled in considerable numbers in Lakerdewani,i.e., Handwe and Belpatta, two tracts lying outside the hills. They had made their way there from 'Birbhum' where they appear to have brought in to clear the country. 'Birbhum' is meant no doubt that portion of the district now included in subdivisions Deoghar and Jamtara.( Page 30 of Mr. H. McPherson's *Final Report of the S.P.Settlement*, 1898-1907) According to Sir William Hunter:—'The permanent settlement for the land tax in 1790 resulted ina general extension of tillage, and the Santals were hired to rid the lowlands of the wild beasts which, since the great famine of 1769, had everywhere encroached upon the margin of cultivation. This circumstance was so noticeable as to find its way into the London papers, and from 1792 a new era in the history of the Santal dates' By 1818 the Santals had made their way further North into the forests below the hills in the Godda subdivision, and even into the Damin-i-koh; for Mr. Sutherland, writing in that year, noticed their presence in toppas Dhamsai and Jamni Harnipur and also in tappa Sarmi of pargana Handwe, and in tappas Marpal and Daurpal, which are included in the Dumka portion of the Damin-i-koh. By 1827 the Santals had got as far as the extreme north of the Godda subdivision, Mr. Ward when demarcating the Damin-i-koh finding three Santal villages in Patsunda and 27 villages in Barkop. His first impressions of the Santals are interesting. " (Man, 1983(First Indian Edition))There are', he wrote, 'within this described line two or three villages established by the race of people called Santars. These people are natives of the Singhbhum and adjacent country; their habits and customs are singular; they are of no caste, extremely hardy and industrious, and are upon the whole considered an extraordinary race of beings…"

"It will be noticed that in the above extract Mr. Ward referred to Singhbhum as the place of origin of the Santal immigrants he met, and from depositions which he took it appears that they had left and were still leaving Singhbhum because of disturbances there. The part of Singhbhum from which they migrated was probably Dhalbhum, in which the Santals are still very numerous, and its neighbourhood. It is not known what were the disturbances alluded to, but the account of the Santals in Midnapore, of which Dhalbhum then formed part, given( in 1820) in Hamilton's *Hindustan* may help to explain the circumstances which would lead them to emigrate: 'Some parts of these jungles are occupied by poor miserable proscribed race of men called Sontals, despised on account of their low caste by the inhabitants of the plain country, who would on no account allow any one of them to fix himself in their vilages. The peasantry in the vicinity, by way of distinction, call themselves good creditable people, while they scarcely admit the Sontals within the pale of humanity; yet the latter are a mild, sober, industrious people, and remarkable for sincerity and good faith. The zamindars give them no leases, yet on the whole treat them well; for such is their timidity that they fly on the least oppression, and are no mre heard of. Notwithstanding they hold their lands on such easy terms, and scarcely ever have their verbal tenures violated, they are said to naked, half-starved, and apparently in the lowest stage of human misery; a result we should not have expected from the character above assigned them…" (Chaudhury, 1965, pp. 861-62)

E. G. Man (Man, 1983(First Indian Edition)) in his book "*Santhalia and Sonthals*" (1867), however, gave a somewhat different theory regarding the origin of the Santhals on the basis of the information gathered from a Santhal *manjhi.* According to him the word *Sonthal* or *Sonthar* is quite a mongrel epithet. This tribe first came from a place called 'Chai Cumpa' in the Nagpore district, but having been greatly oppressed by a certain Mahadeo Sing, they were obliged to quit and retreated into the jungles lying to the north-east of their former habitation. They went ahead, cleared and cultivated their lands until they settled in this area. A small tribe originally united for self-protection, they first called themselves, and were called *Shaitals* which in course of time became corrupted into *Sonthar* and *Santal.* Some of them state that they were originally *kewars* and while in the jungle, suffering from great privation, a *Deh* or spirit put it into their heads to eat rats, snakes, field mice and other vermin. The physical and general characteristics of the Santals given by Man still continue. The complexion of the Santals is dark but not very dark. (Chaudhury, 1965, p. 871)

## Traditions

Regarding the traditions of the Santals the old District Gazetteer of Santal Parganas (1938, pp-108-10) has mentioned as follows:

"The traditions of the Santals represent them as a race wandering from one country to another until they found their present home in Chota Nagpur and the adjacent districts. Starting with the creation, these traditions tell us how the first human pair came into existence, how they fell into sin, i.e., had sexual intercourse with one another, after having been taught to brew and drink handi by Lita, and how they begot seven sons and seven daughters, who ended in marrying one another, whereupon the human race greatly multiplied, also became very wicked. This happened while they were living in Hihiri-pipiri. They then came to a land called Khoj-kaman, where God called upon them to return to Him; but they would not. Thereupon He decided to exterminate the race, sparing only one holy pair—whether the first pair or some other is forgotten—who were ordered to enter a cave in the mountain of Harata. They obeyed, and then for seven days and seven nights it rained fire( or, as some say, water), so that all the rest of mankind and all animals were destroyed. After the rain of fire ceased the pair came out and a new human race sprang from them. They lived for some time close to Harata, but moved from there to Sasan-beda, i.e., a flat riverside land(beda) with turmeric(sasan). Here the race was divided into nations and tribes having the same tribal names as the children of the first pair with five more added. From Sasan-beda they came to Jarpi. As they wandered on they encountered a high range of hills, in trying to cross which they nearly lost their lives. It was so high that it was long into the forenoon before they saw the sun—a proof, be it noted, that they were travelling east. Here they started worshipping Marang Buru (the big mountain); till then they had worshipped only God. Through the Sin pass and Baih pass they came to Aere, from there to Kaende, thence to Chae(Chai), and finally to Champa. (Chaudhury, 1965, p. 853)

"In Champa they lived in prosperity under their own kings for a long time. At first they dwelt in peace with the Hindus, because they had helped Rama against Ravana, but later on they had fights with the Hindus and among themselves. In Champa several races (the Mundas, Birhors, Kurmis and others), separated from what was, according to the traditions, till then the common Kharwar race. From Champa they came to tore Pokhori Bha Bandela, where the people after twelve days' or twelve years' discussion—tradition has forgotten which—decided to give up certain old customs and to adopt new social customs. Thence they migrated to various places, e.g., Shikhar and Sant, and at lenghth came to their present homes. (Chaudhury, 1965, p. 853)

"On the basis of these traditions several theories have been put forward to account for the origin of the Santals. The Revd. L. O. .Skrefsrud has conjectured that they lived successfully in Persia, Afghanistan and Chinese Tartary, and entered India from the north-west, that they settled in the Punjab and made their way thence to the Chota Nagpur plateau. Colonel Dalton believed that the Santals came from North-East India, and found their way to the Chota Nagpur plateau and the adjoining highlands by the line of their sacred stream, the Damodar river. In support of this theory he cited certain remarkable coincidences of custom and language between the Santals and some of the aboriginal tribes on the north-eastern frontiers of India, from which he inferred a connection in the remote past. This theory of a north-eastern origin was also accepted by Sir William Hunter in the *Annals of Rural Bengal*. Colonel Waddell, again, regards the Santal tradition of their wanderings "as a record of actual tribal progress from the central alluvial valley of the Ganges south-westward to the the hills, under pressure of the Aryan invasion of the valley from the north (Chaudhury, 1965, p. 854)

Dr. A. Campbell asserts: "The theory which seems to me capable of proof is that the Santals , or rather the people of whom they are a portion, occupied the country on both sides of the Ganges, but more especially that in the north. Starting from the north-east, they gradually worked their way up the valley of the Ganges till we find them in the neighbourhood of Benares, with their headquarters near Mirzapur. Here the main body, which had kept the northern bank of the river, crossed, and heading southwards, came to the Vindhya hills. This obstruction deflected them to the left, and they at length found themselves on the tableland of Chota Nagpur." He further believes that the traditions point to a remote past and not to recent migration inside the Chota Nagpur plateau (Campbell A., 1894). (Chaudhury, 1965, p. 854)

Sir Herbert Risley does not accept this theory, in whose opinion the legend of the Santals does not appear to deserve serious consideration as a record of actual wanderings. "A people whose only means of recording facts consists oof tying knots in strings, and who have no bards to hand down a national epic by oral tradition, can hardly be expected to preserve the memory of their past long enough or accurately enough for their accounts of it to possess any historical value. If, however, the legends of the Santals are regarded as an account of recent migrations, their general purport will be found to be fairly in accord with actual facts. The same authority then proceeds to point out that it is clear that there was once a large and important Santal colony in parganas Chai and Champa in the Hazaribag district, and that there is some evidence that a fort of theirs was taken by the Muhammadans. 'If the date of the taking of this fort by Ibrahim Ali were assumed to be about 1340 A. D., the subsequent migrations of which the tribal legends speak would fill up the time intervening between the departure of the Santals from Chai Champa and their settlement in the present Santal Parganas.." (TriVo)'

"On this subject Mr. Bodding writes: 'It is as yet very difficult to say anything definite as to the origin of the Santals, or rather of the race to which they belong. They have had no written records of their own. To come to a conclusion, therefore, we have to examine and rely upon other materials. These are their traditions, their customs, their language, their anthropological features and what may be found in foreign records. As to their traditions, it is possible to accord them too high a value; but I feel sure no one who has got a true knowledge of them will be inclined to despise them. When you hear part of the story of the creation, you are reminded of myths of the same kind prevalent, e.g., in Southern Burma. Much is childish. But on the other hand, it is difficult to avoid the impression that below the surface there are remnants of true facts. (Chaudhury, 1965, p. 855)

## Dress and Ornaments

It has been observed that the Santal women generally wear bordered saris not less than seven cubits in length. Half of this serves as the lower garments being knotted at the waist; the other is passed over the left shoulder and hangs in the front. They use no veils for their heads of raven dark mass of wavy hair. They keep them combed in a nice knob at the back of their head and decorate them with flowers of all hues and frequently with tufts of red silk.

It is a practice amongst the Santals that the Female childrenup to the age of five wear a very short loin cloth, worn around a coulered string tied at the waist (*danda jbinjbir*). They call this cloth *gendre*. Girls after ten years wear a thick cloth called *panhand* in Santali. Some of these have a bright violet border. Such saris reach only up to the knee as they measure three cubits in length and one and half cubits in wide. But they take care to cover the upper part of their bodies with another part of measurement called *gamcha*. But the dress of santal women varies from place to place. But women still retained their primitive style intact, makes several pleats in the portion bound round the waist at the front and the end thrown over the shoulder from behind falls over the breast, and the edges are tucked in one either side into the portion round the middle. A second dress is of *katntha* cloth (pieces of old cloth sewn together) which is bound by women round the waist and completed with other pice of cloth thrown over the shoulder and covering the breast. As far as the dress of The Santal Menis concerned, the Santal men are scantily dressed. We can generally see them wearing a short cloth tied at the waist, the end being passed on and secured near the end of the spine to free movement. Santals wear loin cloth, which they call *Panchi* at home but they put on long sheet of thick cloth five cubits in width which they term *kutcha*.

It is very enchanting to see the Santal womenstruck colourful flowers to their hair, and over their ears but those who can afford use ornaments of various kinds, the special features mentions are as follows. These ornaments are made of nickel and silver, which are frequently used. The average woman wears convex-shaped anklets (*paina*). They also use on their feet ornament call *kharua* and with a ring on her first finger of the toe. Their wrist has ornamented wristlets called *phora sakom*. They use several verities of rings like *takamudam, tunki mudam*. While some well to do santal wear a head ornament called *jhipjhipi* a silver tiara- like ornament, with a crescent moon glimmering a locket. Next is the *danda jhinjhir* decorated on the wrist. They decorate their ear lobs with *jhinka*. And the upper ears sparkle with *khutla* with five chains of silver swinging from it. Where as the necks have beautiful aids in the shape of *hansulis*.

## Internal Structure of the traditions of the Santals

According to the *District Gazetteer of Santal Parganas*(1938), pp. 129-130 :

"The tradition of the Santals is that the parents of mankind were Pilchu Haram and Pilchu Budhi, who sprang from two eggs laid by a wild gander and goose. *Pilchu*, it may be explained, means 'original'; *haram*, an old or elderly man, or a married man; and *budhi*, an old woman or a married woman; while *haram budhi* is used to denote a married couple, or a pair living together as husband and wife, except those recently married. The traditional names do not mean more than that the human race sprang from one pair, hatched from two eggs laid by a pair of swans or geese. *Hans* is the name for the gander, *hasil* for the goose; but the words, which are of Aryan origin, may also mean swans. This first pair has seven boys and seven girls; the names of about half of these are mentioned in the traditions, and are also probably of Aryan origin. When they were married and had children, the seven parents (and the grand parents) decided that henceforth brothers and sisters should not marry. They therefore divided themselves into seven exogamous septs, called (1) Hansdak, (2) Mumu, (3) Kisku, (4) Hembrom, (5) Marandi, (6) Saren and (7) Tudu. When the first race was exterminated in Khoj-kaman, only one righteous pair being saved in the cave of Harata, the new race which sprang from this pair was again divided into seven exogamous septs with the same names as the original septs, to which five more were added, viz., Baske, Besra, Paunria, Chore and Bedea; the last sept has been lost.These names are all sept names, not *nomina propria*..

"There is a diffuse kind of traditional story relating how the sept names were given after a big hunt, but they are really totemistic in origin. Each sept (*paris*) has a pass-word peculiar to itself and is divided into a number of sub-septs (*khunt*). No Santal may marry within his father's sept or any of its sub-sept, a Santal proverb saying —'No one heeds a cow track or his mother's sept'. The pass-words, which specially belong to the original septs (*nij-Hansdak, nij-Murmu*, etc.) and frequently are unknown to other sub-septs, are generally names of ancesters, chiefs or other important persons or places, forts, etc. They refer to places and persons in Champa, and are thus of no very great antiquity." (Chaudhury, 1965, p. 872)

## Santali Rites, festivals and ceremonies

For the Santals, rites, customs and festivals are all integral part of culture as well as Dhorom. P.C.Hembram (Hembram P. , 1988, p. 43) feels that a Santal settlement has always been constructed in a place replete with plemty of natural resources as is clear from the early stage study that man was solely dependent on nature, believing that behind every resource an unseen powerful embodiment exists. In order to appease the unseen power called 'bongas', the Santals celebrate puja and organize pleasure festivals. Hembram further remarks that in the Santal community the festivals are both seasonal and occasional in nature. The Santal's festival calendar begins from the month of Fagun (Feb-March) and most of the puja festivals are agriculture-oriented.

According to J.Troisi (Troisi J. , Tribal Religion: Religious Beliefs and Practices among the Santals, 1978, p. 119)the annual community festivals of the Santals such as Baha, Erok Sim, Hariar Sim, Iri-Gundli-Nawai, Janthar, Sohrae and Magh Sim are all connected with agricultural operations. The annual hunt is also a festive occasion for the Santals. Besides these agricultural festivals, the Santals also have other festivals which are neither performed regularly nor associated with agricultural activities. The Santals' religious worship is mainly congregational in nature and there is no individual approach to the bongas, but fellowship with them is maintained through sacrifices, offerings and libations made on behalf of a particular unit, be the village, the subclan, or the household. Likewise the celebrations which accompany such collective rituals, in which people participate for the welfare of the entire group, are truly occasiobs for collective action. It is important to note here that these rites, festivals and ceremonies are channels through which cultural tradtions are expressed and affirmed.

It has been observed that it is generally on the occasion of such collective seasonal rites and the dances and festivals associated with them that the Santals experience a religious feeling, seeing in these festivals an occasion to forget the worries, stresses and strains of day-t-day life. And it is under the mutual stimulation of collective public worship, the Santals feel themselves to be in touch with their spirits upon whom they depend. In this way they are inspired with confidence and hope and with a certain sense of security amidst the uncertainties of their lives. Most importantly, as a result of such communal worship, the feeling of community-belonging is intensified, thus strengthening also their solidarity.

For Joseph Troisi (Troisi J. , Tribal Religion: Religious Beliefs and Practices among the Santals, 1978, p. 121) Santal seasonal rites and festivals contain two strands: the religious and the secular. The Santals being agriculturalists, their religious rites have the social urge of fertility, fecundity, generation, and all that is connected with their existence. The Santals are highly ritualistic people and they rarely doubt the efficacy of their rituals, being convinced that these most produce the expected results. And if the expected results are not achieved, they believe that the lack of success is either due to some hostile forces or that the ritual prescriptions were not properly observed. Thus they are very particular about their time and place of the sacrifices and about the person who is to officiate at the rite. The sacrificial offering is clearly at the centre of every Santal ritual. It is believed that the sacrifice is a meal in which the worshippers who offer it share it along with the god to whom it is offered. According to their belief sacrificial banquets have the object of making the worshipper and his god share the same sacrificial meal so as to form a kinship bond between them

According the Santal belief, the purpose of Santal sacrifices is twofold: to seek protection and prosperity from the benevolent *bongas* and to control the malevolent *bongas* of their malign influence. Thus, on the one hand, through their sacrificial offerings, the Santals make a kind of bargain with the spirits so that they may be protected and on the other hand, the malevolenr spirits are persuaded to turn away from the Santals and not to trouble them any more. One cannot deny the instrumental efficacy believed to be inherent in the rituals. Thus the Santals do hope that rain rituals for example will cause rain and that harvest rituals will produce crops.

The secular aspects of the Santal seasonal rites and festivals provide entertainment and diversion to the Santals . Culshaw (Culshaw, Tribal Heritage: A Study of the Santals, 1949, p. 39) remarks that 'the word *raska*meaning 'pleasure' is often on the lips of the Santals , and it is dear to their hearts'. Their behavior is characterized by a carefree, uninhibited attitude and a joyous frame of mind. Men and women, adults and children all gather together for the occasion to indulge themselves and to meet their friends and relatives.

It is pertinent to mention here that dancing and singing hold a very important role in almost all the festive occasions for the Santals and it would not be wrong to assert that a social feature of Santal dancing and singing is their social character. From the time a girl can toddle, she joins the line of dancers, while little boys ape the antics of the drummers (Troisi, 1978, p. 124). The Santals have a large number of different dances according to the special seasons and festivals. According to Mukherjea, 'These dances…are a part and parcel of the tribal religious life' (Mukherjea, 1962, p. 365) Bodding (Bodding, 1993 (First published in India)) mentions thirty-one types of dances, most of which are performed by men and women together though some are reserved for either of the sexes. For example, 'the *lagre* is the most common of the Santal dances and may be danced at any time, though preferably during moonlight. *Don* is usually danced during marriage festivals. *Jatur* is performed during the *Sohrae* and the *Baha* festivals. *Danta* is also danced during the *Sohrae*. Women generally do not join in this dance. On the other hand, only women dance the *Baha* dance which, as the name implies, is performed during the *Baha* festival. During the *Karam* festival, the Annual Hunt and *Bitlaha*, the menfolk perform special dances' (Troisi, 1978, p. 124).

J.Troisi comments that drumming plays a very important part during dancing since the rhythm and style of the latter depends much on the way in which the drums are played. The Santals essentially use two types of drums during their dancing—the tamak or kettle drum which is made of iron and is shaped like a big bowl nd covered with buffalo or bullock hide, and the tumdak or dancing drum made of burnt clay and conical in shape, the narrow end being covered with goat's skin and the broad end with bullock, buffalo or goat's hide. The tumdak which is played with the hands sets the rhythm while the tamak, played with small sticks, echoes and adds to the rhythm (Troisi, 1978, p. 124) Dancing is often connected with singing. Raha (Raha, 1967) rightly observes, 'when any new event is marked by the Santals they at once give it a poetic expression and sing spontaneously on their way to or during any festival'. As the Santals have different dances for different festive occasions, so also they have elaborate song cycles for various festivals. According to Bhattacharya (Bhattacharya, 1962) the Santals have more than twenty different tunes though most of the songs are ancestral. It is also part of the vitality of Santals to compose songs on the spur of the moment and undoubtedly these songs reflect certain feelings, emotions and sentiments of the Santals (Troisi, 1978, p. 125).

There are essentially two kinds of rites and festivals or ceremonies in the Santal comminty: firstly, seasonal annual rites and festivals concerned with agricultural operations by which the Santal community seeks to ensure safety and prosperity to the village community as a whole at each new stage in its annual agricultural cycle and, secondly, religious rites and ceremonies by which the Santal society marks the physiological phases of human life and above all its crises and transitions.The following undermentioned are the main seasonal Rites and Festivals showing their relation with Agricultural Operations:

***Sohrae*** is celebrated in the month of Dec.-Jan (*Pous*). It is also called harvest festival. Pigs, goats, fowls and eggs are offered by the village *naeke* (priest) in the *jaherthan* (sacred grove).

***Baha*** is celebrated in the month of Feb.-March *(Phagun).* The first fruits of *matkom (bassialatifolia)* and other wild fruits and flowers, mainly the *sarjom (shorearobusta)* flower arebeing offered. The *naeke* and the *kudam naeke* offer sacrifices of fowls at sacred grove in honourof *Maran Buru*, *Jaher Era* and *Moreko-Turuiko*.

***Erok Sim*** is celebrated in the month of *Asar* (June-July). Sowing of rice seeds in the field. The *naeke* sacrifices the fowls to the *jaher bongas* and the *manjhi bonga*, invoking each one of them to make the earth fertile.

***Hariar Sim*** is celebrated in the month of *San* (July-August). It is the time when the Paddy seeds start Sprouting. The *naeke* sacrifices fowls to the village *bongas*, namely *Maran Buru*, *Jaher Era*, *Gosae Era*, *Moreko-Turuiko*, *Pargana bonga*, *Manjhi bonga* and *Sima bongas* for a luxuriant growth of paddy.

***Iri-Gundli Nawai***is celebrated in the month of *Bhador* (Sept.-Oct.). The first fruits of the millet*iri* (*panicummillaceum*) and *gundli* (*panicumfrumentaceum*) are offered to the *bongas*.The *kudam naeke* along with the fruits of the millet offers sacrifices of goat or ram to the *parganabonga* to protect their crops from rats or other pestilence.

***Janthar*** is celebrated in the month of Aghar(Nov.-Dec.), The first fruits of the winter rice crop offering. The *kudam naeke* offers sacrifice of goat or ram to the *pargana bonga* along with the first ears of paddy to protect from stomach disease, to multiply the paddy and also to protect their grains from harm.

***Magh Sim*** is celebrated in the month of *Magh* (Jan.-Feb.), when the *sauri* (thatching grass) is being cut.Fowls are sacrificed by the *naeke* to the village *bongas*, invoking them to multiply their *sauri* crop.

The seasonal rites and festivals discussed above are the ones by which the Santal society seeks to ensure safety and prosperity to the village community as a whole at each new stage in its annual agricultural cycle and the feasting, social reunion and rejoicing that mark their successful termination. Now let us have a look at the various religious rites and ceremonies by which the Santal community marks the physiological phases of human life, its crises and transitions. According to J.Troisi ‘these rites and ceremonies are mainly concerned with securing the active help of the benevolent spirits and the passive forbearance of the malignant ones, so as to ensure the safety and well-being of the individual and his family at the different turning – points in his life-cycle. They are also public and collective occasions which emphasise the relations of mutual harmony and solidarity between the individual and society’. (Troisi J., Tribal Religion: Religious Beliefs and Practices among the Santals, 1978, p. 155) It has been observed that the the turning -points in the life-cycle of an individual Santal are the critical occasions of birth, initiation, marriage and death and the Santals believe that these critical junctures of an individual’s life are replete with danger both for the individual himself and also for others.to control these dangers , guard against any external harm, and satisfy the emotional need of restoring hope nd confidence, these life-crises moments are set off by elaborate socio-religious rituals involving the help of the benevolent *bongas*.

According to Hembrom (Hembrom, 1996, p. 46) every Santal individual in his/her life undergoes through certain rites of passage which unties him/her to the bond of the community and following are the main rites of passage:

***Janam Chatiar***: as per the Santal tradition it is a rite of cleansing and individualization of a new born baby and this ceremony is done on the fifth day after the birth of a boy and on the third day after the birth of a girl baby. Through this ceremony the child is individualized by giving to it a name and is incorporated in the community

***Chacho Chatiar***: This ceremony is performed when a child has reached the adolescent stage. Through this ceremony an individual is admitted as a full-fledged member in the community and after this ceremony he/she is entitled to all the responsibilities and privileges of the community. Unless the ‘chacho chatiar’ has been performed no Santal boy or girl may be married nor accorded the privilege of death ceremony (‘*jan baha*’).

***Marriage:*** To get social recognition to be as husband and wife, the Santal youth must be married ceremonially within the community rule. The general rule of marriage is tribe endogamy and clan exogamy and avoidance of all close relatives from marriage alliance. The whole village community, in a marriage, is involved and they altogether help to establish the new family. The ancesters of the Santals, to help all classes of people to get ceremonial marriage within the community and within its rule, developed or approved of at least seven traditional forms of marriages. It is pertinent to mention here that the generic Santal word for marriage is *bapla*. The seven traditional forms of fthe Santal marriages are as follows:

1. *Kirin Bahu bapla*: it takes place when a man brings his son a bride (*bahu*) for whom he has paid (*kirin*) the bride-price.
2. *Kirin Jawae bapla*: in such type of marriage, a husband is acquired/bought for a girl made pregnant by a man who, either does not want to marry her, or, cannot marry her because he belongs to her clan. Here the cost of acquiring/buying (*kirin*) a husband (*jawae*) is borne by the offender.
3. *Tunki Dipil bapla*: it is also known as the poor man's marriage. The persons who cannot afford the expenses of a regular marriage take resort to this kind of marriage. In this type of marriage the bride gathers all her belongings in a small bamboo basket (*tunki*) and she is brought to the groom's house with the basket on her head (*dipil*).
4. *Sanga bapla*: it is contracted by a widow or a divorced woman, and a widower or a divorced man. The bride-price is half of that given in the case of *kirin* bahu bapla.and this is due to the belief that, after death, a woman will eventually rejoin her first husband because the first *sindur* has given her a special relation to her first husband's *bongas*.
5. *Ghardi Jawae bapla*: this type of marriage takes place in the household of such parents who are having grown up daughters and, either no sons or, if any minor sons are there in the family. In such cases a ghardi jawae is brought in to help in the work of the household. This type of marriage is also arranged in the case of an only daughter or, of one who, for some reason or other, such as ugliness or deformity, has not been sought in marriage by anyone.
6. *Itut bapla* and 7. *Nir bolok bapla* can be classified as marriages by force and are rare. In the case of itut bapla, it is the boy who takes initiative. When the boy is not sure whether the parents refuse to give their consent, the boy, choosing a public place such as a fair or a market, forcibly applies *sindur* to the girl's forehead claiming her as his wife. In the case of *nir bolok bapla*, it is the girl who takes the matter in her hands. By introducing (*nir bolok*) into the

house of the boy who, after having had sexual relations with her, refuses to marry her, she forces him into marriage.

***Death***: The last of the passage of rites in the community is done to thedead. When one dies, the whole community of the village gets involved. All gather at the house of the deceased person. The dead is ceremonially carried out of the house either for creamation or burial, and must be disposed of ceremonially. It is believed that without proper funeral rites a soul of the dead is not received in the community of the *Bongas* in the next world, wher the ancestors and all those who have died reside as *Bongas*. The *Bhandan* a post funeral ceremony is the final farewell to the dead from the world of the mortals. With this ceremony performed the dead is fully granted his/her abode in the next world, in the company of the benevolent *Bongas*, and becomes one of them, and continues his communion with the mortals in their worship.

## Musical Instruments

(i) *Sarpa* is a percussion musical instrument consisting of a vertical pole about fifteen inches high fixed into two crossed horizontal pieces of wood. Holes are bored in the foot-long horizontal pieces and through these holes pass lengths of string to the end of which are attached small circular wooden clappers. With the handle at the top of the vertical pole in the left hand and upper end of the strings held in the right hand, the clappers can be drawn up very sharply against the wooden bars so producing a ringing sound. The workmanship of the *sarpas* varies; some are plain while others display a handle curved in the shape of a dove and geometrical designs on the horizontal bars. The dancers form two lines: the older women form a line in front and sing and dance with their arms linked. Behind them comes a line of younger women, some of the beating the *sarpas*, some with small brass cymbals, while two women at the ends of the line wave the end of their saris to fan the others.

(ii) *BuaE*: It is associated particularly with the month that precedes that in which the Harvest festival is celebrated. This is the month known as dasae from the hindi word dussehra. The *buaE* belongs to a type of musical instrument with a wide distribution in different parts of the world. Its prototype existed when men first plucked the strings of their bows in order to hear a pleasing sound. To the arc of the bow a large hollow gourd is attached and this adds a resonance to the sound of the plucked bow string. The gourd is decorated with paper streamers. One of the songs sung to the accompaniment of *buaE* is in honour of the instrument itself and recounts the birth and growth of the gourd on the manure heap. Some of the dances enact hunting scenes and fights with bow and arrow.

(iii) *Tirio*(flute) : The name tirio is used to denote different kinds of flute as well as the boys' whistle. Flutes contain six holes, and the usual type is the true flute that is held to one side —the instrument associated with Krishna in Hindu Mythology.

(iv) *Banam*: Another instrument in the use of which many men are proficient is *banam*, a one string fiddle. The bowl is hollowed out from a piece of wood or formed sometimes from half a coconut, and it is usually covered with goat skin though occasionally there are specimens covered with monkey skin, which is prized for the purpose. The bowl is pressed against the player's armpit and the bow is drawn across the string at the required point. The string of the fiddle is nowadays made up of metal wire. The whole instrument is about eighteen inches long. It is difficult instrument from which to produce a melody, it is therefore used chiefly to accompany men's songs with somewhat monotonous form of 'seconds'.

(v) *Tumdak* and *Tamak*: W.C. Cushaw (Culshaw, Tribal Heritage: A Study of the Santals, 1949) observes that the most conspicuous of the musical instruments of Santals, both for size and volume of the sound, are the drums. The two kinds in common use are played together. They are known as the *tumda1* and the *mamak*. They are beaten at the dances by the younger men, who drum and leap about in front of the lines of the dancing women and girls. The *tumda1* is made of burnt clay and is somewhat conical in shape. The narrow end is usually covered with goat skin and the wide end with bullock hide. These end coverings are kept in place by narrow leather strips running the length of the drum, and other strips are wound round the drum. It is suspended by thongs from the shoulders of the youth who is playing it. He beats out the main rhythm with his right hand on the narrow end, the left hand beats the deeper note on the broad end to punctuate the bars. The *m amak* is a kettle-drum made of iron in the shape of a bowl and covered with a bullock hide. In addition to being used as an accompaniment for the *tumda1*, it is also the hunting drum. It is slung from the shoulders of the player and beaten with a pair of sticks.

(vi) *Lerda:* A variant of the *tamak* is the *lerda*, which has a flat bottom.

(vii) *dhãk*: The dhãk is a large long drum hollowed out of wood. This drum is in popular use at weddings and also at large dancing gatherings. It has to be carried by two men and is slung from a bamboo pole which they carry on their shoulders. It is the reverberations of this drum which can be heard throughout the surroundings countryside.

## Santali Language, Literature and Culture

Returning, now, to the literary development of Santali language, literature and culture, the European missionaries were the first to take active interest in the Santals and to study their language and culture. J. Troisie (Troisi J. , 1976, p. 3) narrates that on September 26, 1867, a man who was to do so much to promote Santali language and culture, namely Lars Olsen Skresrud, a Norwegian missionary belonging to the Lutheran Church, took up residence at Benagaria (which I visited as part of my field work in May 2017) in the district of Santal Parganas where he died and was buried forty years later (I had a chance visit his tomb as well). He immediately took up the study of Santal language and customs, being thoroughly convinced of the need for knowledge of the culture and institutions of the people. In 1873, Skrefsrud published *A Grammar of the Santhal Language*, a work that has had an important influence on all later treaties on the Santal language. He was an excellent linguist and a practical phonetician. In the beginning he used Bengal characters for Santali but later gave them up for the system which he himself introduced and which, with minor modifications, is still being used nowadays. In 1879, he started a Santali Printing Press at Benagaria which has been most influential in lifting the Santali language out of obscurity.

Chaitanya Prasad Manjhi (Manjhi, 2001) rightly observes that language and culture are the main constituents of the identity of a people.If language, on the one hand, develops with the educational progress of a people, culture, on the other hand, expands its boundary with the changing taste of the people. The language and culture are two ingredients of any society, be it 'modern' or 'primitive' which could be used as yardsticks to determine the 'level' of civilization of that community. While language , which is the vehicle of thought, expression and means of communication among the memebers of that particular social group, has its own domain or boundary to hold its people together making for their identity, the cukture has a tendency to scale the language barrier and expand its frontiers slowly by accepting foreign or alien ones which appeal to its people.The Santals have their own independent language known as *Santali* which belongs to the Munda, Ho, Mahli, Bhumij, and Kharia family of languages. Peter W. Schmidt has classified these groups as the Austro-Asiatic language group. As the Santals belong to the Munda family of languages, they have been classified by Anthropologists as Pre-Dravidians, Kolarians, Dravidians, Proto-Australoids, Nishadies and Austrics. But in the recent year they also have developed their own written script which goes by the name *OlChiki*. Many books have been printed in *OlChiki*. The Santali script, or *OlChiki,* is alphabetic, and does not share any of the syllabic properties of the other Indic scripts such as Devanagiri. It uses 30 letters and five basic diacritics. It has six basic vowels and three additional vowels, generated using the *GahlaTudag*.

Manjhi (Manjhi, 2001) rightly observes that the Santals are very orthodox people with a tendency to cling to the past and their religion '*sarna*' is based on nature's worship. According to the Santal belief, their creator *MaranBuru* has said, "I am everywhere in every form". Therefore they worship the trees in the jaher by installing *Jaher Era*, *Maneka* and *Lita Thakur* under the trees. They believe that the mointains and the hills are the home of gods and goddesses (*bongas*) and the *bongas* live everywhere. The Santals are extremely superstitious people believing that the world is full of spirits-good as well as evil. The good spirits are known as *bongas* and they are said to respond to the call of the humankind when worshipped by any individual or the village community and bring prosperity and well-being to the caller. The evil spirits, on the other hand, known as the '*Bhoot-bongas*', cause harm to the people and the Santals believe that very often illness and disease are caused by their influence. Hence *Ojha* (witch-doctor) is required to drive away the evil spirit.the Santal celebrate various agricultural and traditional festivals as already described earlier in this chapter.

Every village of the Santal community has a sacred grove or *jaher* on its outskirts which is a place of worship of the *bongas*, the village deities and a *gosan* in the village street for the worship of ancient *Manjhi Hadam*. Every religious or social function is celebrated by the community with drinks, dance and music and each function has a particular type of song, song, music and dance forms although thesound and musical instruments remain the same.

Each Santal village is regulated by the village council known as Manjhi-Manchor. The village nominates its headman (*Manjhi*), his deputy (*jog Manjhi*) and his secretary (*Godet*). All the villagers become the members of the Village Council. There of course, is a village priest (*Naeke*) for worshipping the village deities. The village council acts as an institution to settle all communal disputes of the village (Manjhi, 2001).

It can be argued that the Santals have undoubtedly preserved their ancient culture and language but they have tended to remain stagnant, static and obsurantist and beacuase of this they have failed to march with the time. It is trye that the cobwebs of blind faith, superstitions, degenerated, conservative traditions and cistoms have retarded the progress of the community in the spheres of social and cultural life. Moreover, the use of rice-beer in all religious and social functions which is based on superstitions and not on scientific reasonings has become a curse for the Santals. Furthermore, the Santali language has been neglected and discriminated both by the centra and the state government. So far, many Indian languages , which are spoken by people numbering less than Santali-speaking people have received the patronage of the government, but it is unfortunate that the Santali is always relegated to the backyard. The writers of the Santhali literature, therefore, must look beyond the boundaries of ancient orthodox culture and customs and swim in the high seas of knowledge instead of becoming frogs in the wells and today in the age of high technology and internet, the old order must be substituted by the new order (Manjhi, 2001).

Working on Santali myths and legends, Skrefsrud published *Horkoren Mare Hapramko reak Katha* (The book of ancestors) in Santali in 1887, which is a very good collection of Santal myths and legends. It is important to note here that this book formed the beginning of the corpus of Santali literature. As mentioned in the beginning of this chapter that it was taken from the mouth of Kolean, an old Santal guru, whose narrative was based on oral traditions, handed down verbatism by teacher to disciple, from generation to generation. Moreover, this book has been regarded as authoritative on many of the customs of the Santals. In fact, it is frequently referred to in Indian law courts whenever Santal customs are in dispute. It is of priceless value to the ethnologist and the linguist and it is indispensable to all who seek to know the Santals.

Skrefsrud had a mission in his mind right from the beginning to collect Santal words with the object of ultimately publishing a dictionary of the Santli language. He could never, however, spare enough time to complete his work. In 1890 he bequeathed his work, which contained a little more than 13,000 words, to a junior colleague who was an outstanding scholar, Rev. Paul Olaf Bodding, also a Norwegian missionary. In the course of more than thirty years which he passed at Mohulpahari(which I had a chance to visit as part of field work) in the Santal Parganas, P.O.Bodding published more than twenty-five works on the Santals, including books, monographs, articles, two grammars and a Dictionary, covering every aspect of Santal life. There is no denying the fact that his greatest work is without doubt the *Santal Dictionary*, published in five volumes over 1932-36, which is a comprehensive encyclopaedia of everything that concerns the Santals. In fact, the author's intention in bringing out this work was, as he himself remarked, to show the Santal—how he thinks, speaks and understands life. Bodding's last literary work, which he completed before he died in 1938, was the translation into English of Skrefsrud's book *Horkoren Mare Hapramko reak Katha*. He also wrote *Materials for a Santali Grammar* in two parts, published over 1923-29, which is still considered to be the best source for an advanced study of the Santali language. For the use of beginners he published *A Santali Grammar for Beginners* in 1929. In Santal Folktales published in Oslo in three volumes, he made available a rich treasure of genuine Santal folktales. He also furnished the Ethnographical Museum at Oslo with probably the richest collection of Santal implements that can be found anywhere. The Asiatic Society of Bengal published a number of his articles and also a series of two monographs on *Studies in Santal Medicine and Connected Folklore* and a monograph entitled *How the Santals live* which has been included as partIII of *Studies in Santal Medicine and Connected Folklore*. These are, undoubtedly, invaluable contributions to the scientific study of the literature of the Santals.

There is no denying the fact that the contributions of these two missionaries to the knowledge of Santal language, literature and culture are monumental. It is, however, not possible to mention the names of all the missionaries of various nationalities who were also engaged in the cultural upliftment of the Santals. Mention, however, must be made of C.H.Bompas whose book, *Folklore of the Santal Parganas* is a model of folklore research. Mr Andrew Campbell, a Scottish missionary who for the greater part of his life was stationed at Pokhuria in the Manbhum district, edited his *Santali-English Dictionary* in 1899 which was later supplemented by an *English-Santali Dictionary*. This was the second dictionary after Rev. E.L.Puxley's, published in1868. Campbell also wrote quite a number of articles mostly on Santal folklore. The Rev. W.J.Culshaw's book *Tribal Heritage*, and his articles have greatly helped in promoting a better understanding of Santal religious beliefs and practices. Rev. Johannes Gausdal's book, *The Santal Khuts*, is an ethnographical masterpiece on Santal sub-septs. He also published a number of articles on the same subject.

The fact that besides the Christian missionaries there have been quite a number of colonial officers who contributed invaluable material on the Santals cannot be denied. Sir John Shore's article "On some Extraordinary Facts, Customs and Practices of the Hindus," published in *Asiatic Researches*, 1795, contains the earliest mention of the Santals where they are designated as 'Soontars'. Scholars are of the view that the first account of the Santals of the Rajmahal Hills occurs in Montgomery Martin's book *Eastern India* compiled fromFrancis Buchanan's Journal kept during the survey of the district of Bhagalpur, 1810-11. H.C.Sutherland obtained information about the early history of the Santals through investigations into the land tenures of the Paharias of the Rajmahal Hills and from Captain Walter S.Sherwill's notes taken during his tour of the Rajmahal Hills and published by the Asiatic Society of Bengal. E.G.Man, Assistant Commissioner of the Santal Pargans came with another early account of the Santals through his book *Sonthalia and the Sonthals.The Little World of an Indian Officer*, the autobiography of R. Carstairs, who served as Deputy Commissioner and as Settlement Officer, contains a very good description of the land and its people, the formation of the new district, the Census of 1881 and the government of the district. It is on the basis of the nuber of years he served as Deputy Commissioner of the Santal Parganas and later as the person entrusted with the codification of Santal law, that W.G.Archer wrote not less than eighteen articles and four books on the Santals.

With regard to the Santals' early life, there are other sources of knowledge which include the vrious government district gazetteers, Census reports and handbooks and the three settlement reports H.L.L.Allanson, J.A.Craven, J.F.Gantzer, and H. McPherson. L.S.S. O'Malley, H.H.Risley, J.H.Hutton, W. Hunter and Col. Dalton have left us very good accounts of the Santals, their land, customs and habits. R.C.Dutt in 1882 through his article "Aboriginal Elements in the Population of Bengal" gave a very fascinating account of the Santals but it was really with the work of Sarat Chandra Roy that the Indian anthropologists started taking interest in the tribes of the Chotanagpur plateau-the districts of Ranchi, Hazaribagh, Dhanbad, Singhbhum, Palamu and those of the Santal Parganas. With Sarat Chandra Roy, anthropological researches in this area witnessed the beginning of a golden and constructive period. Indian anthropologists, sociologists and ethnologists have by now published quite a number of studies on the Santals.

## The Santal Authors and their publications

It is true that a great deal has been written about the Santals although the Santals have no written record of their own, most of the literature on the Santals, however, is relatively unknown since it has never been systematized. Needless to say that those who know Santal tradition and culture best are the Santals themselves, however, till now there have been very less books on Santals written by Santals. Let us have a look at them: (Gausdal, 1960) (Murmu S. H., 1961) ('Aadivaasi') ('Adivaasi', 1999) ('Armaan', 2009) ('Chaasa', 2003) ('Godet', 2015) ('Santali', 2009) ('Sonali', Bir Baajaal Onol Puthi, 2008) ('Sonali', Jiyon Jhaarnaa, 1995) ('Thakur', 2010) (Bag, 1987) (Besra B. , 1977) (Besra V. , 2010) (Chotrae Deshmanjhi Reak Katha, 1986) (Hansdak, 1994) (Hembram, 1982) (Kisku

D. B., 2001) (Kisku D. , Karam Thakur Samanre, 2001) (Kisku D. , The Santals And Their Ancestors: History, 2000) (Murmu B. C., 2011) (Murmu K. , 2012) (Murmu L. , 2010) (Murmu T., 2010) (Soren '. M., 1987) (Soren J. J., Kubi Gaona) (Soren J. J., Sogoe Pajher, 2002) (Soren N. ) (Soren N., Haarhaam Baabaavaak Gaam Kaahni, 1999) (Soren N. , Jeevet Karam Seren, 1999) ('Sonali', Jiyon Jhaarnaa, 1995) (Soren N. , Haarhaam Baabaavaak Gaam Kaahni, 1999) (Soren N., Jeevet Karam Seren, 1999) (Soren V., Mitten Kukmu, 2006) (Soren V., Taaraal Baasaal, 2010) (Tuddu K. , 1984) (Tuddu S. C., 2002). Of these Stephen Murmu's book, Hor Bapla Puthi, is the most detailed study ever done on Santal marriage customs. Chotrae Desmanjhi's narrative of the Santal Rebellion of 1855-57 is unforgettable in which he himself took part as a boy of fifteen. Of these books, a few contain various Santali songs, folktales, riddles and one is a Santali translation of R. Carstairs novel on the Santal Revolution.

Though the santals may not be having a very advanced or sophisticated civilization, but there is no doubt that they know the art of happy living as can be seen from their songs, dances riddles and folktales. Moreover, the Santals are great story tellers too. The roles which the Santal folktales play to serve the Santals are very important and invaluable. They make the tribe laugh in spite of poverty, illness and daily worries. They preserve tribal knowledge and give sanction to tribal custom. Besides, the Santals are also musical people, and this is evinced from the fact that when any event takes place, the Santals give it a poetic expression and sing spontaneously. They have elaborate song cycles and different tunes for various festive occasions and the agricultural seasons.

Let us have a look at the works done in the respect of Santali Dance, andSongs:

(Archer W. , 'Santal Poetry', June 1943); (Archer W., 'More Santal Songs',, 1944 );(Archer W., 'Santal Transplantation Songs', March 1946); (Archer, W.G., and Soren Gopal Gamaliel, 1943); (Archer, W.G.,and Soren, Gopal Gamaliel, 1943);(Banerji, 1959);(Bhattacharya, 1962);(Bhattacharya, 'Woodland Verses', 1964);(Campbell, 'The Traditions of the Santals', March 1916);(Campbell, 'Santal Legends', June 1916); (Canney, 1928); (Culshaw, 'Notes and Queries. Santal Songs', March 1946);(DasGupta, May 1963); (Majumdar, 1925); (Marandi); (Mitchell, Nov. 1875); (Mitra, Sept. 1929); (Mitra, 'Santali life in a Santali Folksong', 1926); (Mukherjea, 'Santal Folk Poetry', July-Dec 1936);(Raha, 1967); (Satyarthi, 1951); (Sinha, June 1946); (Soren N. ); (Soren N., Maran Din Seren); (Soren N., Sohrae Porob ar Sohrae Seren);(Mitra A. , 1953); (Gausdal, 1960) (Murmu S. H., 1961)

('Aadivaasi') ('Adivaasi', 1999) ('Armaan', 2009) ('Chaasa', 2003) ('Godet', 2015) ('Santali', 2009) ('Sonali', Bir Baajaal Onol Puthi, 2008) ('Sonali', Jiyon Jhaarnaa, 1995) ('Thakur', 2010) (Bag, 1987) (Besra B., 1977) (Besra V., 2010) (Chotrae Deshmanjhi Reak Katha, 1986) (Hansdak, 1994) (Hembram, 1982) (Kisku D. B., 2001) (Kisku D., Karam Thakur Samanre, 2001) (Kisku D., The Santals And Their Ancestors: History, 2000) (Murmu B. C., 2011) (Murmu K. , 2012) (Murmu L., 2010) (Murmu T., 2010) (Soren '. M., 1987) (Soren J. J., Kubi Gaona) (Soren J. J., Sogoe Pajher, 2002) (Soren N. ) (Soren N. , Haarhaam Baabaavaak Gaam Kaahni, 1999) (Soren N., Jeevet Karam Seren, 1999) ('Sonali', Jiyon Jhaarnaa, 1995) (Soren N., Haarhaam Baabaavaak Gaam Kaahni, 1999) (Soren N., Jeevet Karam Seren, 1999) (Soren V., Mitten Kukmu, 2006) (Soren V., Taaraal Baasaal, 2010) (Tuddu K., 1984) (Tuddu S. C., 2002).

## Folk Dances and Folk Songs

The very 'beingness' of folk-dance suggests a sense possessing a certain complexity of development in a world of existence and also by its name implies a distinction based more or less roughly on this complexity whereby the ruder arts of the less cultured members of society are distinguished from the more sophisticated arts of the educated classes (Banerji, 1959).The whole body of persons comprising it, in a primitive community, is the 'folk' and in the best sense of the word it might be applied to the entire population of any community. Such catch-phrases as 'folk-lore' and 'folk-music' are narrowed down to include only those who are mainly outside and beyond the current zone of urban culture and systematic education— the uneducated or little- educated inhabitants of village and countryside. Dance is at once, amongst all arts, the most primitive and the most sophisticated and there is hardly a civilization or a culture where the awareness of human movement as a vehicle of expression of joy and of sorrow is not evident. It would not be out of place to say that perhaps before man began to speak and to paint, he began to dance. Despite great variations and multiplicity of themes, forms and style of folk art, folk dance continues to be a distinct category chracterised by an overwhelming quality of spontaneity, of participation of every one, without an artificial barrier between the creator and actor, the performer and the audience. The intimate relationship of the folk arts with functions of daily life, whether of food-gathering, hunting, fishing or methods of grain cultivation and harvesting, collective activity in the context of rites and rituals connected with these functions and the beliefs of the performers in the propitiation of the spirits, links them to one another (Vatsyayan, 1976).

J.Troisi (Troisi J., Tribal Religion: Religious Beliefs and Practices among the Santals, 1978, p. 124) rightly observes that dancing and singing hold a very important role in almost all the festive occasions for the Santals. Men and women, adults and children all gather together for the occasions to indulge themselves and to meet their friends and relatives. A social feature of Santal dancing ansd singing, as that of other tribals, is their social charater. There is no denying the fact that from the time a girl can toddle, she joins the line of dancers, while little boys ape the antics of the drummers. The Santals have a large number of different dances according to the special seasons and festivals. Charulal Mukherjea (Mukherjea, The Santals, 1962,Revised Edition, p. 365) goes to the extent of saying that 'these dances… are a part and parcel of the tribal religious life.'

Santhali Dance-songs of Jharkhand consist of 'folk-dancing', 'primitive –dancing' and 'aboriginal dancing'. There is, however, a marked distinction between folk-dancing and primitive-dancing. Folk-dancing is that dancing which has developed, and is maintained by them in a fluid tradition without the aid of the professional dancer, teacher or artist; and is not, at least in its particular form, observed and practiced in towns on the stage, or in the ball-room. Folk-dance was made for the sheer pleasure of the performers and not for the entertainment of the public; while the primitive and aboriginal dancing was nothing but a spontaneous and emotional rhythmic expression preparatory to a ritual or battle. Folk-dance, with the progress of civilization, has developed from aboriginal –dancing and this less primitive form of dance discards much of the spontaneity, crudeness and the occasional indecency of the other. Nevertheless, primitive dance was the foundation of folk-dance and folk-dance was the foundation of the refined forms.

Although various studies have been made on social, economic, political and religious aspects of the Santal tribe (vide O'Malley 1938, Mukherjee 1943, Culshaw 1949, Datta-Majumdar 1956, Orans 1965, Bodding 1968, Kochar 1970 and Archer 1974) an intensive study of their music and dance is lacking. Those who worked on Santal music have, in fact, collected, compiled, translated and to an extent interpreted versions of some of their song-forms (vide Mitchell 1875, Majumdar 1925, Archer and Soren 1943a and 1943b, Archer 1944a, 1944b, 1946 and 1974 and musical instruments (vide Vols. I, IV, and V). He has also described some of the musical instruments in connection with the folk tales (vo ide Vol. I, pp. 10-11 and 212-213). Culshaw (1949), in his book *Tribal Heritage: A Study of the Santal*, has devoted a chapter to Santal dancing, music and poetry. Chattopadhyaya (1978) has also given description of Santal musical instruments in her book *Tribalism in India*(Prasad, 1985).

Thus, having gone through the available resources on Santal Music and Dance-Songs, it was felt that an intensive study of their Dance-songs that forms an intensive part of the Santal life be made in their social and cultural context.

## References


(n.d.). *Tribes and Castes of Bengal*, Vol. II, pp. 225-6.

*Chotrae Deshmanjhi Reak Katha.* (1986). The Literature Committee of the Northern Evangelical Lutheran Church.

'Aadivaasi', B. M. (n.d.). *Jhaali.* Dumka: Santali Sahitya Prasarak Sewa Mandal.

'Adivaasi', B. M. (1999). *Disaam Bhokta (Santali Kahani).* Dumka: Santali Sahitya Prasarak Sevamandal.

Archer, W. (1944 , Sept). 'More Santal Songs',. *Man in India*, Ranchi, 24.(3) pp.9-13.

Archer, W. (June 1943). 'Santal Poetry'. *Man in India*, Ranchi, 23 (2), pp. 98-105.

Archer, W. (March 1946). 'Santal Transplantation Songs'. *Man in India*, Ranchi, 26 (1), pp. 6-7.

Archer, W.G., and Soren Gopal Gamaliel. (1943). *Hor Seren.* (Santal Songs), Benageria: The Mission Press.

Archer, W.G.,and Soren, Gopal Gamaliel. (1943). *Don Soren.Hor Seren Reak Dosar Hatin.* (Don Songs. The Second part of Santal Songs), Benageria: The Mission Press, pp. 435.

'Armaan', B. k. (2009). *Pe Pawa Chaawle.* Dumka: Santali Sahitya Prasarak Sewa Mandal.

Bag, D. (1987). *In the Midst of Santals.* Calcutta: Subarnarekha.

Banerji, P. (1959). *The Folk-Dance of India.* Allahabad: Kitabistan.

Besra, B. (1977). *More Soros Kahni.* Kolkata: The Santali Literary & Cultural Society.

Besra, V. (2010). *Vidrao.* Ranchi: Santali Literature Publication Pvt.Ltd.

Bhattacharya, S. S. (1962). 'Santal Songs: Different Types'. *Bulletin of the Cultural Research Institute*, Calcutta, 1 (2), pp. 54-61.

Bhattacharya, S. S. (1964). 'Woodland Verses'. *Bulletin of the Cultural Research Institute*, Calcutta, 3 (3-4), pp. 49-64.

Bodding, P. (1942). *Traditions and Institutions of the Santals(Horkoren Mare Hapramko Reak Katha).* New Delhi: Bahumukhi Prakashan.

Bodding, P. (1942(First Indian Reprint1994)). *Traditions and Institutions of the Santals.* New Delhi: Bahumukhi Prakashan.

Bodding, P. (1993(First published in India)). *A Santal Dictionary: 7 Parts in Five Volumes.* New Delhi: Gyan Publishing House.

Bodding, P. (2001(Second Reprint)). *Studies in Santal Medicine and Connected Folklore: Part I,II and III.* Kolkata: The Asiatic Society.

Campbell, A. (1894). 'Traditional Migration of the Santal Tribes'. *Indian Antiquary*, pp.103-4.

Campbell, A. (June 1916). 'Santal Legends'. *Journal of the Bihar and Orissa Research Society*, Patna, 2 (2), pp. 191-200.

Campbell, A. (March 1916). 'The Traditions of the Santals'. *Journal of the Bihar and Orissa Research Society*, Patna, 2 (1), pp. 15-29.

Canney, M. (1928). 'The Santals and their Folklore'. *Folklore*, London, 39, pp. 329-43.

'Chaasa', B. H. (2003). *Baha Seren.* Dumka: Santali Sahitya Prasarak Sewa Mandal.

Chaudhury, P. (1965). *Bihar District Gazetteers: Santal Parganas.* Patna: Th Superintendent Secretariat Press, Bihar.

Culshaw, W. (1949). *Tribal Heritage: A Study of the Santals.* London: Lutherworth Press.

Culshaw, W. (March 1946). 'Notes and Queries. Santal Songs'. *Man in India*, Ranchi, 26 (1), pp. 66-67.

DasGupta, S. (May 1963). 'A Short Introduction to the Variety of Folk Dances in India'. *Folklore*, Calcutta, 4 (5), pp. 163-91.

Gausdal, J. (1960). *The Santal Khuts.* Oslo: H. Aschehoug & Co.

'Godet', J. S. (2015). *Sirjonpuri Ar Udgau Aran.* Kolkata: Diamond Art Press.

Hansdak, '. B. (1994). *Tiriya Baadoli.* Dumka: Santali Sahitya Prasarak Sewa Mandal.

Hembram, N. (1982). *Austric Civilization of India:Prevedic Kherwal-Santal civilization.* Calcutta: Hari Pada Sahoo Books& News.

Hembram, P. (1988). *Sari-Sarna( Santhal Religion).* Delhi: Mittal Publications.

Hembrom, T. (1996). *The Santals: Anthrropological-Theological Reflections on Santali & Biblical Creation Traditions.* Calcutta: Punthi Pustak.

Kisku, D. (2000). *The Santals And Their Ancestors: History.* Dumka: Hihiri Pipiri Dudhani-Kurua.

Kisku, D. (2001). *Karam Thakur Samanre.* Dumka: Hihiri Pipiri.

Kisku, D. B. (2001). *Maran Thakur Samanre: Religious Literature.* Dumka: Hihiri Pipiri.

Majumdar, S. (1925). Some Santal Songs. *The Visva-Bharati Quarterly III*, pp. 67-9.

Man, E. (1983(First Indian Edition)). *Sonthalia and the Sonthals.* Delhi: Mittal Publications.

Manjhi, C. P. (2001). Santhal Language and Culture . In N. Mathur, *Santhal Worlview* (pp. 89-99). New Delhi: Concept Publishing Company.

Marandi, C. (n.d.). *Hor Hopon.* (Songs of Men), Dumka: Alka Printing Press, pp. 20.

Mitchell, J. (Nov. 1875). 'Santal Songs with Translation'. *The Indian Antiquary*, Bombay, 4, pp. 342-44.

Mitra, A. (1953). *Census 1951. West Bengal. The Tribes and Castes of West Bengal.* Calcutta: Superintendent, West Bengal Government Press, pp. 414.

Mitra, S. C. (1926). 'Santali life in a Santali Folksong'. *Journal of the Anthropological Society of Bombay*, Bombay, 13 (1), pp. 47-51.

Mitra, S. C. (Sept. 1929). 'The "Magical Conflict" in Santali, Bengali and Ao Naga Folklore'. *Man in India*, Ranchi, 9 (3), pp. 173-80.

Mukherjea, C. (1962). *The Santals.* Calcutta: A.Mukherjee &CO. Pr. Ltd.

Mukherjea, C. (1962,Revised Edition). *The Santals.* Calcutta: A. Mukherjee & Co. Private Ltd.

Mukherjea, C. (July-Dec 1936). 'Santal Folk Poetry'. *The New Review*, Calcutta, 4, pp. 220-26.

Murmu, B. C. (2011). *Sabarnakha.* Ranchi: Novelty Art Press.

Murmu, K. (2012). *Lantiti.* Kolkata: Kranti Press.

Murmu, L. (2010). *Golden Passport to Jeret Jivha.* New Delhi: Santali Literature Publication Pvt. Ltd. Ranchi.

Murmu, S. H. (1961). *Hor Bapla Puthi: Pahil Hatin (A Santal Marriage Book).* Benagaria: Benagaria Mission Press.Reprint in 2015.Kranti Press, Kolkata.

Murmu, T. (2010). *Towa Baahaa Maalaa.* Dumka: Santali Sahitya Prasarak Sewa Mandal.

O' Malley, L. (1938). *District Gazetteer of Santal Parganas.* pp.108-119.

Prasad, O. (1985). *Santal Music: A Study in Pattern and Process of Cultural Persistence.* New Delhi: Inter-India Publications.

Raha, M. K. (1967). 'Folk Songs of the Tribals of West Bengal- An Analytical Study of Continuity and Change'. In H. Biswas, *Folk Music and Folk-lore, An Anthology* (pp. 57-81). Vol. 1, Calcutta: Folk Music and Folkl-lore Research Institute.

'Santali', S. A. (2009). *Goso Baahaa.* Ranchi: Santali Litearature Publication Pvt.Ltd.

Satyarthi, D. (1951). *Meet My People. Indian Folk Poetry.* Hyderabad: Chetna Prakashan Ltd., pp. 304.

Sinha, S. K. (June 1946). 'Santal Folk Songs'. *Journal of the Bihar and Orissa Research Society*, Patna, 32 (2), pp. 184-88.

'Sonali', M. S. (1995). *Jiyon Jhaarnaa.* Dumka: Santali Sahitya Parishad.

'Sonali', M. S. (2008). *Bir Baajaal Onol Puthi.* Dumka: Santali Sahitya Parishad.

Soren, '. M. (1987). *Tiriya Baadoli.* Dumka: Dharam Printing Press.

Soren, J. J. (2002). *Sogoe Pajher.* Dumka.

Soren, J. J. (n.d.). *Kubi Gaona.*

Soren, N. (1999). *Haarhaam Baabaavaak Gaam Kaahni.* Dumka: Santali Sahitya Prasaarak Sevamandal.

Soren, N. (1999). *Jeevet Karam Seren.* Dumka: Santali Sahitya Prasarak Sewa Mandal.

Soren, N. (n.d.). *Aasadh Binti.* Dumka: Santali Sahitya Prasarak Sewa Mandal.

Soren, N. (n.d.). *Jawae Dhuti Seren.* (Betrothal Songs), Dumka: Alka Printing Works, pp. 17.

Soren, N. (n.d.). *Maran Din Seren.* (Christmas Songs), Dumka: Alka Printing Works, pp. 16.

Soren, N. (n.d.). *Sohrae Porob ar Sohrae Seren.* (The Harvest Feast and Harvest Songs), Dumka: Alka Printing Works, pp. 16.

Soren, V. (2006). *Mitten Kukmu.* Dumka: Minerva Press.

Soren, V. (2010). *Taaraal Baasaal.* Dumka: Minarva Press.

'Thakur', B. M. (2010). *Dong Seren.* Ranchi: Santali Literature Publication Pvt. Ltd.

Troisi, J. (1976). *The Santals: A Classified and annotated Bibliography.* New Delhi: Manohar Book House.

Troisi, J. (1978). *Tribal Religion: Religious Beliefs and Practices among the Santals.* New Delhi: Manohar Publications.

Tuddu, K. (1984). *Santali Padya Sangrah(Saantarhi Gaathni Gaadel).* Ranchi: Santali Sahitya Parisad.

Tuddu, S. C. (2002). *Taaraas.* Jamshedpur: Sangeeta Printers.

Vatsyayan, K. (1976). *Traditions of Indian Folk Dance.* New Delhi: Indian Book Company.

## Chapter Three

# Social Dancing I: Considering Contextualization

Subhendu Sekhar Bhattacharya(Bhattacharya, 'Santal Songs: Different Types', 1962) argues that there is a wrong perception gaining currency among the general people that there is only one tune for Santali Songs, which is a fallacy. In order to counteract such notions from gaining ground as well as for a better understanding of the Santali Songs it is essential to give just a brief sketch of the description of Santali songs. According to Bhattacharya one can distinguish more than twenty varieties with respect to the Santali songs. Bodding's *Dictionary* Vol. II, p. 331, (Bodding, A Santal Dictionary: 7 Parts in Five Volumes, 1993(First published in India)) lists thirty one dances (or games) practiced by grown-up people: *Baha enec; Buru beret enec; Bhinsar enec; Don enec; Dunger enec; Dharua( or dhaura) enec; Dhumdar bhet enec; Dhurumjak enec; Dahar enec; Danta enec; Dom enec; Gadoe enec; Gidini enec; Golwari enec(or, Gulwari enec; Gunjar enec); Jale enec; Jatra bonga enec; Jatur enec; Jhika enec; Kundur jhagra enec; Kunkal cak enec; Kutun pota enec; Lagre enec; Lauria enec; Loboe enec; Mander enec; Marak enec; Matwar enec; Pak don enec; Rinja enec; Sohrae enec; Taini enec*. Each tune has got its musical notation on *madol* and *nagara* current among singers and the scientific notations have been created by Christian Missionaries. A local Santali tribe Ramdas Tuddu has, in fact, written a book entitled *Kherwal Bonsa Dhorom Puthi* where he has created musical notation for five varieties of Santali Songs namely Soharae, Baha, Don, Karam and Lagre .

W.J.Culshaw (Culshaw, Santal Songs, 1979) describes Santal songs to be 'spontaneous' and 'ephemeral'. He says that on any moonlight night, when work is slack, the younger adults of a Santal village gather together to sing the songs classed as "Lagre" and "Porob" and that most of the songs are classified according to the rhythm of the type of dance or dance cycle with which they are associated. Culshaw is making a very important point further in saying that 'by means of songs, the Santals keep alive the memory of past events. Many classes of songs might almost be described as history in memorable form. One can analyse "history" into component tradition legend or myth, but it is not at all clear how far the Santals themselves differentiate these differing elements or whether they do so at all. This is true of many of the songs sung at the time of different festivals, particularly the great festivals of Springtime and Harvest, and the songs sung at the crises in individual life, such as initiation and marriage. Each festival and each occasion has its own appropriate cycle of dances, with characteristic step and rhythm, and consequently its own type of melody.

Sunity Kumar Sinha (Sinha, June 1946)feels that a song reflects more directly the feelings and passions of men than words however poetic they may be. It is true that passionate throbbings of a human heart seek artistic expression for which songs form the most suitable vehicle and it is not the monopoly of the rich only, the poor may as well sing and so the poor, simple and innocent Santals sing and dance to forget their woes and miseries. Song plays a very important part in their life. They are born singers and at every step of their life there is song. They sing when a child is born, they sing when he is married and sing the mourning song when one dies. Songs are the most essential features of the festivals of the folk, wherein are sung the praises of spring, the union of youth and joy and the like.

I'm reminded of W.J.Culshaw (Culshaw, Tribal Heritage: A Study of the Santals, 2004 (Published in India), p. 39) who, talking about Santal dancing, music and poetry says that 'the word *raska* meaning 'pleasure' is often on the lips of Santals, and it is dear to their hearts. They turn from their difficulties and sorrows to find solace in one or other of the many ways in which they can experience *raska*. Among these dancing is the most important'. The Santali word *eneœ* is used for dancing and dancing is indeed the play of the tribe. In every village there is a dancing floor, an open space that is well cared for. At festival times it is swept and freshly plastered with cowdung by young unmarried girls, and when it is not used for dancing it is used for meetings where the young men gather in the evenings to discuss their affairs and interests.

As far as the dances are concerned, Culshaw adds that some of the dances are connected with particular festivals and they are performed only at those times or during the whole of the month of the festival. There are other dances which are suitable at any time during the year. Some are dances for women alone and others for men alone, while in a few both women and men dance. The chief element of variety is introduced by means of varying the rhythm; to the casual observer most of the dances look the same. To perform a dance, a group of men or women dance together, forming a line with their arms linked, stepping sideways or forward and then backward, keeping time to the beating accompaniments of the drums, moving either in a circle or from one side of the dancing-floor to the other and from time to time breaking out into song.

Whenever there is an occasion for rejoicing there will be dancing. It is much in evidence during the celebrations and ceremonies after the birth of a child or at his fuller reception into the tribe, and again during marriage festivities. The General type of dance on all these occasions is known as *doE* , which has within it many variations. At these times it is the women who do the dancing, while the men furnish an accompaniment with drums and flutes, and many of the songs refer directly the purpose for which the folks have gathered together. During marriage ceremonies bapla, or type of dance specifically associated with marriages is also in evidence. The *doE ge[* is the dance of the men on the night of the annual hunt. It is a wild type of dance, when there is much leaping in the air. Two of the young men stripped of the clothing dance about in front of the lines, and the dances are preceded and ended by the shouting of obscene words.

Sunity Kumar Sinha (Sinha, June 1946) is of the view that the Santals are hedonists and the philosophy of their life is ' Eat, Drink and be Merry', for life is short and after death there is no merriment. Here are a few songs that convey this reflection towards life like those of Omar Khayam and Epicurus:

(i) We shall eat drink and be merry
For our souls are of air and body of clay
And there is no happiness after our death.
There is happiness so long we stand here on this earth.
Our life is ephemeral like the water in an Arum-leaf.
The morning dew drop will not linger.

(ii) The whirlwind will rise up in
A moment and will reach the up-countries.
The water in the Arum-leaf will fall in a moment.
Similarly our life will extinguish
In the twinkling of an eye

(iii) You will go to the same place
From where you have come
Clouds rise from the sea
And fall as rains, making
The river full to its brim
The water of the river flows gently and slowly
And reaches the sea
From where it came.

Charulal Mukherjea (Mukherjea, The Santals, 1962,Revised Edition) rightly observes that any new-comer delving into the folk-songs of the Santals will be, I'm quite sure, stuck by the extraordinary simplicity and naivete of their songs. Closer acquaintance with them reveals that these songs are replica of the joys and sorrows of the countryside and glorify nature in her beautiful manifestation of leaves and flowers. That the Santals have elaborate song-cycles for festive occasions like the *Sohrae*(the December Harvest Home), the *Baha*( the Spring Festival), the *Pata* (the Santal Cx[xk or Hook-swinging festival) and marriages is not generally known to everyone. In addition to these, the sowing of the seed and the various stages of the different harvests are celebrated with special songs by the men and women of the tribe amidst tribal dances and ceremonis.

## Dance-songs

By now it is evident that ***Santali songs*** are of various types and some of them are accompanied by music and dance. The songs which are accompanied by dance are Lagre, Dou,Guluari,Dahar,Daha, Rinja,Vinsar, Jhika, Humti, Gunjar, Soharae, Loboe,Dunger, Durumjak, Tundum,Thabur and Jatur. The Songs which are not accompanied by dance are Bir, Horo,Rohoe, Bapla Binti and Morna. Your attention is drawn to the fact that the composers of the songs are not known and some of the songs are very old and at times the songs are either highly philosophical or vulgar. Some of the songs are spontaneous overflow of powerful feelings and full of deep thoughts, emotions and sentiments.

Since my research work is confined to dance- songs, I will, therefore, be focusing on songs accompanied by dance. It has been observed that most songs are accompanied by dance and I have proposed to deal with them as they form the overwhelming majority among Santali songs.

According to Bhattacharya (Bhattacharya, 'Santal Songs: Different Types', 1962) there are nine principle varieties of songs with dance:

(i) LAGRE SEREN, (ii) PATA SEREN, (iii) DONG SEREN, (iv) SOHRAE SEREN, (v) DAHAR SEREN, (vi) BAHA SEREN, (vii) KARAM SEREN, (viii) DASAE SEREN, and (ix) BIR SEREN.

### (i) Lagre Seren

P.C.Hembrom (Hembram P. , 1988, p. 49) very categorically and etymologically describes the term 'Lagre' as being derived from 'la' and 'more'. He explains that 'La' means scraping or removing the grass from surface of the earth and here it stands for *akhara*(centre of a village or meeting place of villagers). According to Hembrom 'More' means five standing for whole village group including Majhi, Jog-Majhi, Paranik, Godet, and other village folk and 'More' is degenerated as 'ngre' or 'gre' and compounded with 'la' to form 'Lagre' or 'Langre'. At the initial stage the head of Moreko(village five) called Majhi and assistant head called Jog-Majhi engage two virgin maids to scrape off the grasses of *akhara* and erect a small alter and the maids then purify the spot with 'cow dung water'. Thereafter with solemn swearing and chanting of Mantras they start a pleasure dance believing that the dance would invoke shower for agricultural work.

'Lagre' is the commonest dance tune and is suited for all odd occasions. W.G.Archer (Archer, The Hill of Flutes: Life , Love and Poetry in Tribal India, A Portrait of the Santals, 1974, p. 65) records that the Lagre dance has a standard form called *tahri*. The girls form a curving line facing the drummers. They begin with a song to 'bind' the akhra or dancing ground after that they slowly edge along its rims. Then the drums quicken and a jerking oscillation starts. The right foot goes slightly out and edges right. The left foot joins it. Then the right moves a little to the side and the left goes out and edges near it. At the same time the knees bend and straighten, the clasped hands sway gently in and out and the buttocks bob roundly up and down. The heads go nodding to the drums and as the line of bodies sets up a vertical undulation, the songs rise calmly through the din.

The distinctive characteristic of these songs is that these songs have almost always romantic connotations. Birds such as fly-catchers, peacocks, doves and pigeons stand for girls; monkeys and porcupines for boys. Making love is suggested by phrases such as 'drinking a river-full of water', 'crying for water', 'swaying in the dew', 'picking cotton on a hill' and 'losing a ring'. Seduction is implied by the phrases 'striking with a flute', 'shooting an aarrow' or 'climbing a fig tree'. An unwanted pregnancy is described as 'making a citron fruit fall', and places of assignation are referred to as 'a gully with the plantain' or 'the foot of the mountain'. It has been observed that direct allusions to sex are never made. 'Four-letter' words are scrupulously avoided and it is rather by means of symbols drawn from daily life that the singers make their point.

Talking about Lagren enec, Charulal Mukherjea (Mukherjea, The Santals, 1962,Revised Edition, p. 366) writes that this is the most common of Santal dances and may be held at any time, but a moon-light is the favourite occasion for it. When the moon glimmers, men beat the drums and *madals* to attract the youths and maids of the tribe by the music. Soon a sufficient number assembles at the spot; they make a complete circle with a radius of seven to ten feet .The steps of the 'Lagren' dance are regular all through. The feet , they wave forward making an angle of 45° (degrees) and swing to the right, while the circle appears to move in an anti-clock-wise direction. So they dance merrily for half an hour, when comes an interval. Now they sit and rest for about ten minutes. Some crack jokes, while men sing and women reply in chorus. So they go on till about 3 a.m. in the morning. Charulal further adds that 'Lagren' is a very stimulating dance, and on these occasions the youths and maids of the tribe get plenty of opportunities for love-making. Even the steps of the dance provide facilities for courtship, as the couples face side-ways and talk as they dance. And after the dances, parties in love retire into the woods. "In Lagre dance", says Sadhna Prasad DasGupta (DasGupta S. P., 1979), "the beating of the *Madal* is slow. Similar slow is the movement of the bodies. The women join hands, form a semi-circle and dance in swinging movement inright side and in left side. In this dance the body from waist to foot swings much."

Giving detailed description of Lagre dance, P.O.Bodding (Bodding, A Santal Dictionary: 7 Parts in Five Volumes, 1993(First published in India)) explains that this is the most common of all Santal dances and may be danced at any time or occasion. The girls take hold of each other by their hands( so that one girl's right hand is clasped by the other's left hand(fingers); there may be as many as convenient for the space in one row, generally upto some twelve or even more. In front of these there are three boys, two belabouring dancing-drums and one a kettle-drum. The boys move drumming towards the girls and jump back again, while the girls move backwards and forwards, the slightly semi-circular row gradually altering its position, so that they little by little turn round. The girls also move the middle of their bodies backwards and forwards. With short intervals they may continue until long past midnight. He further writes that this dance gives the young people an occasion to have sexual intercourse when not actually dancing. Even old women will dance this dance when they are drunk with beer; as the girls and young men are at present wild with lust they dance every night in the village street outside the headman's house.

The songs, sung on these occasions, are mostly love-songs. Consider for example the following love-song:

**(I)**

Nadiaka dhare dhate
Kahar bansi baje,
Hai hai xntare kandiche.
Akhite dekhini, kanetx sunini,
Haihai, amar xntare kandiche.

**(Translation)**
On the banks of the river,
Whose lute plays?
Alas! the heart weeps.
I haven't seen with eyes,
Nor heard with ears.
Alas, my heart weeps ! (Mukherjea, The Santals, 1962,Revised Edition, p. 367)

When there are no rains, there are certain 'Lagre' songs in invocation to the rain god, which are sung to make the skies yield rain:

**(II)**

Svarager hur hur
Prithimite dhula chilu urilx
Dhaner sisx chilu marilx
Mnuser chati chilu phatilx he.

**(Translation)**
In the sky, clouds rumble, Oh god!
On the earth, dust flies.
Oh god! the ears of corn dry up.
The hearts of men are breaking, Oh god! (Mukherjea,1962, p.368)

**(III)**

There are ten drummers
There are twenty girls
The dancing ground is big and wide
Do not rouse me, drummer

Or I will make you drink
A river-full of water

**(IV)**

The fly-catcher, elder brother
Is crying out for water.
All things are bad, girl.

**(V)**

At night I slept on a verandah
And in a dream I found you
How lovely you were
Swaying in the dew.

**(VI)**

O you peacock in the peacock forest
I will make you fly
On your feathers I will put
Golden sindur.

**(VII)**

To the high lands
Went the cattle
To the muddy swamp
The buffaloes.
Middle brother,
The mud is heaving.
In the gully with the plantains
Is a spring with a bonga

**(VIII)**

Monkey, from branch to branch you sprang
You strolled from path to path
Take care, monkey
Or the citron fruit will fall

**(IX)**

In the middle of the street
Is a dancing ground

Go quickly, girl
For though you are frightened
I shall look inside your heart

**(X)**

With a gold umbrella
You have gone away, my son
But do not cross
The five mountains
Let me go, mother
Go I will
For a girl is standing

Lovely as a flame. (Archer, The Hill of Flutes: Life , Love and Poetry in Tribal India, A Portrait of the Santals, 1974, pp. 66-67).

Manis kumar (Raha, 1967) gives some examples of Lagre songs in order to assess the rhythm of the song:

**(XI)**

Hor Kad Diku kad
Sona Chandom Ematk
Ench Da Chamdo Bam Emadinch
Mati Re Han Biti Re Han
Ench Da Chando Emanch Me
Iji Ge Chando Sona Huyutinch

**(Translation)**

(You were ploughing the stony plot below the tank. You must have been very eager for the rice-gruel. You took up the goading stick and displayed it towards me. I got afraid-perhaps you were going to beat me (Raha, 1967)).

Manis Kumar, furthermore, describes that not only this light-tuned song is present in Lagre type, but we also see different other types of tunes in Lagre. In his view the Santals are often seen to sing the Lagre songs concerning natural conditions. Let us see examples:

**(XII)**

The cuckoo sings on the Peepal tree at the end of the road
Summer is on
Bull frogs croak in the tank below the vegetable plot
Rains are coming.

**(XIII)**

When tigers growl on the low mountains
We may clearly presume the hot summer days are in view;
Tigers go away to higher mountains
That indicates the approach of rains.

According to Manis Kumar Lagre songs are not only restricted to such themes only but often contain themes of their social life also. When the spring appears in the young hearts, when the young boys and girls come closer to each other in their day-today- contact, when they fall in love with each other, they sing:

**(XIV)**

Har Khanad Fich Red
Tingun Mese Eha Mairi
    Sedai Reya Kathayan Kuli Me
Har Khanad Fich Red
Bayanch Tingun Eha Mairi
    Sange Rege Juri Menaya (Raha, 1967).

**(Translation)**

(You are my life, Jiban,
I am your life, Jiban,
    Our lives have been bound together, Jiban.
As leaves never fall from the date-palm tree,
So I am not going to relinquish your mind;
    So we would support each other for ages.) (Raha, 1967)

Lagre type of songs were used by the Santals as inspiration to fight against the Britishers. When Hul rebellion broke out amongt the Santals against the British rule in 1855, the Lagre type of songs inspired the Santals much to fight against the injustice and the torture they suffered from. Manis Kumar Raha gives example of the song sung by the rebel Santals:

**(XV)**

Saheb rule is trouble full
Shall we go or shall we stay?
Eating, drinking, clothing
For everything we trouble
Shall we go or shall we stay?

Sido, why are you bathed in blood?
Kanhu, Why do you cry, Hul Hul?
For our people we have bathed in blood,
For the trader thieves
Have robbed us of our land (Raha, Santal Folksong, 1979, p. 257).

Sido and Kanhu fought against the British rule very bravely with their own bows and arrows. They created a terror among the British army with their native bows, arrows and tangi. Fear they did not know, death they did not care while singing the following heroic song:

**(XVI)**

Saya Chetan Kuri
Lipir lipir sari
Hayate Hila Kan Hipir Hipir
Rath Nakich Bagiben
Gech Gurich Chetben
Bangben Sahao Leda Hiram Sikir (Raha, Santal Folksong, 1979, p. 257).

**(Translation)**

(We shall eat, drink and make ourselves merry. This body, this lump of earth will not stay on. Life slides along, like water on an arum leaf. This body, this lump of earth will not stay on.)

## (II) Pata Seren (Hook-Swinging Festival) also known as Dharua Seren

Subhendu Sekhar Bhattacharya (Bhattacharya, 'Santal Songs: Different Types', 1962) gives an account of what pata seren is. He writes, "The Word Pata Seren literary means song sung at Pata festival (i.e. Chaitra Snkranti or Saiber Gajan). But actually is not confined to that occasion only. These songs can be sung at any time and at any place". Pata seren is a simple tune and approximates Jhumur tune which is extremely popular as the principle folk tune of songs. In Pata the words occupy the principle position and dance is controlled by it. Sri Rjendra Nath Majhi narrates: "*Karam Puthi* (Introduction) Nitre Ho Kono Kono Disomra Pata Tandi Ki Chata Tandikere Apan Apan Ato Piche Sanam Arak Renge, Ayoteko Hoponko Misera Kimin Hopon Laite Patae Them. Deko Horko Talare Kono Atoren Do Lagre Ko Akhrawakada Kono Atoren Do Dharuako Akhrawakada ar Ayoteko Do Deko Horko Then Dakar Dakar Ko Enec Etkoa Ni jer Man Bhoromko do Bako Hudiseda". "Even at present in some part of the country they dispatch the entire population of the village to the Pata festival. On Chat festival—mothers, sisters, songs and daughter-in-laws. In some villages they set up the dancing ground in the hamlets occupied by Hindus. The mothers leaping and frisking before the eyes of Hindus- they neither feel shame nor loss of prestige."

For P.O. Bodding (Bodding, A Santal Dictionary: 7 Parts in Five Volumes, 1993(First published in India)), Pata is 'the hook-swinging festival of the Hindus( in honour of Mahadeb). This festival is celebrated on the last day of C t(the last (twelfth) month of the Hindu year (last half of March and first half of April)). But the local low-caste Hindus and aborigines actually have the festival at any time during the whole of Baisak(up to the middle of May). Now even Santals celebrate it ; and where it is held, Santals will attend in crowds and dance, etc., during the night. They dance the whole night at the place where the *Pata* is held; at present Santals observe the hook-swinging festival.'

W.W.Hunter (Hunter, 1979, p. 274) in his article entitled 'Ten Santal Festivals' asserts that Pata(hook-swinging) festival, though stopped by the Government, is still in practice among northern Santals in April or May, lasting almost a month. He describes Pata festival saying that young men used to swing with hooks through their back, as in the Charak puja of the Hindus. The swingers used to fast the day preceding and the day following the operation, and to sleep the intermediate night on thorns.

Charulal Mukherjea (Mukherjea, The Santals, 1962,Revised Edition) argues that the Santals, in addition to their orthodox festivals, associate themselves with the various Hindu ceremonials like the Durga Puja, Kali Puja and others. From their evidence, however, it is not clear as to when they began their association with the Hindu festivals, but looking at the *Pata*, it seems to be pretty old. According to her the orthodox meaning of the word *Pata* is stated to be "a festival in honour of *Mahadeo*". She elaborates that the customary practices in connection with the *Pata*, vary in different areas. It is believed by the Santals that there are some amongst Santals who show signs of supposed spirit possession(the Santal Jhupar) with the arrival of the festival and they go here and there like Tagore's maniac('khepa') in eternal search for the "touchstone." They dive in a pond, ransack the forests, search the hills, and at last coming upon a stone shout, "Eureka"("We have found."). And the admiring audience see that they have unearthed a stone, which they all acclaim as the symbol of *Mahadeo*. These people called *Bhxktas*, then run to the conveners of the Hindu festival *Cxrxk* and prevail upon them to worship the images ceremonially , and if listened to , they are permitted to join with the devotees and take part in the ceremonials.

There is another saying, as Charulal Mukherjea goes on to describe, that there are others who arrange their festivals. Such people go begging from house to house for three days previous, and with the proceeds, they buy milk. Then they , on the eve of the Pata, assemble at a field, where the Bhoktas( devotees) erect a hut-temple with subscriptions collected from the tribe; and offer milk, rice and ghee to the deity Mahadeo with a good deal of ceremony, a goat being sacrificed in a place away from the improvised temple. The ceremonials conclude with special songs and dances in which the Santals take part with a great deal of gusto.

For Charulal Mukherjea (Mukherjea, 'Santal Folk Poetry', July-Dec 1936) Pata is equivalent of the Bengali Charak puja or Hook swinging festival. There is no available evidence to suggest that Pata is originally Santali festival, since no mention of it is made in the Hapram Reak Katha, the institutes and traditions of the Santals. However, one of the songs sung on this occasion woul seem to suggest that the festival was formerly celebrated in water. This song Pahil Pahil ko pata kadac, may be thus rendered:

In water was Pata held in times old and early,
In water was fixed a post,
Where swung the Pata-host,

The wheel revolved, revolved the wheel merrily (Mukherjea, 'Santal Folk Poetry', July-Dec 1936, p. 245).

Another song sings of the swinging-wheel and cracks a joke about the bhaktas, the devotees who are possessed by the spirit of Pata-bonga(the deity of Pata) and act their parts during the festival as if they were gods themselves:

The Dan is six yards long,
Six and half the post,
On the Dan swings along,

Sir Bhakta merrily tossed (Mukherjea, 'Santal Folk Poetry', July-Dec 1936, p. 245).

W.G.Archer (Archer, The Hill of Flutes: Life , Love and Poetry in Tribal India, A Portrait of the Santals, 1974) holds a different view with respect to the *Pata* festival. He is of the view that the Pata or hook-swinging is the first spectacle that sometimes leads to extra-village romances. This festival which is Hindu in origin occurs only in certain villages and takes place either in mid-April or when a Santal Bhogta or devotee discovers a new 'Mahadev' stone. If a man is fishing and stumbles on a smooth 'bonga-like' stone and if he then scratches it and it shows white, he cries out that it is Shiva and that the stone is giving milk. He then puts the stone in a new pot containing sun-dried rice and hangs it in the cattle shed. Each evening for seven days he goes down to a pool or stream, takes a bath and offers frangipani flowers, milk and sweets. He takes a thin cane with him for driving away evil spirits. Then on the seventh day a gathering of other bhogtas is held and swinging is performed.

Giving a very detailed account of Pata festival, W.G.Archer, further maintains that 'when the swinging is done as a festival, crowds from all the neighbouring villages come in. Lines of girls and women perform Lagre dances throughout the night . Pet quails are brought in their cages. Little stalls are set up. Rallying poles poke up above the heads and the celebration has all the excitement of a fair. The devotees who are chosen , one or two from each village , must not have eaten oil or salt... (Archer, The Hill of Flutes: Life , Love and Poetry in Tribal India, A Portrait of the Santals, 1974, p. 134).'

It has been suggested by W.G.Archer that in the earlier days, to employ hooks was usual and the ritual has been described in the following way: "At the ceremony observed in honour of Pata Bonga and which is performed before the raised mound and stone outside the village, the same ordeal is gone through as when the Jatra Bonga is celebrated, but at the finish the Sonthals formerly used to have the Churruck Pooja, or swinging festival; the hooks for suspending the devotee being inserted in the muscle of his back , who was generally an enebriated oracle. He was then suspended in mid-air and swung round, apparently hanging by the hooks. I have, however, seen a good many of these revolving martyrs, and although to a casual observer it appears very dreadful to behold a man thus pendant, it is not quite so bad as it seems, for his friends take the precaution to tie a girth of strong cloth round the victim's body, in such a manner that his weight rests upon the cloth rather than on his muscles (Archer, The Hill of Flutes: Life , Love and Poetry in Tribal India, A Portrait of the Santals, 1974, pp. 134-35)."

W.G.Archer further shows that hooks, among Santals , are now dispensed with and after the bhogta has again poured milk on the mast, he takes his basket in one hand and goes out in the air, sailing round three times, first in one direction and then three times in the other, scattering frangipani flowers and sinjo leaves as he goes. He then comes slowly to rest and his place is taken by another. As the bhogtas swing solemnly and gently round, the crowd cries 'Mahadev, Mahadev,' the drums beat and Lagre dancers go circling round the field. The actual swinging is done only by bhogtas and the number is limited to one, three, five or seven. Each bhogta swings not only for himself but for his village (Archer, The Hill of Flutes: Life , Love and Poetry in Tribal India, A Portrait of the Santals, 1974, p. 135).

In 'Santal Songs: Different Types' Subhendu Sekhar Battacharya discovered that there are songs which condemn Pata songs in unequivocal terms. Examples of two such songs are as under:

> "we shall not go out for dance in the field where 'Ind Porbo' is being held. We shall not dance before assembly of other communities. We shall dance doE , Lagre, Baha and Karam inour village. We shall dance only in our village."(Lagre)

> "Sounds of madol, nagra and horns are being heard in the common meeting ground. Gils and youth will dance and sing in the common ground.we would no longer dance the Pata dance.we would no longer sing Jatra song.we must not tarnish our clear and pure social life." (Pata)

In Subhendu Sekhar Bhattacharya's view free mixing with Hindus is full of dark forebodings. He believes that young girls may succumb to their wiles or may be unable to resist the lure of their wealth. This is slightly hinted at the last line of the previous song and expanded in detail in the song given below. Though some Pata songs depict Hindu influence on Santal culture, this intrusion of Hindu culture, the Santals utterly dislike:

> Pikhuree Pittare Babla Butare
> Cheda Hili Han Ya Jung Kana?
> Ra Bangkhang Chekaya, Hamar Bangkhand Chekaya
> Dadam Baburey Heroman Kan (Raha, Santal Folksong, 1979, p. 258).

> **(Translation)**

> "Stuffing your mouth with betels, looking now to right and now to left, wearing sari trailing along the ground— you, Jhari move about in the market place. You sing songs in the language of the Hindus.You are such a fool that you do not feel that you are abandoning your religion. You smile at Hindu youths. Never do you care that you are turning your back to the community. You will move about cawing like a market

crow. You will never get settled anywhere, I can see it with my eyes." (Pata) (Bhattacharya, 'Santal Songs: Different Types', 1962).

Charulal Mukherjea (Mukherjea, The Santals, 1962,Revised Edition) gives example of one of the songs, sung in the festival , which would seem to show that Pata was formerly celebrated in water. This verse is as follows:

Pahil pahilko patakeda dak
Talare khunti latarre,
Radha corokko nacurena.
(Translation)

In the first Pata festival, a post was fixed in the water. Under it a *Radha Corok* ( a swinging wheel) began to swing round.

There is another song that sings of the swinging wheel and cracks a joke about the *Bhokta*s, the devotees who are possessed by the spirit of Pata-Bonga ( the deity of Pata), and act their parts during the festival as if they were the gods themselves:

Barohat dan dada terohat khunti,
Dan upor bhoktago rahigel
Bhokta pujai mahasoy.

**(Translation)**

The dan is twelve cubits long
Thirteen cubits the post,
On the dan swings along,
(Sir) Bhokta merrily tossed. (Mukherjea, The Santals, 1962,Revised Edition, pp. 268-69).

Charulal Mukherjea recounts how the joy of the Santals during such festivals knows no bounds. Lagre batches of men and women go from place to place and the men play on pipes. The women decorate their hair with beautiful flowers and entwine their arms round one another's shoulders. The kettle-drums, the cymbols and the wine, produce an atmosphere in which these simple people forget their mundane existence in the pursuit of their primitive practices and observances. The *joie de vivre* is reflected in the following song in which a woman requests her sister to accompany her to winess the Pata festival for three days to their heart's content:

Certan disomre pe maha jargon pata hoyok;
Dar ge didi ge songe jaibo,
Pe maha jargon sobay jaybo.

**(Translation)**

In the uplands for three days they keep awake for the Pata;
O sister, do wait for me, I shall go with you;

For three nights they keep awake; we all shall go (Mukherjea, The Santals, 1962,Revised Edition, p. 269).

## (iii) DONG SEREN

Rev. P.O.Bodding describes *do1 ᒪE* as 'a kind of dance, drumming and singing connected with marriage'. According to him this dance is performed in the following manner: 'a number of women form a row, standing close together so that the arms of those standing at each other's side are in line together from the elbows; they clasp each other's hands; two men are in front each having a dancing drum, while a third man has a kettle-drum (tamak). When they commence, the women "trot" , with an up and down motion of their bodies, backwards and forwards for a few paces; meanwhile , the men beat the drum and follow the women to and fro' (Bodding, A Santal Dictionary: 7 Parts in Five Volumes, 1993(First published in India)). Dong seren are the songs sung to the tune of do1 ᒪ E . There are quite a number of don songs sung by women going to fetch firewood, etc., from the forest and are also used at the *horok* ceremonies, at the marriage and at *bahraota*.

For Subhendu Sekhar Bhattacharya (Bhattacharya, Santal Songs: Different Types, 1979) Don seren is 'one of the most commonest types and is used at all social functions e.g. Marriage and Chatiar. It may be called functional song par excellence.' He collected around 750 folk songs and, as per his statement, most of the songs—out of 750 folk songs— belong to Don songs. This fact justifies the great popularity of the Don songs. The fact that it has got high frequency of usage has given rise to several sub-varieties such as Sohoria, Dangua, Budhi and Jhika. In Bhattacharya's view Jhika has diverged so far from the main tune structure that it is now recognized as a separate variety. In addition, slight variations occur in different parts of the Santal territory and such tunes are known by the tracts such as Jharkhand, Mayurbhanj and Raipuria. Of these Jharkhand tracts have attained special celebrity as being explosive songs.

Charulal Mukherjea is of that don dance is danced during marriages generally in which mixed men and women choose their groups and form a lively circle. The women interlock their hands gracefully, whereas men with Nagera and Madal stand in the centre forming an inner circle. After the music continues, the dancers advance two steps to the right in a general motion. Then they gracefully extend each feet forward. They dance for twenty minutes or so while women sing in unison. Charulal Mukherjea further narrates that when the dance finishes, it is now men's turn to sing while women reply in a musical chorus. This continues for some time when again the drums resound; so they dance on and on in a non-stop manner and may continue for two days (Mukherjea, The Santals, 1962, Revised Edition, pp. 368-69).

Mukherjea says that this dance takes place as a mark of joy when volunteers help a Santal farmer who has no helping hand to help him in his agriculture. She asserts that such help is, according to custom, always extended, and the farmer entertains the co-villagers at a thanksgiving party when don is danced after a liberal drink of rice-beer. Charulal is here suggesting us that any scholar studying the don dance may easily find out the fact that the suggestive hip and body movements, special to the dance, can have only one meaning that is recreating in artistic forms the human urge to procreation, where the married pair might unite in love and affection and get children so that the Santals might increase in number (Mukherjea, The Santals, 1962, Revised Edition).

P.C.Hembram (Hembram P. , 1988) says that 'Dong' is a very popular term for the marriage-dance but the term signifies the marriage itself. According to him the Santals have their own definition about the origin of the notion of 'Dong' which they occasionally express in the form of a song as follows:

Dong do okaredo janam len,
Dong do okaredo busar len,
Dong do dong lisai-lasai,
Dong do Hihirire janam len,
Dong do pipirire busar len,
Dong do dong lisai-lasai." (Hembram P. , 1988, p. 57)

**(Translation)**

(Where a marriage is originated,
Where a marriage is come into being!
The marriage is attractive and enchanting.
A marriage is born at Hihiri,
A marriage is come into being at Pipiri,
The marriage is beautiful and grand.)

A few examples of Dong songs:

**(i)**

I saw her in a dream and rose up,
My mind wandered away,
Only the body was left behind
Beyond the cattle shed and under
The cover of the Jam trees my mind
Moved onward—to the spot
Where my beloved was. (Raha, Santal Folksong, 1979, p. 258)

**(ii)**

Inch Juri Kuri Hank Janwayen
Inch Krutum Kara Hank Bahuyan
Inch Krutum Chaole Bandi Huti Ko Lagaoyen
Inch Ge Minayanch Bejuri Har

**(Translation)**

(The clouds are forming in the distant sky
Black clouds are rising up
Perhaps father and mother are going
To bring a dark son-in-law for me) (Raha, Santal Folksong, 1979, p. 258).

**(iii)**

Five mango leaves and a pot of water
I do not know if you really sprinkled water over me
I do not know if you really wetted me or not
But you made me a prisoner for entire life.

**(Iv)**

Chikate kuintti Sunumana
Chikate Matakam Rasawanan
Chikate Kara Macha Geya
Chikate Kuri Macha Chinkar Geya

**(Translation)**

(Yes, yes give me up
My parents will be highly pleased
They will be able to settle marriage

Over and over again
But give me, throw over to me—
My maiden Mind.)

There are other varieties of Don songs apart from above given love and social songs. During Transplantation the following songs are sung:

**(v)**

In Jeth the wind
Is coming with the rain
Where are you, headman?
Bring the two Bullocks
Put the red one to the yoke
And we will plough
The field below the palm-tree. (Raha, Santal Folksong, 1979)

**(vi)**

Wealth, wealth
O, mother wealth
Where was your birth?
I was born
In the soil
I was born
In the splash of rain. (Raha, Santal Folksong, 1979)

Often called the sons of nature, and being inspired by the love of nature, the Santals compose the following Don songs in praise of nature:

**(vii)**

Baru Jharna Re Nakar Baha
Atti Manderate Kander Akan
Taber Taker Tianch Sit Leda
Durup Durup Tianch Baha Leda
Beret En Torage Masat Ena

**(Translation)**

(The flowering tree in our yard
Has produced flowers in abundance
We sweep the yard even at mid-day and in the afternoon
Still the flowers continue to drop down on the ground) (Raha, Santal Folksong, 1979, p. 259).

Subhendu Sekhar Battacharya (Bhattacharya, Santal Songs: Different Types, 1979) gives five beautiful examples of Don songs of different types. Of five examples that he gives the first song is a Chatiar song sung at the birth of a Santal child expressing the joy and latent philosophical truth present in the form of contrasting nature of yearning and attainment:

**(viii)**

> "The brilliant tail indicates that it is a young parrot. It may be a young parakeet. When you bring it down it looks like a young parrot, when it reaches my hand, it is a young parakeet."

The second song is an example of a Dasigua Don% a lament song for a single life by a bachelor:

**(ix)**

> "You said previously: 'when my son grows up I shall find out a wife for him. Alas! I have grown up. I am getting old. I have withered away like a fibrous ribbed gourd left on the fence."(Dasigua Don).

The third example is also a lament song for a single life, however, not by a bachelor but this time by a maiden:

**(x)**

> "All my girl companions have been married away. All youths earmarked for me have obtained wives. Paddy stored up in straw bundles for being used on the occasion of my marriage is being bored through my weevels. I stay on a spinster."

The fourth song is an example of a marriage song put in the mouth of a bride and has a caustic fling at the lover of pre-nuptial days:

**(xi)**

> "I am getting up on the bridal basket. You remain in a melancholy mood. If you have so much love for me, why do you not draw me down from the basket?"

The fifth and the last one is a beautiful example of a dream-fancy(Budhi Don) composed by Sarada Prasad Kisku, the most powerful poet in the language:

**(xii)**

> "I saw her in a dream and rose up. My mind wandered away, only the body was left behind. Beyond the cattle shed and under the cover of

the Jam trees my mind moved onward to the spot where my beloved was."

Marriage songs:

A bride sings:

Nin nutum do baba bargere mad waepe,
Guric mandere khunti bidme,
Nin nutum baryatko hor rege daram kope,
Ninren jurido natorege.

**(Translation)**

O father, build the canopy in the field(near the house, not in the court-yard).
Fix the post(of the canopy) in the cow-dung heap.
And when the bride-groom's party comes, meet them on the way(and make them return),
Because my (life's) mate is in the village. (Mukherjea, The Santals, 1962,Revised Edition, p. 349)

You can sense that here is presumably a case of a girl being given marriage without her consent; the bridegroom is prescribed a humiliating reception because the bride's lover is already in the village.

Another song describes the marriage dances thus:

Cameda latarre mandewa latarre,
Lid lupur lidar lupur baihar rote,
Leka mersa mersi.

**(Translation)**
They are dancing beneath the canopy
Under the branch of the tree;
They are hopping up and down and cheek
By jowl, like frogs in the field. (Mukherjea, The Santals, 1962,Revised Edition, p. 350)

In the next song the singer addresses the caged-bird as to the time when the bridal party is expected to arrive:

Cetan disom khon ninidin
Darakan disadaram ben nasul
Miru, najani din con, najani ninda con,
Pasen con dinman tala ninda.

**(Translation)**

They are coming from the up-country to take me.
O bird, do tell me when they will come?
Keep awake and tell me when they will come.
They might come in day-light or at night,

They might come at midday or mid-night. (Mukherjea, The Santals, 1962, Revised Edition, p. 350).

In the following song a reference is made to a humorous song about a bride-groom's party:

Cetan disomren sange baryat,
Bare butarebon deraket ko;
Jomak nuniak do timinrecon
Bare hongor hatar metakope.

**(Translation)**

We have a big bride-groom's party from up-country.
We have given them a resting place under the banyan tree.
It is not known when we can serve them dinner.

Let them in the meantime eat the banyan fruit. (Mukherjea, The Santals, 1962,Revised Edition, p. 351)

Charulal Mukherjea describes that marriage ceremonies in Santal villages are red-letter days in the life of the women of the tribe. The following song expresses the joy that infects the life of the community:

Tehenge sindo, tehenge nindado
Matkom gelere nelerasa
Dose lsiskope, rasi nato kuri kora
Doko neljon ma
Matkom gelere nelerasa.

**(Translation)**

This day is a day of all days,
This night is a night of all nights.
In *mohua* flowers there is honey.
Go and tell the youths and maids of populous villages;
Let them come and see

The *mohua* flowers are full of honey. (Mukherjea, The Santals, 1962,Revised Edition, pp. 351-52).

Next is a farewell song in a very pathetic tone giving us a tragic touch in the separation:

Beker beker yamgim janamlidin,
Konor konor yamgim haralidin.
Batire basan dak' malire sunum
Koto jotonte yamgim haralidin,
Bam dayalenayo bammayalen,
Tala ninda minhun merom
Leka yamgim chutikidin.

**(Translation)**

As a babe you brought me forth on this earth,
You have reared me up in your arm ( always);
With a bowl of tepid water and oil in a vessel,
With what a care have you reared me up!
O mother, where is your affection for me?

You are now sending me in midnight like a cow or goat. (Mukherjea, The Santals, 1962, Revised Edition, p. 352)

Songs of Love

In the following song, a man thus speaks of his love for a lame girl:

Burure sinarak' legec' legec' sinarak,'
Jibon calak rehoin sidgeya,
Natore kuri konrse kata kuri
Hirom cetan rehoin agueya.

**(Translation)**

Sin leaves are soft and away on the hill;
My life may go, but I must pluck them.
There is a maid in the village, she limps as she moves.

Though I have a wife, I must marry her. (Mukherjea, The Santals, 1962,Revised Edition, pp. 353-54).

In the following song there is exact counterpart wherein a woman sings of her love for a lame youth in exactly the same language with only slight variations:

Burure sinarak' legec' legec' sinarak,'
Jibon calak rehoin sidgeya,
Natore kora konrse kata kora
Hirom cetan rehoin boloygeya.

**(Translation)**

Sin leaves are soft and away on the hill;
My life may go, but I must pluck them.
There is a youth in the village, he limps as he moves.

Though he has a wife, I must have his love (even as a co-wife). (Mukherjea, The Santals, 1962, Revised Edition, p. 354)

In the next song a girl is in a dilemma into on seeing her lover at a distance:

Gaten triyoy noron buruma cetanre
Ninma dak' in lolo jojo jharnare
Thilin bagirema horkororora
Norakin ruarrema gaten khinsok'a
Horko rororbacha in sahaokeya
Gaten kahis dote bangin sahaoke.

**(Translation)**

My lover is playing on his pipe on a hill;
I am gathering water from Jaja-spring.
If I go to my love, leaving my pitcher here,
People will criticize me.
If I return home, my lover will be pained.
I can stand what men may say (gladly enough)

But I can never bear the pain in my lover's heart. (Mukherjea, The Santals, 1962, Revised Edition, pp. 354-55).

In the next song we witness a new attachment formed by a youth. Here the former sweet-heart of a girl is being addressed by her to get rid of his infatuation:

Sedae sedae do gate lan tahenkan,
Sedae leka ror landa rorem namkan,
Ne kaira sakam re maya redme,
Ne natu got' kam jonom jonom.

**(Translation)**

At first we were friends.
(Now) should you want the same smiles and talk,
Wrap the love in a plantain leaf
And let it drift in the current. (Mukherjea, The Santals, 1962, Revised Edition, p. 355).

The following song illustrates the truth that in love there is no distinction between the high and low:

Namdo kisar hopon nindorengec,
Hopon ceka leka tem bulau
Kidin nalo sarim rag, sari nalo
Sarim homora, bana horge conlan conlan soman geya.

**(Translation)**

Girl: You are a rich man's son,
I am a poor man's daughter.
How could you charm me so?

Boy: Really, do not weep,
Don't feel wounded (my dear),
We both equal are. (Mukherjea, The Santals, 1962, Revised Edition, p. 356).

W.G.Archer (Archer, Santal Poetry, 1979) quotes few marriage songs:

**I**

You petted me like a pet parrot
You petted me like a tame pigeon
Father, Oh when did you give your word?
From my friend's love you parted me.

**II**

My mother on the stool
My father on the chair
Oh they sit at ease
You are tired of rearing me, milk tree
So stary as you are.

**III**

Seeing a tall tree
And its thick leaves
The little bees have settled
Seeing a big house
And a high roof
The strangers chose it
From birth on to birth
They are our kinsmen.

### IV

With such a big pond, O lotus
Why have you come where water flows away
Come to the spider's country, O my lotus
And the rain is drizzling down.

### VI

O two white doves of the white mountain
What was your sorrow that you flew away?
It was the heat of the day
It was the dew in the night
It was the dew that made you fly away.

### VII

At the end of the street
The sound of violin and flute
To the spring I had gone for drawing water
Hearing and hearing,
Listening, listening at the spring
O friend, I left behind my pot of water.

### VIII

In what a lovely way you flaunted
O you true one, how I loved and fondled you
My heart is a glass and I look at you in it
But how dimly I see you now.

### IX

The tank, the tank
Who dug it like a sea?
The chain of gold
The ring of silver
The mother linked them to the sky.

### X

On the big mountain, the fat rabbit
On the small hill, the peacock with its tail
Scamper away, O you fat rabbit
Fly away, O peacock with your tail.

**XI**

In the upper land the clouds have gathered
And the storm is coming up
O dark girl, we will take a leaf of a palm tree
And stop the wind and rain. (Archer, Santal Poetry, 1979, pp. 9,10 and 11).

W.G.Archer gives examples of Santal Transplantation songs:

**I**

Wealth, wealth
O mother wealth
Where was your birth?
I was born
In the soil
I was born in the splash of rain.

**II**

Wealth, wealth
Where is your mother
Where is your father?
My mother and father
Are wind and rain
My milk is water trickling.

**III**

Paddy, for so long we kept you
In a big house
Now you are going out
To a fine field
We shall scatter you
Paddy.

**IV**

In Jeth the wind
Is coming with the rain
Where are you headman?
Bring this two bullocks
Put the red one to the yoke

And we will plough
The field below the palm tree.

**V**

In our fields
In our lands
Is a house of wealth

**VI**

The paddy is weeping
The paddy is asking
When will be my wedding?
When the water of the sky
Drenches the earth
Then will be your wedding.

**VII**

Lukhi , lukhi
You have come from the house
Where will you stay?
Mud is my dwelling
Rivers are my parents
Water is my milk.

**VIII**

Put on your clothes, girl
And comb your hair
Let us go
To the house in the fields.

**IX**

My lover sits by the river
Give me the fishes
O my lover
If there is any love in you

I will cook the fishes for you. (Archer, Santal Transplantation songs, 1979, pp. 19-20).

S.C. Majumdar (Majumdar, Some Santal Songs, 1925) gives ample examples of different types of dong songs such as nature songs, marriage songs and songs of love:

**I**

Do not play your flute, Badan, by the bank of the river.
Why trouble the water that lies beneath the rock?

**II**

Early in the morning, mother, I was going to fetch water,-
Looking back, I found someone had broken the young tips of the castor-plant
When I had taken my bath, sitting on the big slab of stone, and washed my hair
I peeped into the water, and saw my shadow
My youth has passed away!

**III**

Father you dug a pool at the bend of the road across our village
On its banks you planted trees of tagar flowers
Father, I also have grown up like those trees;
But while their flowers have faded, this blossom of yours
Is trembling in the breeze.
My sweetheart has his decoration of gold, and his ornaments of silver
Their vision haunts mu mind.
Let me hang my dreams high up on the branches
Of the tamarind tree at our door;
For they make me neglect my sweeping of courtyard.

**IV**

The tamarinds are swaying to the breeze in the orchard,
The mango branches are heavy with their clusters of fruit.
Come, mine own, to eat mangoes at our place;
I left my full pitcher by the pool in the sands,
To hasten to you, love, when I saw you coming.

**V**

There's a voice and a smile in the banam, Muni,
There's a heart in the flute.
I am in your heart, Muni, you are in mine.
On the webs floating in the sky, which bind everything together!

**VI**

Numberless are the mahua trees in our land,
Their flowers they keep dropping through the day and in the evening.
The breeze is envious, the sun is languid,-
What harm, my love, if in this day of the hot wind
You do not gather mahuas?

**VII**

I have no girl of my age here, unwedded still I am.
Needs must I go from here too some other land;
Or let me rather lean against a tree, raising my eyes to the moon,
Entreating him to find me my mate.
My other is dead and so is my father.
Who is there to call me: "come and sit here, child?"
There's only the plantain tree in our courtyard.
It is my father and my mother as well,-
It calls me: "Child, come and sit here!"

**VIII**

O mother, the drums, little and big, sound in the village.
As I listen and yearn, listen and yearn,
My body rocks like a lotus leaf on the water.

**IX**

The river bank is full of kambir flowers
The day wears on as I climb its steep side,
The night grows dark as I gather the blossoms,
The sun rises while I weave them into a garland.

**X**

My parents are like the moon,
My brother and sister are like the stars.
I was born under the yellow sirguja blossoms,
And my name is little sunflower. (Majumdar, Some Santal Songs, 1979, pp. 139-40).

Mitchell Murray J (J Murray, 1979) in an article entitled 'Santali Songs: With Translations and notes' cites few example of Santali songs from which I am quoting two marriage songs:

3. Dini tale, mai tale, dini tale bite tale
Sadom re la dejeya, chhater tale numule tale

**(Translation)**

Give to us our daughter , give to us our daughter
We shall place her on horseback, and shade her
With an umbrella.

4. Napum, mai, chanda taka, neugam nenga netat:
Chet: hirir garir mai, chet: bam maro.

**(Translation)**

Daughter, your father has received piled
rupees. Daughter, your mother too
has received her present.
Why run hiding hither and thither, daughter?
Why so reluctant?

## (IV) Sohrae Seren

In common practice the songs sung during the Sohrae festivel is known as *sohrae seren*. According to P.O.Bodding (Bodding, A Santal Dictionary: 7 Parts in Five Volumes, 1993(First published in India)) Sohrae is a name commonly given by the Santals to what is otherwise called *kartik* (end of October and the first half of November). P.O.Bodding maintains that it is the principal festival of the Santals. According to tradition, the Sohrae festival was formerly observed in the month of Sohrae. P.O.Bodding asserts that 'it is very likely a harvest festival. When the people cultivated jungle grain, the month of Sohrae would be time when these were harvested. Now that rice has become their principal food, the harvest festival has to come later, it has consequently been moved to the latter half of the month of Pus(just before or after our New Year's day), when all paddy is reaped. It should regularly be started on a Wednesday, but this is not always observed. All people bathe and have their clothes washed; sacrifices are offered by the village priest outside the village, (not in the *jaher*), near water, and in every house by the master of the house to the house-gods (*orak bongas*). The young men go from house to house to bless the cattle (*jagao*); the girls do the same in their respective cow-sheds….' During the Sohrae dance the girls and young men go dancing from one end of the Village Street to the other, and return in the same way, singing Sohrae songs to Sohrae tunes, while the young men drum using a peculiar time.

P.C.Hembram(Hembram P., 1988, p. 47) points out that the festival celebrated during the Autumn season is called 'Soharay'. This is not only a festival of man but also of cattle. It is for their protection and security of cattle that Santals worship the cattle-deity at 'cow-shade'. Besides, 'got sim' puja is held at Jaher. Moreover, Santals worship their house-hold deities for welfare and prosperous life of family. Hembram maintains that Sohrae is one of the grand festivals of the community which accompanies songs and dances. As far as the origin of the word 'Sohrae is concerned, Hembram states that according to Santal tradition, the name Soharay has been derived from 'sohey' and 'ray'. 'Sohey' means to surrender or to agree and 'ray' means the pact of the treaty. Thus, the name bears a history of turmoil between Santals and invaders.

There is a profound belief among the Santals that after a great struggle Santals won the war resulting into the invaders surrendering themselves to Santals. And before entering into a treaty, arrangement was made between two groups through messengers for communicating the schedule of treaty in the form of burning candle. The alliance was fixed to be held in the dead dark night of new moon through a celebration of burning candle. 'One burning candle means an item of a treaty as communicated earlier. Thus it originates Dipawali festival.'

E.G.Man (Man, 1983(First Indian Edition), p. 56) reports that 'the Soharai, or harvest joy, is their longest and one of the most important festivals.' This festival, according to him, is celebrated and continued almost for five days and nights and dancing, eating, drinking, singing, and every imaginable kind of debauchery are the main activities towards which the people are devoted. Man remarks that 'for the whole of that time the village street is alive with noisy groups of both sexes; the elder ones smoking and drinking, while the young people are flirting, romping, and dancing.' He further describes, "On one day in particular the confusion becomes worse confounded, the brute creation being pressed in as unwilling sharers in the commotion. The cattle are brought out and tied to ornamented posts in front of their several owners' compounds: men and boys then fling at them bits of sticks, baskets, and the youngsters rush between the animals from one side of the street to the other, carrying in their hands skins and cloth which they wave before the eyes of the baited prisoners. This combined with the beating of drums, the shouting of many voices, the reeling figures of the drunken, and the shrill chantings of the women, make up a series of Bacchanalian orgies which baffle description." E.G.Man draws our attention to one part of the ceremony which in its performance was, in view of E.G.Man, similar to the Egyptian myth of the "Bull and the Egg."

According to J. Troisi (Troisi J. , Tribal Religion: Religious Beliefs and Practices among the Santals, 1978, p. 126) among the Santals , the

Sohrae or Harvest Festival is one of the most important and the principal celebrations as per the tradition. The Sohrae festival also happens to be their 'largest and merriest' annual event when the Santal people hailing from different villages gather to enjoy themselves by indulging in dancing and singing. In J Troisi's view this festival is held in the month of *Pus* (December-January), immediately after the crops have been reaped, threshed and stored. The Sohrae includes the blessing and baiting of cattle, a fishing expedition and a village hunt. In addition, the spirits are not forgotten for the Sohrae offers the Santals an occasion to thank their spirits and the rituals performed include sacrifices of fowls to the village spirits, and the ancestral spirits. Moreover, kinsmen from different villages are cordially invited; married daughters are expected to return to their father's household for the occasion; relatives bring gifts along with them. Troisi remarks that this is the festival which binds together the whole tribal Santal community and all—human and divine, living and dead—take part in the celebration of all the festivities directly or indirectly.

Sunil Kumar Dasu (Dasu, 1979, pp. 28-29) has drawn his observations regarding the Sohrae festival held among the Santals on the basis of the data placed in the form of a chart and I am further giving descriptions of the Sohrae festival given by various research scholars who figure in that chart. N.Dutta-Majumdar (Majumdar N. , 1956, p. 49 & 103) reports that the Sohrae or Banda Parab is a harvest festival of the Santals. It is the largest and merriest of the festivals celebrated for five days in the month of Pous (December-January). Martin Orans (Orans M. , 1965) is of the view that Sohrae is the most important festival of the Santals connected with harvest held in December for three days. Mahendra Nath Banerjee and Ajit Kumar Sarkar (Sarkar, 1964, pp. 52-61) remark that the Sohrae is held in the month of *kartik*(October-November) on the new moon day and on that day the presiding deity of cattle is worshipped. The Sohrae is known by other agriculturist groups as Bandhana or Khawa Ceremony. W.J.Culshaw (Culshaw, Tribal Heritage: A Study of the Santals, 1949, pp. 110-12) contends that the Sohrae is connected with harvest and is held during the period between the dark night of October-November and middle of January, and that it may last for three days. It generally takes place at the time of Hindu Kali puja and during the ceremony sacrifices are offered to *ange* spirits. P.C.Biswas (Biswas, 1956, p. 138) asserts that Sohrae is a Harvest festival of the Santals and is held during the month of *Pous*(at the beginning of January). According to Biswas the first three days are most important and the last two days are meant for merry-making.

In a study about the Santal seasonal rites or feasts and festivals and particularly about winter harvest-the Sohrae feast Mohan K.Gautam (Gautam, 1977, p. 181) remarks that in the long awaited month of *Pus*( middle of December to middle of January), after the Santals in our villages have reaped, harvested and threshed the 'new paddy', believing that the *Bongas* have been so kind and helpful in providing sufficient sunshine , rain, good weather, fertility of land and unity among the villages, and realizing that now that they have sufficient food, they would like to thank the *Bongas* and specially the Sohrae deity in whose name the festival is held. Mohan K.Gautam is of the opinion that this is the time when the Santals should wind up their reciprocal obligations, exchange gifts, visits,and discuss the future plan of their community.

W.J.Culshaw (Culshaw, Tribal Heritage: A Study of the Santals, 2004(Published in India), p. 138) points out that *Sohrae* or *Banda parab* or harvest festival is one of the chief festivals of the Santals connected with agricultural operations, celebrated in the Bengali month Pous after the rice crop of the has been harvested. This festival, in his view, lasted for five days. As far as fixing of date of its celebration is concerned, Culshaw argues, that previously there was no fixed date and the villagers of one locality would perform the festival one day whereas the others would perform the festival on some other day. Now-a-days, howver, the Deputy Commissioner of the Santal Parganas fixes the date for this festival , and this date is proclaimed by a man with a *sal* branch in his hand in every *hut*. Joseph Troisi (Troisi J. , Tribal Religion: Religious Beliefs and Practices among the Santals, 1978, p. 89) offers his views telling us that some people worshiped their *abges* during the Soharae festival and he further quotes O'Malley and Gausdal's views about it. O'Malley (O' Malley, Bengal District Gazetteers, Vol. 22, Santal Parganas, 1910, p. 122) records that there was no fixed date on which these sacrifices( for the bongas) were to take place,'each man performing them when it suits his convenience.' According to Gausdal (Gausdal, 1960, p. 25) these sacrifices were offered during the month of *Asar* (June-July) or during the month of *Aghar* (November-December).

According to W.W.Hunter (Hunter, 1979, p. 274) The Sohrae festival is a rice-harvest and it is held after gathering in the month of December. Hunter suggests that this festival lasts for five days in each village; it, however, is generally prolonged for a month by fixing different days for it in neighbouring villages. Hunter further explains that during the ceremony 'an egg is placed on the ground; all the cows of the village are driven near to it and the animal that first smells at the egg is honoured by having its horns rubbed with oil.'

In the view of V.Manuel Raj (Raj, 1990, p. 36)who has worked with the Santals and published extensively on the Santals, Sohrae is the principal feast of the Santals as their principal food is rice. This festival, according to him , is celebrated in the mnth of Pus(December-January). He is of the view that unlike the other festivals , it involves much preparation—houses are renewed, new clothes are bought, plenty of rice-beer prepared and as many as possible kin and kith are invited for the celebration. Most importantly, the entire land of the Santals bubbles with joy and gaiety on this festival. It is also the festival of thanksgiving of love, brotherhood and sisterhood.

For Subhendu Sekhar Bhattacharya also (Bhattacharya, Santal Songs: Different Types, 1979, p. 24), as we have seen with other scholars, Sohrae is the greatest festival among the Santals. He is also of the similar view that it lasts for five days but he adds that on all these five days of celebrations ban on home-brewing of rice beef is lifted in the respective areas. What is interesting here is to note the fact that in actual practice these dates are not followed and each village fixes five consecutive days according to its convenience. And only the date lines fixed for kali puja and Pous Sankranti are observed. In addition, songs and dances go on night and day during the festival, and a considerable quantity of rice beer is drunk and some amount of laxity between young men and women is tolerated. He adds that all five days have got five individual names which indicate the observance for the day concisely and precisely. Bhattacharya gives the details of the names of each day:

"1st day (*Um Hilok*- Day of Bath) ceremonial is taken on the day, clothes are washed and house cleaned.

2nd day (*Dakae Hilok*-Day of rice) married daughters, near relatives and friends are invited to partake in the feast.

3rd day (*Khuntao Hilok*- Day of cattle poking) Cattles are worshipped in the morning.They are tied to the ropes and men tease them to fury so that they charge at the persons with their horns. This appears to be the core of the religious function. Songs and dances also reach their height on the night.

4th day ( *Jale Hilok*- Day of begging)- young men and women go dancing from house to house begging for rice etc.which is finally cooked into a hash and eaten by the whole community.

5th day (has got no special name) the feast is terminated in the morning by a drink of a cooled rice beer and the elders in council over particularly objectionable behavior by the younger folk if any."(p.24).

In fact Charulal Mukherjea (Mukherjea, The Santals, 1962,Revised Edition, p. 242) in her analysis about the *Sohrae* festival of the Santals particularly of the Santal Parganas calls Sohrae *the winter Harvest Home* and it has been described to be the biggest annual event of their tribal life. This particular day is assumed for the Santals to be an important day of thanksgiving to such gods as rain, the sun and fair weather for their invaluable contribution to a bumper crop. Also known as *Bundhna* in common parlance, Sohrae has no fixed date in the tribal calendar. Each village decides the date of the festival as per its own convenience. Sometime dates are fixed by the Deputy Commissioner and the Excise Department to have easy regulatory mechanism to control the arrangement. There is, however, a unanimous agreement that the festival must conclude before the last day of the Bengali month, that is, *Pous* (mid-January).

The following is a folk-song sung on the field on the first day of Sohrae, with water near about:

Kò nàhi sirijala
Boma prithima ho;
Kò nàhi sirijala
Gàia jo yo re;
Kò nàhi sirijala
Gàia jo.

Thàkuràhi*n* sirijala
Boma prithima ho;
Thàkuràhi*n* sirijala
Gàia jo yo re;
Thàkuràhi*n* sirijala
Gàia jo.

Tirmuti sirijala
Kànureb Gowala;
Purubàhi*n* daharali
Gàia jo yo re;
Purubàhi*n* daharali
Gàia jo.

Kaha*n* bàbu hèralòn
Danda ka bàsi ho;

Kaha*n* bàbu hèralix
Gàia jo yo re;
Kaha*n* bàbu hèralix
Gàia jo.

Batèhi*n* hèralxn
Danda bàsi ho;
Gòtèhi*n* hèralio
Gàia jo yo re;
Gòtèhi*n* hèralio
Gàia jo. (Mukherjea, The Santals, 1962,Revised Edition, pp. 243-44)

The sense of the above folk-song may thus be rendered in English:

Who has created this world?
Who has created the cattle?
Thàkur(God) has created this world.
Thàkur has created the cattle.
The hawk created Kanu Gowala.
He used to feed cows in the east.
Well, my son! (Kanu) where have you lost your
Flute which you always keep in your loin?
Kanu replies:
I have lost my flute in yonder field;
I have lost my cattle in yonder pasture.

On the day of worship of cows (Gohal Puja), when all are sleeping, young men of the tribe keep vigil and go from place to place to awaken the cows, beginning with the Headman's house, playing on pipes and kettle drums.

The following is a song sung on the occasion:

Gàini cxlilo siribinda bxnè ho,
Màhisini carae ganga para jo yo re,
Màhisini carae ganga para jo.
Gàini awae adha berena ubayete,
Màhisini awae adha rata jo yo re,
Màhisini awae adha rata jo.

Kòn singe debo telare sindura,
Kòn pithe debo dhubi dhana jo yo re,
Kòn pithe debo dhubi dhana jo.

**(Translation)**

The cows have gone to Sree Brindaban
The buffaloes are grazing on the bank of the
Ganges, on the other side, look there!
The buffaloes are grazing on the bank of the Ganges, on the other side.
The cows are returning at sun-set.
The buffaloes return home at mid-night,
The buffaloes return home at mid-night.
On which horn shall I apply oil and Vermilion?
Oh! On whose back shall I place grass with Paddy?
On whose back shall I place grass with Paddy?

Charulal Mukherjea further describes that while the young men sing the song given above, the maidens form a batch on the other hand. They deck their hair with flowers and entwine their arms with their sisters. Thus they march in the procession to the tribal Headman's house, where, with fresh paddy , grass and lamps, they sing special songhs round the cattle and thus visit all the cow-sheds of the village. Furthermore, cattle are anointed with oil and daubed with vermilion, and a share of rice-beer given to each. The following folk-song is sung on the occasion:

Hate lela arwa cal
Gocha lela pakal pan
Càli bela àmki devi
Gàiye cumbài.

Eka cumbài cumbài lagal
Dui cumbài barare
Pàri gela sirà barda
Akeka lo.

Kae barda kanda sè
Kae barda khèja sè
Dèbore putà
Rila malare pan.

Dhire calae dhire calae
Bàburè barada
Kaise tò kambe sindur.

Though it is difficult to translate to bring out its sense, all that appears is the fact that the worshippers have taken sun-dried rice in their hands. The sun has gone down. The cows are kissed. The horned bullock falls down. They are in a puzzle as to which bullock they will give the pan (perhaps water). Next they feel that the bullock is slowly going. How can vermilion be applied(while in motion)? (Mukherjea, The Santals, 1962,Revised Edition, pp. 247-48).

Let us have a look at a song sung by those who possess female-buffaloes in their cattle-shed:

Tòkòerèn gàiko ho, gàiko borot' borot';
Tòkòerèn bitkil ho, bitkil nàhum dàrum.

Phalnarèn gàiko, gàiko borot' borot'
Phalnarèn bitkil, bitkil nàhum dàrum.

Bitkil janga ho, dama domo,
Huhàr janga ho, tilmàn talman.

Neke dòko calaoen sinÞegxr bire,
Neke dòko calaoen manegxr bire.

Dotè amka ho, nàcur leko,
Dotè amka ho, bihur leko.

Siñègòr birerè kule gò menae,
Manègòr birerè tàrube hòpòn.

Neko dòko nàtiña car cur carèc'
Rehda hasa ho jarapè lòyò.

**(Translation)**

Who has got so many cows which look bright and beautiful?
Who has got so many female buffaloes black and bulky?
So ans so's cows look bright and beautiful.
So and so has female buffaloes black and bulky.
The legs of the female buffaoes are very plump,
But green pigeon's feet are very light and soft.
These buffaloes went to the forest of Siñ,
These green pigeons went to the forest of Man.
Well, young men, go and bring them(female buffaloes) back from forests;
O, young men go and bring (them).

The young man replies:

In the forest of SinÞ, there is a lion;
In the Man forest there is a small tiger.

These buffaloes graze and eat this and that,
And drink saline water and mud from springs. (Mukherjea, The Santals, 1962, Revised Edition, pp. 248-49).

Charulal Mukherjea further maintains that, in the morning the fixing of posts all over the village upto the Headman's house takes place, that after the midday meals cows and buffaloes are tied to these posts with strings, and that the feet of these animals are then washed and their horns decorated with garlands and cakes are made of treacle. She explains that the young sportsmen of the village thereafter come in a body and begin poking these animals and dance round them, all the round trying to snatch away the cakes.

W.G.Archer (Archer, The Santal Sohrae, 1979, pp. 1-3) remarks that the Sohrae, the harvest festival of the Santals, takes place in the month of January when the paddy harvest is in. In his view, this festival includes the blessing and baiting of the cattle, a fishing expedition and a village hunt. Married daughters come home and during the seven days of the festival there is dancing and relazation. 'The milk of the black cow' is the pot of the rice- beer which a married daughter brings home. He had a beautiful collection of Sohrae songs:

**(XV)**

Elder sister, elder sister
Go out , o elder sister
The festival like an elephant
Is coming near
You with a lota of water
I with a cup of water
Let us go and bring it in
The festival like an elephant
You with a plate and water
I with a long tailed cow
With the tail of that cow
We will fan and bring it in

**(XVI)**

Elder sister, elder sister
Go out, o elder sister
The festival like an elephant has come
How shall we welcome it

How shall we receive it
Sister, o elder sister
How shall we bring it in?
With a glad heart
And a sound of joy
We shall open our heart's door
And take it to our hearts.

**(XVII)**

Elder sister
I will catch it by the hand
I will pull it by the leg
The festival like an elephant
Is going away.

**(XVIII)**

Sohrae, Sohrae
It was good while you were here
It was different while you stayed
Come again in time
Joy, do not cry
Joy, do not mourn
On the due day come back.

**(XIX)**

Uncle, at Sohrae
Call us and invite us
Uncle, we are yours
Uncle, bring us leaves of lar
And leaves of tamarind
Uncle, we are many
Brothers and sisters
Put what you like in our hands
But, Uncle, we are yours.

**(XX)**

Father,
For twelve years is the festival
For thirteen years, Sohrae
It goes away and wanders back

Lovely as gold, father
Is the life of a man
But, it goes and never returns.

**(XXI)**

Boy, take a stick in your hand
Tie the cloth round your waist
And go and bring your sister.

**(XXII)**

Boy, you are walking in the village street
You are strolling up and down
To right and left of you are the marigolds
But do not take then in your eyes.

**(XXIII)**

Sit down, stand up
O friend we have no food or drink
But in the eyes meeting there is pleasure

**(XXIV)**

A leaf cup for meat
A bowl for rice beer
You have invited
Your daughters and sisters

**(XXV)**

Girl, while your mother and your father live
Bring them the milk of the black cow
When your mother is no more
And your father dead
Your heart will burn
From heaven down to hell.

**(XXVI)**

Wife, there is rice and curry
Give it to our daughters and grand-daughters. (Archer, The Santal Sohrae, 1979, pp. 1-3).

W.G.Archer (Archer, The Hill of Flutes: Life , Love and Poetry in Tribal India, A Portrait of the Santals, 1974, pp. 195-213) outlines a detailed account of how the Sohrae festival is celebrated and what are the common songs sung during the celebration. At the Sohrae festival, married daughters are expected to return to their parents and a number of songs express the excitement of the visit:

253

Boy, take a stick in your hand
Tie the cloth round your waist
And go and bring your sister.

254

A leaf-cup for meat
A bowl for rice-beer
You have invited
Your daughters and sisters.

255

Wife, there is rice and curry
Give it to our daughter and grand-daughters.

257

From over the mountain
The twelve mountains
We have called
The daughters, the sisters
Girl, give them enough rice

Give them plenty of curry. (Archer, The Hill of Flutes: Life , Love and Poetry in Tribal India, A Portrait of the Santals, 1974, p. 196).

W.G. Archer maintains that during the visit, rice-beer is brewed, household chores are forgotten and for a single charmed week, the code of sexual conduct is deliberately relaxed. At Sohrae a newly married woman is free to meet her lover even if her husband is present and the girl is not deterred from seeking out her friend. See the following example where she is seeking out her friend:

262

There is moisture on your hands
Sweat on your eyes

O my love, who are you?
Feel with your hands
Touch me with your thighs
I am your former lover.

263

We are going on the road
There are limes in the way
One I have eaten
Two I have tucked away
O take them for yourself
For once you were my lover. (p. 198).

Sohrae songs deal mainly with the ways of lovers and provide a running commentary on what is happening behind the scenes—girls encouraging the boys, boys running after girls, clandestine engagements occurring, husbands and wives keeping out of each other's way. Marriage itself is mocked, brides are jokingly consoled and over everything there is an air of laughing relaxation, modest fun and sportive daring. See more examples:

278

Sit down, stand up
O friends, we have no food or drink
But in the eyes' meeting there is pleasure.

279

In the thick forest, father
A dove has been decoyed
In the middle of the village
The headman was enticed.

280

In the upper village
O you two girls
A green boy
Is playing on a drum
Girl, we will dance
Out of the house
Swinging our legs
Holding our cloth.

281

Aunt, the jamun buds are scarlet
The tip of the plantain sways
So long as I have no husband
I shall nod and sway my body.

282

Boy, beat the drum
And like a plantain
Sway your body
Play the flute
Make it sound
Like the calling of a quail.

283

There is a gander
That wanders in the streets
The gander has a necklace
What will you do with it, girl?
For like a tall bamboo
Your husband comes.

284

Brother, brother, elder brother
Give me a turban
And I will go
And tease the girls.

285

Sister-in-law
From thetree
The parrot cried
In the locked house
The fiddle sounded.

286

Because of our love
You keep a comb in your hand
You get up
In the morning

You comb your hair
O my love
Wait this year
Wait next year
The year after
I will make you mine.

287

Spider, spider
Spin me a thread
Tie the heart of my parents, spider
And I will put a silver bangle
On both your wrists.

289

Mother, father
The drum sound in the village
And like a lotus leaf in water
My body trembles as I hear them.

290

Father, from the east
And the west
A bridegroom comes
With ornaments of gold.

291

Elder brother
The little sways
The tasseled hat falls down
O little girl
Do not let the tears fall.

294

Under the flowering tree
My lover wanted
Twelve rupees
I wept five nights and days
My lover wanted
Twelve rupees of me.

295

O my love, come and talk in our village
If you want milk, I will give you milk
If you want curds, I will give you curds

But only with a pigeon's soup will you be happy. (Archer, The Hill of Flutes: Life , Love and Poetry in Tribal India, A Portrait of the Santals, 1974, pp. 205-08).

The following two songs are sung at the end of the Sohrae as goodbye songs to Sohrae festival:

298

Elder sister
I will catch it by the hand
I will pull it by the leg
The festival like an elephant
Is going away.

299

Sohrae, Sohrae
It was good while you were here
It was different while you stayed
Come again in time
Joy, do not cry
Joy, do not mourn

On the due day come back. (Archer, The Hill of Flutes: Life , Love and Poetry in Tribal India, A Portrait of the Santals, 1974, pp. 212-13).

Manis Kumar Raha (Raha, Santal Folksong, 1979, p. 260) is of the view that in Sohrae song love and religion have taken more prominence. Consider for examples the following songs of love: I.

My heart is on fire where shall I keep my heart?
Cut down logs of wood into shape,
Construct a building and
Keep your heart therein.

**II**

Aben Da Juri Kuri Atte Ben Hisalee
Enchren Juri Ben Hatao Akan

Chetan Tolare Kamar Menay Latar Tolare Sonhar
Sikari Kay Tam Na Sanat Janwaya.

**(Translation)**

(Dear lover, please do not take hold of my arm,
Dear lover, do no throw your arms across my neck,
I have silver ring in my finger
I have a garland of silver beads on my neck.)

**III**

My husband is sleeping by my side
My secret lover is lying in wait
Please go away secret lover
How can I come out?
My husband stretches himself
Over the flank of my Saree
He has interlaced his thigh with mine
Please go away secret lover
How can I come out?

**IV**

Chanak Chetain ReTirio Sattekan
Siri Muhan Ye Muruli Sattekan
Muruli Lante Ganch Lab Ena
Juri Tahen Te Ench Attang Ena.

**(Translation)**

(Formerly you said that you would
Retain me for ten years and
Remember me for twenty years more
Where are those ten years?
Where are those twenty years?
You have abandoned me
Before the year is over.) (Raha, Santal Folksong, 1979, p. 260).

The following are some examples of ritual (religious) Sohrae songs:

"To-day we have taken (ceremonial) bath
In the Duldali tank
Tomorrow we shall offer sacrifice
To Gods in the specious Pavillion"

Sohrae , Sohrae
It was good while you were here
It was different while you stayed
Come again in time
Joy, do not cry
Joy, do not mourn
On the due day come back.

Father
For twelve years is the festival
For thirteen years Sohrae
It goes away and wanders back
Lovely as gold, father,
Is the life of a man. (Raha, Santal Folksong, 1979, p. 261)

### (V) Dahar Seren

According to Subhendu Sekhar Bhattacharya (Bhattacharya, Santal Songs: Different Types, 1979) to understand what Dahar is it is important to have a glimpse of the mythological background and he narrates, "Pilchu Haram and Pilchu Budhi got in course of the time seven sons and seven daughters. The couple was afraid that they might form an undesirable alliance. So Pilchu Budhi got charge of the seven daughters and went to Sukrue forest with them. Pilchu haram took charge of the boys and lived with them in the Khanderae forest. One day the boys shot at a deer and in pursuit of the deer they chanced upon the spot where the girls were swinging upon pendulous roots of banyan tree. The surprise of the girls on seeing living shapes similar to them yet dissimilar in pursuit of a deer with an arrow pricking on its back found expression in the song and this song was in Dahar tune . The story goes on to say how they got united and the earth was populated with their children."

Dahar songs have now become a pendant to the Sohrae festival. When the group of dancers, during the Sohrae celebration, reach the end of the road, it is customary to sing some Danger songs and then start on the return journey. So also at the other end of the road. Thus an intimate connection has developed between Dahar songs and the Sohrae festival and some are inclined to treat them as one of the variety of Sohrae songs.One of the distinctive characteristics of the Dahar dance is that this dance is performed exclusively by the women only; almost all other dances are performed by men and women.together. Among the Dahar dances handed down to us, some are pointed as being the original songs which sprung on the lips of the sons and daughters of the primeval ancestors of mankind. Dahar dances are, generally speaking, sketchy and are intentionally put into archaic language. Consider for example the following song:

**I**

> "Mohua flowers come like claws on the paw of the cat. Sal flowers sway in the freeze. When I collect them and tie up in my lap nectar falls in drops. It emits a smell somewhat like fish-soup somewhat like loin juice."

W.G.Archer (Archer, The Hill of Flutes: Life , Love and Poetry in Tribal India, A Portrait of the Santals, 1974, p. 68) records that 'side by side with Lagre, Santals also dance the Dahar which resembles a forward-moving Lagre, the girls taking two steps to the side and then a pace forward. As with Lagre itself, the songs are chiefly concerned with village romance:

**II**

In a bush of thorns
Two pigeons
Are busy with a nest
Boy
Do not shoot an arrow
For the two
Are calling to each other.

**III**

On the mountain the flames spread
On the hill the fire
Goes mounting in a line
Look at that old man
Running and stumbling
Look at that boy
And the lily
Straining into bud,

**IV**

Climb on the thatch, girls
See him on his way
For he goes
To the foot of the mountain.

**V**

Mother
On the small hill
I gathered cotton
And my ring
Slipped from my finger.

**VI**

Behind an ant-hill is a porcupine
We will stone him from above
We will pelt him till he falls.

**VII**

Beyond the mountain
The ring dove is cooing
Under the mountain
The boys are with the cattle
With a flute they struck the dove
O my friend, go slowly
Very slowly.

**VIII**

Durgi
Your brother-in-law
Has climbed a fig tree
Durgi
Your brother-in-law

Is being chased by bees. (Archer, The Hill of Flutes: Life , Love and Poetry in Tribal India, A Portrait of the Santals, 1974, pp. 68-69)

**IX**

Mother, the ants
The ants are swarming
Under the branches
Of the banyan

**X**

Under,under the banyan is a young deer

Mother, look at the young deer, the young deer. (Archer, Thc Hill of Flutes: Life , Love and Poetry in Tribal India, A Portrait of the Santals, 1974, p. 263).

Charulal Mukherjea (Mukherjea, The Santals, 1962,Revised Edition, p. 374) tells us that 'Dahar ènèæ takes place between the first day after the new moon of "Magh"(Jan-Feb) and the full moon of Falgun(Feb-March) beginning with evenings and ending with mid-nights. She further describes that happy and cheerful men and women make a circle with their hands entwined, the musicians standing in the centre. In Dahar dance we can see the circle formed by men and women taking two steps forwards, and then changing the direction to the left with one steo, and next to the right again with a single step. The circle can be seen moving on and on in the dreamland of a moon-lit night. Men sing and women reply jointly and this continues for near about ten minutes. Teasing belles sing again after taking a short rest. Men and women form the circle again automatically proceeding the dance afresh, while the musicians display their skill to the admiring bystanders. Charulal Mukherjea is of the view that Dahar dance is a religious dance considered to be a prelude to the forthcoming Baha festival and the songs are also devotional referring to the deities of the Holy Grove.

Manis Kumar Raha (Raha, Santal Folksong, 1979, p. 261) seems to be having the same views as Bhattacharya and remarks that Dahar songs have much more importance in the lives of the Santal people and these Dahar songs have mythological connections having some connections with Sohrae songs as well. He gives an example of Dahar song:

**XI**

Nai Nare Narete
Bugite Tale Jiling Jhinga
Jalite Gath Da Maya Gi Sanai
Nutu Kate Jam Da Natti Sibil

**(Translation)**

(Such a lonely place. Even the stumps of
Tree strike me in terror. The roots make
Me afraid. Everything here is against me
And then the young man on the 'Mas Kalai'
Plot eating boiling frog. He looks menacing.)

## References

Archer, W. (1974). *The Hill of Flutes: Life , Love and Poetry in Tribal India, A Portrait of the Santals.* London: George Allen & Unwin LTD.

Archer, W. (1979). Santal Poetry. In J. Troisi, *The Santals: Readings in Tribal Life, Volume III: Myths and Folklore* (pp. 9-13). New Delhi: Indian Social Institute.

Archer, W. (1979). Santal Transplantation songs. In J. Troisi, *The Santals: Readings in Tribal Life, Volume III: Myths and Folklore* (pp. 19-20). New Delhi: Indian Social Institute.

Archer, W. (1979). The Santal Sohrae. In J. Troisi, *The Santals: Readings in Tribal Life* (pp. 1-3). New Delhi: Indian Social Institute.

Bhattacharya, S. S. (1962). 'Santal Songs: Different Types'. *Bulletin of the Cultural Research Institute*, Calcutta, 1 (2), pp. 54-61.

Bhattacharya, S. S. (1979). Santal Songs: Different Types. In J. Troisi, *The Santals: Readings in Tribal Life, Vol.III: Myths and Folklore* (pp. 21-30). New Delhi: Indian Social Institute.

Biswas, P. (1956). *Santals of the Santal Parganas.* New Delhi: Bharatiya Adimjati Sewak Samaj, Kingsway Camp.

Bodding, P. (1993(First published in India)). *A Santal Dictionary: 7 Parts in Five Volumes.* New Delhi: Gyan Publishing House.

Culshaw, W. (1949). *Tribal Heritage: A Study of the Santals.* London: Lutherworth Press.

Culshaw, W. (1979). Santal Songs. In J.Troisi, *The Santals:Readings in Tribal Life, Volume III: Myths and Folklore* (pp. 109-10). New Delhi: Indian Social Institute.

Culshaw, W. (2004(Published in India)). *Tribal Heritage: A Study of the Santals.* New Delhi: Gyan Publishing House.

DasGupta, S. P. (1979). Santhali Folk dances. In J. Troisi, *The Santals:Readings in Tribal Life, Volume III: Myths and Folklore* (pp. 111-12). New Delhi: Indian Social Institute.

Dasu, S. K. (1979). A Note on Important Festivals among the major Tribals of West Bengal. In J. Troisi, *The Santals: Readings in Tribal Life, Volume I: Religion and Magic* (pp. 24-55). New Delhi: Indian Social Institute.

Gausdal, J. (1960). *The Santal Khuts.* Oslo: H. Aschehoug & Co.

Gautam, M. K. (1977). *In Search of an Identity:A case of the Santal of Northern India.* Leiden.

Hembram, P. (1988). *Sari-Sarna( Santhal Religion).* Delhi: Mittal Publications.

Hunter, W. (1979). Ten Santal Festivals. In J. Troisi, *The Santals: Readings in Tribal Life, Volume1: Religion and Magic* (pp. 274-75). New Delhi: Indian Social Institute.

J Murray, M. (1979). Santali songs with translations and notes. In T. J, *The Santals: Readings in Tribal Life, Volume III: Myths and Folklore* (pp. 141-43). New Delhi: Indian Social Institute.

Majumdar, N. (1956). *The Santal: Memoir 2.* Deptt of Anthropology, Govt. of India, pp. 49& 103.

Majumdar, S. (1925). Some Santal Songs. *The Visva-Bharati Quarterly III*, pp. 67-9.

Majumdar, S. (1979). Some Santal Songs. In J. Troisi, *The Santals: Readings in Santal Life, Volume III: Myth and Folklore* (pp. 139-40). New Delhi: Indian Social Institute.

Man, E. (1983(First Indian Edition)). *Sonthalia and the Sonthals.* Delhi: Mittal Publications.

Mukherjea, C. (1962,Revised Edition). *The Santals.* Calcutta: A. Mukherjee & Co. Private Ltd.

Mukherjea, C. (July-Dec 1936). 'Santal Folk Poetry'. *The New Review*, Calcutta, 4, pp. 220-26.

O' Malley, L. (1910). *Bengal District Gazetteers, Vol. 22, Santal Parganas.* Calcutta: Bengal Secretariat Book Depot.

Orans, M. (1965). *The Santal: A Tribe in Search of a Great Tradition.* Detroit: Wayne State University Press.

Raha, M. K. (1967). 'Folk Songs of the Tribals of West Bengal- An Analytical Study of Continuity and Change'. In H. Biswas, *Folk Music and Folk-lore, An Anthology* (pp. 57-81). Vol. 1, Calcutta: Folk Music and Folkl-lore Research Institute.

Raha, M. K. (1979). Santal Folksong. In J.Troisi, *The Santals: Readings in Tribal Life, Vol III: Myths and Folklore* (pp. 255-63). New Delhi: Indian Social Institute.

Raj, V. (1990). *A Santal Theology of Liberation.* New Delhi: Uppal Publishing House.

Sarkar, H. B. (1964). A Study on the Agricultural activities and ritualistic performances among the Santals of Belpahari. *Bulletin*, Vol III, No 1, pp. 52-61.

Sinha, S. K. (June 1946). 'Santal Folk Songs'. *Journal of the Bihar and Orissa Research Society*, Patna, 32 (2), pp. 184-88.

Troisi, J. (1978). *Tribal Religion: Religious Beliefs and Practices among the Santals.* New Delhi: Manohar Publications.

# Chapter Four

# Social Dancing II: Considering Contextualization

### (VI) Baha Seren

According to P.O.Bodding (Bodding, A Santal Dictionary: 7 Parts in Five Volumes, 1993(First published in India)) 'baha' literally means 'The flower festival' and this is the second great festival of the Santals. Rev.Bodding points out that the 'Baha'festival is celebrated in the month of Phagun (February-March) when the moon is in the last quarter. The Santals are of the opinion that it is a festival to mark the turning of the year soon after which a new year begins, that the sal tree blossoms, and the sal blossoms play important part in the festival. Bodding further recorded down a narrative told from the mouth of an old guru, named Kolean whose narrative was based on oral tradition handed down verbatism by teacher to disciple, from generation to generation, a practice which 'has now fallen into disuse.' Bodding (Bodding, Traditions and Institutions of the Santals, 1942(First Indian Reprint1994), p. 150) submits that in the words of Kolean: "Baha (the Flower festival) is our other great festival. This comes in the month of Phalgun (middle of February to middle of March) at the third quarter of the moon. This is a festival in connexion with the turning of the year.The Sal trees blossom at this time, the icak and the murup also blossom, and the Mahua gets flowers. Before we have the Flower festival, we do not suck the icak flowers or the muru flowers, and we do not deck ourselves with Sal flowers, and we do not eat the Mahua either. If anyone sucks or eats these before this festival, to their houses the village priest will not go, and he will not eat or drink anything of theirs until the Flower festival is held. The Flower festival is our righteous festival, not licentious like the Sohrae" (Bodding, Traditions and Institutions of the Santals, 1942 (First Indian Reprint1994), pp. 150-51).

T. Hembrom (Hembrom, 1996, p. 43) in his study on the main festivals of the Santals remarks that Baha festival is celebrated in the beginning of the spring (Feb-March) when most of the trees begin to put on new leaves and bring forth blossoms indicating the renewal of life in nature. Philosophicalyy one may think of the renewal of creation connected with this festival. It is worth noting that this festival marks the end of an agricultural year and the beginning of a new agricultural year, giving the Santal people rays of new hope and new life as manifested in the natural phenomenon. It is important to note that during the festival *Sal* and *Mahua* flowers are offered to the benevolent *Bongas* at the *Jaher Than* (the village sacred grove) by the village priest, *Naeke* and the he sacrifices fowls as thanks offerings, and offers supplications to them to protect the village on behalf of all the village community.Most importantly, people express their joy for the arrival of new life with new hope with dancing and singing.

V. Manuel Raj's study (Raj, 1990, p. 37) records that Baha Porob is the second great festival of the Santals which is celebrated in the month of Phagun (Feb-March). It being the flower festival marks the bloomings of 'matkom' and 'sarjom' trees. He concludes by saying that at this festival the Santal land is adorned with the flowers of these trees with the Santal new year too blooming with it marking the commencement of the Santal new-year and the use of 'sarjom baha' and 'dak' at this festival expresses certain sacredness about the festival.

P.C.Hembram (Hembram P. , 1988, p. 44)belives that as per the tradition Baha is a main puja festival in Santal society and it is celebrated in the spring season when trees particularly 'Sal' and 'Mahua' bear new flowers and the surroundings are echoing with bleething song of cuckoos, and that 'Jaher place and Majhisthan' are decorated with thatched shade one day before the day fixed for the puja. The word 'baha' implies flower but it also stands for a virgin maid. The earth place of celebration looks like a holy-maiden when seen the surroundings covered with decorated with flowers and green foliages.

During the puja, flowers and new fruits, particularly mango and Mahua, are offered to the deities. Baha songs are very inspiring and enthusiastic and the dances accompanying are equally attractive with both males and females participating in dance. Men form a separate row, rhythmically move their bodies and jump at the rhythm of 'Jathur don'. After the puja is over, in the afternoon, villagers escort Nayke back home from Jaher and the villge women move on dancing in village lanes encircling Nayke who holds a winnowin fan full of Sal flowers accompanied by a young man who shoulders a new earthen pitcher full of water. In the process, every housewife washws the feet of Nayke and the young man while crossing the respective house and they collect holy water. The dance continues till they reach his house and thereafter the villagers leave the house of Nayke (Hembram P. , 1988, p. 44).

E.G.Man's book (Man, 1983(First Indian Edition), p. 49) reveals that the Baha Parub is celebrated on the return of the spring season. He shows that on the occasion of Baha festival the worship and sacrifices are conducted in the following manner: "The six stones at the foot of the six trees in the sacred grove are first marked with red paint (*Ara Hera*) by the village priest, who s generally an old man. He then cuts off the heads of six fowls over the *gahi*, or sharp Sonthali battle axe, and having accomplished it, immediately allows the blood to drop from their necks over the six stones. After this he appropriates the half-dozen heads as his own share. The villagers claim the bodies, and all partake of the sacrifice in company and on the spot and then follows the drinking of their home-brewed *Hanri*, which invariably terminates every public or private sacrifice, whether it has taken place inside or outside of their houses" (Man, 1983(First Indian Edition), pp. 49-50).

That the Baha Parab or Flower festival is the second great festival of the Santals held after the full moon in the month of Phagun (February-March), when the *Sal* and the *Matkom* or Mahua trees begin to blossom has been the view held by Joseph Troisi (Troisi J. , Tribal Religion: Religious Beliefs and Practices among the Santals, 1978, p. 134). He asserts that the Baha festival lasting two days marks the beginning of the Santal New Year. There are some scholars who consider this festival as spring festival of the Santals. It has been their tradition that no Santal will gather the *matkom* blossoms which provide them with both food and drink until this festival has taken place. There is no denying the fact that this festival is characterized by drinking, dancing and eating, it is, however, also true that it is as Kolean says and Bodding writes, "a righteous festival not licentious like the Sohrae" (Bodding, Traditions and Institutions of the Santals, 1942(First Indian Reprint1994), p. 151). Joseph Troisi argues that there is no fixed date for this festival as such, as this festival is held on different days in different villages with a reason behind it being that people may visit their relatives and friends. He believes that this festival is meant to appease the major *bongas* who are believed by the Santals to have kept the village free from any sickness or witchcraft and have preserved the crops and cattle.

Giving us a detailed portrayal of Baha ènèc Charulal Mukherjea (Mukherjea, The Santals, 1962,Revised Edition, p. 375) remarks that Baha ènèc, as its name suggests, is danced during Baha festival (Flower festival), when on the second day of the celebration men and women go to the Holy Grove (Jaherthan) to accompany the village priest to invoke the deities over there. Charulal Mukherjea is calling this dance to be a devotional dance having women participation only. The distinctive characteristic of this dance is the fact that women during the dance do not interlock their hands and form no circles as in other dances. They, however, proceed in a tripping marching order with musicians in a separate groupand with men singing and women replying in chorus. Charulal comments: "it is picturesque to see the dancers waving their right hands upwards, up to the shoulders, which are swung down soon to be folded beautifully. When the right hand is raised, the right foot takes a step. Next advances the left foot, and the folded hands are raised up with a devotional beam in their eyes. So they go on till they reach the Holy Grove and thus dance round it thrice" (Mukherjea, The Santals, 1962,Revised Edition, p. 375).

Dealing with the subject of Baha festival which Charulal Mukherjea calls 'the Santal Sal'-Blossom Festival' (Mukherjea, The Santals, 1962,Revised Edition, p. 257), he states that the Santals celebrate Baha, their sal-blossom season towards the latter part of February. This is an occasion for their rejoicing and merry-making with sprinkling of water and its special songs and dances. According to the Traditions and Institutions of the Santals, as he quotes, the aim of this festival is to celebrate the advent of Spring, which sees the efflorescence of their favourite *sal, polas, mohua,* and *icak* flowers. It is a practice among them that no Santal will suck the honey of these flowers or eat them, nor will their women wear them in their hair until Baha festival is over.He writes, "The festival begins with a day of purification called *Um*, when the young men of the village assemble at the *Jaherthan*, (the Holy-Grove) in the village....this is followed by a general incarnation of the gods" (Mukherjea, The Santals, 1962,Revised Edition, pp. 258-59).

W.G.Archer takes a different view of the nature and paradigm of Baha festival displaying a deep connect between 'marriage', 'fertility' and the Baha festival (Archer, The Hill of Flutes: Life , Love and Poetry in Tribal India, A Portrait of the Santals, 1974, p. 237). He argues that after the marriage when a Santal couple have settled down and start a separate house, the house will need a child-'to give it life'.The family feels incomplete without a baby. A wife wil be handicapped in running the household if there is no daughter to assist her and similarly a husband will find it difficult to cultivate his fields if there is no one to graze the cattle or assist with ploughing while in old age a son is his principal if not his only support. In

Archer's view to have a child before marriage or not to have a child after the marriage –these are among a Santal's greatest dreads which are easily visible in their Baha songs:

**I**

When sal trees are in leaf
On the mountain
How lovely they look
Wealth in the house
A door in the doorway
But without a child
There is no beauty(p.237)

**II**

The mother set me up with money
The father gave me a tank
But I have no children
To whom shall I give
A share in the tank
Cando, if you will give me children
Give me a child of gold(p.237)

What W.G.Archer wants to convey here is the fact that even for ensuring this family objective of having children, the Santals essentially are dependent upon their bongas, depending on certain aspects of Thakur Jiu, the Bidhi Bidhanta: 'Unless these will it, no child can come'—this is the strong belief that the Santals carry on in their community. Hence, for Archer, to ensure children as well as to promote prosperity, the major bongas must therefore be honoured and the first means to do that is the Baha feastival or feast of flowers, held in the month of March.

According to W.G.Archer there are three Santali narratives of how and why Baha festival is celebrated. First, 'In olden times, when all the forests were thick and dense, the great trees were the abode of bongas. The Tudus were iron-workers and everyday went to the forest for charcoal. One day two Tudu boys were making charcoal when they saw some bongas approaching. They were struck with fright and ran away. At a short distance, they found an atnak' tree. The trunk was hollow and in their fear they went inside. Since their home was near the tree, the bongas gathered by it and began to dance together. The Tudu boys stayed trembling in their hole. Then they resolved, 'This is the haunt of bongas and whatever we do we are bound to die. But before we die let us dance with them.' Thinking this, they came out of the hole and, since all the bongas were naked, they began to call out. As they called, they ran among the bonga boys and girls holding out a flower for them to sniff. As a bonga girl smelt the flower, the Tudu boy fondled her breasts. The girls were filled with confusion and began to dance bending low. As the hands of the Tudu boys were smutty with charcoal, the breasts of the bonga girls became black. From that time on the nipples of women have been black like the ends of a drum.The bongas were delighted with the two Tudu boys and taught them everything about dancing and bonga service. They also taught them their names%Jaher Era, Maran Buru, the Five-Six, Gosae Era, Pargana bonga, Manjhi Haram, and the the bonga girls, Hisi, Dumni, Chita and Kapra. By the grace of the bongas, the two boys learnt all the ways of singing and of bonga service and became the gurus or teachers of the twelve clans. They went round the twelve countries and made disciples from all the people. When people heard their skill in singing and saw their knowledge, they were amazed and even today their prowess is celebrated' (Archer, The Hill of Flutes: Life , Love and Poetry in Tribal India, A Portrait of the Santals, 1974, p. 238). Archer writes that from the day they got this knowledge of the bongas, the Santals are observing Baha as their first festival. People remember them in their songs:

**III**

O you two drummers
Playing the drum
You do not know
The beat of the songs
Give your drums to the two Tudus
And they will beat the tunes.(p.238-39)

The second narrative goes as follows: 'When there were only Santals, the clan of Tudus did the work of blacksmith. Two brothers went to the Urmi forest to make charcoal. It became night. They started to go back. In this way they saw three bonga girls dancing. Behind them, the Five-Six were dancing sogoe fashion, with their clothes rustling. The bonga girls had sal flowers in their hair. The clothes were tied. There were no buffalo horns or drums. The two brothers were afraid and hid in a hole in a fig tree. The bonga girls with the Five-Six came near them. They danced round the tree. The younger of the brothers said "Our lives are gone. There is no chance of saving them. Let us go and dance with them." So the two brithers came out. The younger went dancing, sogoe fashion, with them round the tree. He went round three or four times. His hands were black with charcoal.

He caught a breast of one of the bonga girls and his touch made it black. The girl saw the black on her breast and bowed low. The other two bowed down with her. They danced until cock-crow, bending their bodies and swaying their arms. The Five-Six danced with them when it was dawn the bonga girls told the Tudu boys to start a festival because they had danced with them. The Tudu boys said, "What shall we call it?" The bonga girls said, "Call it the Baha festival because we danced with flowers in our hair." Then the Tudu boys left them and went to their village. In the village they called the villagers and asked them to start the festival. They told them about the bonga girls but the villagers did not believe them. That evening a buffalo horn sounded in the priest's house and a drum began to beat. No one was playing the horn and the drum was beating of itself. As they sounded, a man was possessed with the Baha bonga and rushed to the forest. At that time, there were no jahers or sacred groves. He swept a patch of trees and went round and round it. The priest followed him with a vessel of water. They made the first grove. The next day they put stones by the trees in the name of the Five-Six and all the village girls came and danced round them, bending down their bodies. They did this once a year for five years. After five years the Baha bonga came on a man and said that they must sacrifice a black calf to the Five-Six every five years and take a new dhoti, a new broom, a new basket, bonga bells, a new earthen pot and a bow and arrow, an axe and an iron chain when they went to the grove. Since then they are doing this" (Archer, The Hill of Flutes: Life , Love and Poetry in Tribal India, A Portrait of the Santals, 1974, pp. 239-40)

The third and final narrative tells us about Gosae Era, the lonely figure who is a member of the company but is kept slightly apart. According to the third narrative: " At the time of the first ancestors there were five brothers who lived in the forest. Their mother was with them. They used to hunt the whole day and bring back peacock and any game they killed. Their mother stayed home and cooked for them. One day they were hunting and came on a Hindu girl of the Kamar caste. She was lovely as a flame. The youngest of the five brothers set his heart on her and sai he would take her with him. He asked his brothers and took the girl away. It was then the practice that on returning from the hunt the eldest brother would give their mother the same number of arrows as there were hunters and the mother would give out rice as many times as there were arrows. Their mother said, "For whom have you given me an extra one?" They said, "We have brought another with us. We have brought a Kamar girl back as a wife." Their mother said, "Do not bring her here. She is not of our caste." That night they gave her rice and kept her. The next day they put up a separate shed a little apart and she lived with them there. As they had brought her they did not send her away. The mother of the boys is Jaher Era. The Kamar girl is Gosae Era. The five brothers are Moreko Turuiko (the Five-Six). Because of this, Gosae Era is always kept apart' (Archer, The Hill of Flutes: Life , Love and Poetry in Tribal India, A Portrait of the Santals, 1974, p. 240)

W.G.Archer, however, contends that although the Baha festival is propitiation of the major bongas, its ritual is a miming of fertility. He observes that on the forst day, sheds are erected, the Baha hunt takes place and the grove is swept. On the second day, trees are shot at, the flowering forest is celebrated, flowers are thrown into the aprons of the women and a water-battle is waged in the village streets. He conceds that children are not expressly demanded but everything is done— by symbol, poetry and action—to simulate their gift.

Let us now consider some more examples of Baha songs (Archer, The Hill of Flutes: Life , Love and Poetry in Tribal India, A Portrait of the Santals, 1974, pp. 241-43):

**IV**

Under the rafters
Who is sitting
Who has taken his seat?
The priest is sitting
Under the rafters.

**V**

Who will cut
The wood for Maran Buru?
Who will thatch
The shed for Jaher?
The priest will cut
The wood for Maran Buru
The priest will thatch
The shed for Jaher.

**VI**

What has the priest brought?
What things has he set down?
He has brought
A bowl of oil

He has put down
A box of scarlet powder
He has brought
A winnowing fan of bamboo
He has set down
A basket of bamboo

**VII**

Ja Gasae
We have washed
And cleaned our heads
In whose courtyard do you sit today?
In whose courtyard do you sit erect?
In the priest's courtyard I am sitting
By the small path I sit erect
In the priest's courtyard
Is liquor made from flowers

**VIII**

Chita, why are you late?
For whom do you delay?
Ja Gosae
For whom do you delay?
My father's kinsmen are away hunting
My brothers beat the jungle
Chita, because of this you dallied
For this you made delay

**IX**

On the top of a pipal
The barbet calls
On the branch of a banyan
The woodpecker sings
The year has turned
The year has come again
The woodpecker calls
Turning it has turned
The barbet sings
Coming it has come

The woodpecker calls
The weevils have gone
Away with the river
The insects have gone
Into the sea.

**X**

In the shade of a pipal
At the foot of a banyan
A barbet sings
The land is aflame
The land is burning
The woodpecker calls
The year is new
The year has come again
The barbet sings
Who chose the spot for dancing?
Who made the dance start?
The woodpecker is singing
The Five chose
The spot for dancing
The Six have made the dance start
The barbet sings
The place for dancing
Is chosen, chosen
The dance is starting
The woodpecker sings
The dancers are starting.(p.243)

According to W.G.Archer after the bongas have left, rice beer is drunk, dancing starts and songs are sung throughout the night. These songs have a variety of themes, some of them being celebrations of the hot season and the flowering forest:

**XI**

On the rol mountain
The rol tree is in flower
And the flowers hang.
On the rol mountain
The rol tree is in fruit

And the fruit swings.
On the meral mountain
The meral tree has flowered
And the flowers sway.
On the meral mountain
The meral tree has fruited
And the fruit hangs.
The blooms, the blooms are white
And the fruit hangs
The fruit has filled the branches
And the fruit hangs.(p.244-45)

**XII**

The pipal leaves sway 'hipar hipar'
The banyan leaves go 'nohar nohar'
The pipal tree, the banyan
The pipal leaves
Are a red sari
The banyan leaves
Are a silk cloth
The pipal and the banyan
I went below the pipal
And its sap dripped on me
I went below the banyan
And its sap fell on me
The pipal tree, the banyan.

**XIII**

In the pipal tree the barbet sings
On the branch of the banyan
The woodpecker calls
The year is turning
The barbet sings
The year has turned
The woodpecker calls.

**XIV**

Ja Gosae
The Five, the Five brothers

The woodpecker calls
The Six, the Six sisters
The woodpecker sings
The Five have chosen
The place for dancing
The barbet is singing
The Six hav said
The dance must start
The woodpecker sings
The place is chosen
The barbet sings
The dance is starting
The woodpecker sings.(p.245)

W.G.Archer gives examples of the following songs that refer to the earlier ablutions and dwell on washing and fishing:

**XV**

Gosae, O elder sister
The river is full
The river is in flood
'Seke seke' sounds the water
'Rule rule' goes the stream
The fish has risen
The fish has come
Let us make a net
And pull it to the shore.(p.246)

**XVI**

The river has filled
The river is in flood
Parrot, go back
My heart is in my lover
My husband's brother has my life.

**XVII**

'Titriti rankilo'
A ring was on the finger
'Titriti rankilo'
A ring was on my toe
Wher, elder sister

Is the ring on the finger?
Where, elder sister
Is the ring on your toe?
Golden sister
The ring on the toe
I was washing my body
At a pool in the sand
The ring was on the finger
I was drawing
Water at the spring
The ring was on my toe
In thepool in the sand
The ring fell from my finger
In the spring water
The ring slipped from my toe
My lover has found
The ring of my finger
My husband's brother
Kept the ring of my toe
Tell him to return
The ring of my finger
Tell him to give me
The ring of my toe
The ring of my finger
Is not with my lover
The ring of my toe
Is not with my brother-in-law.(p.246-47)

Look at the following songs describing the Baha hunt:

**XVIII**

The two hunters on Logo Buru
The two beaters of Ghanta bari
Come to the hunting
Go to the chase.

**XIX**

The hunters have hunted
The beaters have beaten
In what forests did they hunt
Where was it that they beat?

They have hunted the Sin forest
They have beaten the Man forest
They have caught a new-born tiger
Ja Gosae

**XX**

The young dog loiters in the forest
The curled hawk rests on the hand
Let us go to the hunt
Go to the chase
The young dog noses in the forest
The curled hawk rests on the hand
Let us go to the hunt
Go to the chase
Let us lead the young dog
Let us carry the curled hawk
Let us go to the hunt
Go to the chase.
Throw the ringed stick
Leave the milk, the parched rice
Let us go to the hunt
Go to the chase
The young dog returns from the trail
The hawk has soared out of the hand
Come and return.(p.247-48)

For W.G.Archer the second day is the climax of the festival. The godet is sent to collect the bonga fowls; the priest's wife prepares some wet flour and the priest himself chooses a new fan and puts it some oil, flour, rice, vermilion and a wedge of wet cowdung and throughout tis time a line of girl goes slowly round the courtyard , their bodies bending and their arms swinging slowly in the baha dance. Later as the priest goes to the grove , the boys and girls dance behind him and a little later girls and women come dancing to the grove. At the grove they form a single line and then dance slowly by the trees, rounding their haunches, bending their bodies and swinging their arms so that they almost touch the ground. They dance and sing the following songs:

**XXI**

Chita, beneath a pipal give me oil
Kapra,below a banyan bring out oil

Chita, under a pipal
Bring water for my feet
Kapra, under a banyan bring me oil
Yesterday I brought rain
But the well is dry
I gave you rain two days ago
But the spring is dry
Wher the girls wash their hair
Whose share of water
Has dried in the well
Where the girls wash their hair?
Whose water
Dried in the spring
Where the girls wash their hands?(p.250)

**XXII**

Kapra, do not wash
In the water of my well
Do not clean your hair
In the water of my spring
Go to the river
Stand in the middle
Wash your body
Clean and rinse your hair.

**XXIII**

The trees
The forest
Has decked itself in beauty
I will go for leaf-cups
And make my body
Beautiful with flowers.

**XXIV**

Gosae, Gosae
Who will wear the flowers?
Gosae
Who will put them in a basket?
Jaher Era

Will wear the flowers
Gosae Era
Will put them in a basket.(p.250)

### XXV

'Tiriri rankure'
A ring on the finger
'Tiriri rankure'
A ring on my toe
'Tiriri rankure'
Rings on all the fingers
'Tiriri rankure'
Rings on all my toes(p.251)

Cahrulal Mukherjea (Mukherjea, The Santals, 1962,Revised Edition, p. 260) gives an example of a duet Baha song:

### XXVI

Semi-chorus:

On the Pipul tree, the woodpecker is twittering,
Under the banyan tree, the *gutrut* is singing.
Has the Spring arrived?

Second semi-chorus answers:

The seasons have changed, so the wood-pecker twitters;
The Spring has come back so the *gutrut* babbles.
The Spring has come back to us.(p.260)

P.O.Bodding (Bodding, Traditions and Institutions of the Santals, 1942(First Indian Reprint1994), pp. 152-53) cites few Baha songs:

### XXVII

High up in the Pipal tree,
There, Lord, the Crimson-breasted Barbet is singing;
In the hanging branches of the Banyan tree
There, Lord, the Wood-pecker breathes.

The country has turned round,
Lord, the Crimson-breasted Barbet is singing;
The country has turned back again,
The Woodoecker, Lord, breathes.

It has certainly turned round,
Lord, the Crimson-breasted Barbet is singing;
It has certainly turned back again,
Lord, the Woodpecker breathes.

Who of you cared for him?
Lord, the Crimson-breasted Brbet is singing;
Who of you was anxious for him?
Lord, the Woodpecker breathes.

The Five cared for him,
Lord, the Crimson-breasted Barbet is singing;
The six were anxious for him,
Lord, the Woodpecker breathes.

He did certainly care for him;
Lord, the Crimson-breasted Barbet is singing;
He was certainly anxious for him;
Lord, the Woodpecker breathes. (p.152)

### XXVIII

In accordance with custom I have put
On my hand a ring;
In accordance with custom I have put
On my leg an anklet.

Where have you, my elder sister,
On your hand the ring?
Where have you, my elder sister,
On your leg the anklet?

In the water of the hollowed-out hole I let it fall,
O mother, the ring on my hand.
In the water of the pool I let it slip down
The anklet on my leg.

Why, my friend picked up
The ring on my hand;
Why, my companion took up
The anklet on my leg.

Tell him to give
Thering on my hand;
Tell him to hand over
The anklet on my leg.

With your friend is not
Thering on my hand;
Nor with your companion is
The anklet on your leg. (p.153)

Following immediately after the village priest the young men and girls dance and sing the following songs as they pass along:

### XXIX

The hard verandah, the verandah of abstinence
To-day the village priest spent the night on a bamboo mat,
To-day the village priest lay abstinent on the floor on a bamboo mat.

### XXX

Of the house, of the house,
Of the stately house,
Of the homestead, of the homestead
In the leaf-cup mustard.

Who of you will put it down
In the stately house?
Who of you will receive
In the leaf-cup mustard?

The Moreko will put it down
In the stately house;
The Jaher era will receive
In the leaf-cup the mustard.

They first take omens
For the forest country;
They wander round about
In the villages, the hamlets.

It is there, it is there,
The cow with the black female calf.
It is there, it is there
The speckled pullet. (p.154).

Later at the time of invocation, the village priest makes the bongas sit down on a mat under the shed, and he himself sits down in front of the bongas and sacrifices fowls. During the invocation the priest inserts the words, "in the name of the Flower festival" followed by the priest putting down one flower bud and one Mahua at each of the bongs of the sacred grove. Thereupon they sing:

**XXXI**

The Môreko are five brothers
The Turuiko are six brothers

The rainy season rain comes peltingly,
The rain of Sita's valley comes drizzingly.

What will they use for plastering?
What will they use for leveling?

Milk they will use for plastering
Cream they will use for leveling.

Here, please, is your oil, your sindur;
Here, please, is your eye-paint, your rora bark.

Receive your oil, your sindur,
Accept your eye-paint, your rora bark. (p.155)

After Jaher Era's washing the feet of the priest and splashing water on each oher, the dancing girls ask the priest for flowers. They sing:

**XXXII**

We two shall ask, my elder sister, we two shall ask
The Môrek for Sal flowers. (p.155)

The girls and young men each separatlely receive flowers from the priest and bow to him. Thereupon they sing dancing:

**XXXIII**

The wild cow, the wild cow
Runs out, runs in;
Very nice is the wild cow.

The Bison cow, the Bison cow
Runs out, runs in;
Very nice is the Bison cow. (p.155)

The young men and girls then return to the village, dancing the whole way. They sing:

## XXXIV

The blind buffalo wallowed
In the Siñjo river,
In the Siñjo river, girls, the two girls
In the big river. (p.156)

After the girls and young men of the village have splashed water on each other, and elderly men and women also splash water on each other, thereupon they dance in the court-yard of the priest. They sing:

## XXXV

Who is it, girls, in the court-yard,
The reddish white horse?
Who is it, girls,in the place outside
The reddish companion mare?

The priest is in the court-yard, girls,
The reddish white horse;
The priest is in the place outside, girls,
The reddish companion mare.

Moving up and down, moving up and down girls,
Is the reddish white horse;
Swaying, swaying girs,
Is the reddish companion mare.

Bind on him the bells, girls,
On the reddish white horse;
Tie on to her the jingle-belt, girls,
On the reddish companion mare. (p.156-57)

Giving us a detailed recorded account of Spring festival W.J.Culshaw (Culshaw, Tribal Heritage: A Study of the Santals, 2004(Published in India), p. 105) gives examples of Baha songs:

## XXXVI

Hesak ma cotere
Tude doe ragele;
Des ma nacuren
Disom ma bihuren

The above words are followed by these as a kind of chorus:

Naejom jomme naeke ere!

High up in the pipal tree
Sings the crimson-breasted barbet;
It wanders through the country,
It flies over the land.(p.105)

## XXXVII

Sokrare hat baha daina
Sokrare hat baha daina
Gutuialan jhamka jakur daina
Bahaealan dalae dalae

Down in the valley blooms the hat tree, sister;
Come let us make flower chains, sister;
Come, let us wear the flowers,dangling. (p.105)

## XXXVIII

Halanalan najin matkom,
Bahaealan najin sarjom baha
Nuilan najin matkom rasa.
Translation
Let us gather, O elder sister, the *matkom*;
Let us wear the *sarjom* flowers, elder sister, in our hair;
Let us drink, O elder sister, the juice of the *matkom*.(p.107)

## XXXIX

Ne tora nepe tora;
Murum panja;
Ne tora nepe tora
Sosan panja.

Toka birte boloena
Murum panja;
Toka birte soroena
Sosan panja.

Man birte boloena
Murum panja;
Sin birte soroena
Sosan panja.

Translation
Look here, look at this,

The footprints of the nilgae;
Look here, look at this,
The footprints of the wild buffalo.

In what forest have they entered
The footprints of the nilgae?
To what forest do they lead,
The footprints of the wild buffalo?

Into the forest of Man have they entered,
The footprints of the nilgae;
To the forest of Sin have they lead,
The footprints of the wild buffalo. (p.108)

According to Mohan K Gautam (Gautam, 1977, p. 193) the word Baha in Santali means a flower and the the arrival of Baha porob (the flower festival) is the start of thr Santali new year and the festival must be observed somewhere in the month of phagun (middle of February to middle of March). In his view there is no fixed date or day on which it is to be celebrated; it depends on the blossoming of the sala tree. In fact its date is announced by village council after seeing the natural growth of the trees in consideration of the exact time of the start of the spring season.

He argues that the Baha feast is held to honour the arrival of spring and it is essential that it takes place before the Sala flowers touch the ground. It is strongly believed the offering of the sala flowers to the bongas shows an intimate relation between the Sala forest and the Santal village life. Moreover, it can be denied that the Sala on the whole is a very indispensable object in their material culture. The fact that it is an event of Santal's leisure season helps them to celebrate the Baha festival with great pomp and show. Mohan's contention is that it is the Sala trees which once attracted the Santal ancestros to migrate to this area which was fully occupied by the Sala forests. He states that the Baha festival of the Santals coincides with Hindu festival of Holi(festival of colours and spring) which also marks the end of the winter harvest and a change in the season.Like other scholars he is also of the view that no Santal dares to use the flowers either to decorate the hair, for consumption , or suck the honey, until the Baha festival is observed, and he is likely to get severe punishment if found guilty.

According to N Dutta Majumdar (Majumdar N. , 1956, pp. 50,103), his study on the Santals reveals that the Spring festival is held in the month of Phalgun(February-March). For him the Baha festival is celebrated with gaiety and enthusiasm which includes singing, dancing and drinking in the village. Martin Orans (Orans M. , 1965, pp. 74-75) points out that the Baha festival is essentially a Spring festival held in the month of March and lasts for two days. His submission is that the Spring festival is celebrated with requests to deities to prevent the occurrence of disease and to provide good crops.This festival observed as the second in ranking in importance among the annual ceremonies.

Hemendranath Banerjee and Ajit Kumar Sarkar (Sarkar, 1964) in Bulletin, C.R.I., Vol. III, No.1, 1964, p. 57 remark that the Baha festival among the Santals is celebrated in the moth of Phalgun(February-March). On this day mahua flowers are offered to the village deities for general welfare and success in cultivation. W.J.Culshaw (Culshaw, Tribal Heritage: A Study of the Santals, 1949, pp. 102-107) points out that the Spring or Flower festival is held after the full moon in the month of Phalgun(February-March) on March 17th -18th. He argues that it is held on different days in different villages and the first day is observed as the purification day. For P.C.Biswas(Biswas, 1956, pp. 141-42), the purpose of the Baha festival for the Santals is to celebrate the new year and it is held in th month of Phalgun(February-March) when the Sal trees begin to flower and this festival continues for two days.

W.W. Hunter (Hunter, 1979) seems to suggest that Baha (Flower) festival is celebrated in the month of March for two days. He explains that every house washes the Naikki's(priest's) feet, and he distributes flowers in return. Ceremonies take place in the grove of trees outside the village. Four chickens are offered to Marang Buru(the great god of the Santals);one coloured chicken to Jaher Era (the primeval mother of the race); one black chicken to Gosai-Era (a female divinity residing, like Jaher-Era, in the Sal grove); and a goat or a chicken to the Manjhi Haram(the late head of the village).

Subhendu Bhattacharya's study (Bhattacharya, Santal Songs: Different Types, 1979) shows that Baha festival seems to be the most sacred festival of the Santals and is the second great festival among the Santals., and that it is held immediately after Dol Purnima i.e. at the approach of spring. Neither Mohua flowers are collected nor Sal Flowers worn, nor ICA flowers sucked till Gods are invoked in this festival. Unlike others he contends that Baha festival lasts for a single day only. He argues that there is of course a rehearsal of Rumm on the previous night which need not be considered. He maintains, "Offerings and sacrifices are made to the Gods at the sacred grove before noon after which two persons take up the roles of Maran Buru and Jaher-Era. It is believed they are 'possessed' by the Gods. Such phenomena are called runnin Santal, 'Jhupar' in local dialect and 'Bhor' in standard Bengali. Maran Buru plucks flowers from sal trees and Jaher-Era staying at the bottom collects the flowers. The village priest takes the flowers from her and moves from house to house with flowers and a pot of water. He offers flowers to the girls in each house and sprinkles little water over their heads. Soon it turns into a general merriment of sprinkling water and pelting with flowers"(p.26-27).

Bhattachrya contends thatsprinkling of water and pelting with flowers bear remakabke similarity to throwing of coloured water during Dol festival which is observed by Hindus almost at the same time. He argues that this is a ceremony connected intimately with Krishna cult. He tells us that songs are sung at various stages of the Baha ffestival. Most of them are ceremonious litanies, except a few which deal with secular topics such as fishing, hunting and dancing. All Baha songs are in an elevated style and contain delicious tunes.

For Manis Kumar Raha (Raha, Santal Folksong, 1979) also Baha songs are mostly ceremonial litanies. He gives example of few Baha songs as mentioned below:

**XXXX**

Songs are going on over the fence,
Music is being played beyond the courtyard.
How can I attend now?
How can I go out?
My bracelets would tinkle when I move,
My anklet would jungle.
How can I attend now?
How can I go?
The father-in-law is in the house,
The mother-in-law is at the door,
How can I attend now?
How can I go?
A lamp is burning within the room,
A cord of hair is fastened to the door,
How can I attend now?
How can I go?

**XXXXI**

Music is proceeding in Lungu Hills
Bells are ringing ding-doing at Ghantabari
Why is music going on now?

Why are bells ringing now?
Music is going on so that
Men may assemble there
Bells are ringing so that
Men may assemble there,
Why still music is going on?
Why still bells are ringing?
Music is going on still so that
Young hens may be killed.
Bells are ringing still so that
Castrated goats may be destroyed

To conclude with it can be stated that Baha songs are, as P.C.Hembram (Hembram P. , 1988, p. 99) records, mainly religious and puja songs.These songs are sung during Baha and Mamore puja and festival. Number of songs express various incidents and effects of nature directly related to the community life. A few songs have ethical significance and others are of agricultural and natural phenomena. Rest are hymn type.

## (VII) KARAM SEREN

According to Charulal Mukherjea (Mukherjea, The Santals, 1962,Revised Edition, p. 237) *Karam* festival is celebrated in the month of September-October in compliance with the following practice: 'the males of the village go after nightfall and cut a branch of a *Karam* tree(Adina Cordifolia) which they fix in the village lane and round which the young people dance till morning, when *Karam* branch is thrown into a tank. No sacrifices are offered, but a libation of liquor is poured out to the manes of the village-chief and to Maran Buru"(p.237).

Jeseph Troisi (Troisi J. , Tribal Religion: Religious Beliefs and Practices among the Santals, 1978, p. 141) points out that Karam festival concerns the Santal story of the origin of man and the division of the tribe into clans and subclans. And this peacitice is observed and recited by the elders in villages on certain occasions and one of those occasions when it is celebrated is known as *Karam* festival. He argues that this festival is not an annual ceremony, nor one that the village as a whole must perform regularly. In fact, this festival is, as he believes, sponsored by an individual household and the villagers are free to assist This festival is likely to take place in the month of *Asin* (September-October). J Troisi contends that this festival was not originally a Santal festival but it is believed to have been borrowed (by the Santals) from their neighbors In Culshaw's view (Culshaw, Tribal Heritage: A Study of the Santals, 1949, p. 114) many of the songs sung during the festival contain references to various heroes of the Ramayana. For J Troisi the aim of this festival is to seek an increase in wealth and progeny and to ward off any evil through the worship of the *Karam* tree.

J Troisi further remarks that during the celebration of this festival no sacrifices are offered but rice-beer libations are poured out to Manjhi Haram and Maran Buru and the villagers give themselves up to merry-making, dancing and singing. The festival starts usually in the evening in the dark with two unmarried men of the village who bathe and go to the nearby forest from where they bring two branches of the karam tree (Adina cordifolia) and plant them in the *Kulhi* outside the house where festival is to be celebrated. The villagers accompany the youths to the forest, dancing and singing dhurumjak tunes to the accompaniment of drums. Dancing and singing continues around the two branches, then the household elder, at whose instance the festival is performed, approaches the branches and he sprinkles the tree with water, puts a piece of cloth over the branches and a small light infront of them, thereupon he marks the branches with *sindur* and pours three rice-beer libations in front of them, each time invoking Manjhi Haram and Maran Buru to bring prosperity to his household. Thereafter, a village elder starts reciting the Karam binti, which is the history of creation, the origin of man, and the division of the tribe into clans and subclans, When the recital is over, those present start dancing and singing again till about sunrise when the branches are taken and immersed in the village water tank. Thereafter everyone returns to his house.

It is noteworthy to mention here—and the Santal society deserves a note of appreciation for this—the fact that the Santal society was gender neutral,accommodating towards embracing different kind of sexes from the community, promoting life-long friendship between young unmarried people of the same sex, be it the alliance between two boys or two girls both were accepted by the Santal society. Joseph Troisi points out that 'according to Santal tradition, young unmarried people of the samr sex who want to enter into a friendship alliance formalize this life-long friendship during this festival. The alliance between boys is called *Karmu Dharmu* and among girls *Karamdar*. It is brought about by the parties concerned exchanging karam buds and fixing them in each other's hair in the presence of the villagers gathered for the festival. Besiades linking two friends who promise each other mutual economic assistance, especially in times of crisis, the alliance also puts each one of them into new relationship with the other's family. Thus, in the case of boys wwho address each other as Karmu and Dharmu, the alliance gives each one of them the status of brothers while girls become sisters' (Troisi J. , Tribal Religion: Religious

Beliefs and Practices among the Santals, 1978, p. 142). J.Troisi remarks that 'parallel to this type of friendship there is the *Phul* type of friendship which is usually solemnized at Sibrat Melas. Another type of friendship is called *Baha Phul* among girls and *Jom-nu Gate* among boys. And in this latter type of friendship relation, there is no obligation of economic aid nor do the parties enter into any kinship relation' (p.142).

According to P.C.Hembram (Hembram P. , 1988, pp. 53-54)*Karam* and *Dhorom* concepts are ancient in origin and an integral part of tribal tradition and they are celebrated as a part of ritual ceremony. As per the Santal folk tradition —and there is also a parallel story in Santal society described in 'Karam-Binti'—'Karmu and Dharmu'were two brothers who sacrificed their life for the cause of peace and happiness in the society, travelling many places and suffering a lot to bring back 'Karam gosae' the deity of activities and wealth who left them for a far away place on dissatisfaction with their neighbours. 'Karam gosae', however, was pleased by their sincerity, devotion, and patience and because of which these two brothers managed to meet her at distant place far away of their native village beyond the seven seas and thirteen rivers (sat sammundar tero nadir pare). Thereupon, they expressed their strong desire to take her back to their native village.Upon being asked as to how they would take har back as she had no desire to go on riding an elephant or a horse nor she would like to use any other conveyance, they replied to her that they would take her back on their shoulders and waist, signifying that the abilities, sincerity and devotion had overcome all miseries and troubles, depicting a theme of patience, devotion, sincerity and diligence.

In his dictionary (Bodding, A Santal Dictionary: 7 Parts in Five Volumes, 1993(First published in India)), explaining the meaning of the word 'karam', P.O.Bodding offers a different argument that 'Karam' refers to several festivals such as *i) guru(or cela) karam; 2) manjhi( or jivet) karam; 3)mora (or goc) karam; 4) upas karam; 5) mak more karam.* He says that at the three first-mentioned festivals the village men , in the evening, go to the forest, and two unmarried young men cut two branches of the *karam* tree and then carrying the branches to the village with the accompanying crowd drumming at the time of both going and coming. They also dance around the tree from which the branches are taken. Having brought the branches in the village , the branches are planted in the street outside the house of the principal host, a bit of ordinary cloth is put over the branches and a small lamp is placed in front of the branches. During this time a number of men dance round the place drumming and singing. Further, a guru recites the karam binti which is, according to the Santal traditions, a history of the world from the creation and through the ages, followed by the crowd dancing round the place, some women dancing round the branches, and the men dance turning in a circle outside, singing and drumming.

Elaborating on the other karam festivals, P.O.Bodding reports that the *guru(or cela) karam* is performed by the *ojha guru* and his disciples(v.dasae kora) and ut is celebrated in the month of Aghar. The distinctive characteristics of this festival are the beer being brewed from the grains collected by the guru and his disciples, and the branches being planted outside the *ojha guru*'s house. In his view, the *manjhi (or jivet) karam* entails this being performed by the newly-appointed headman and the branches being planted in the street outside his house. *The mora(or goc) karam* is generally performed by people who can afford it along with the Bhandan, the last funeral ceremonies for for a dead person.This *karam* is diffenrt from other karam festivals in the sense that apart from the performance of the ordinary *bhandan* with sacrifices to the deceased, the branches are brought and disposed of as at the karam; the host places at the branches brass cups and plates and even a drum in some cases, which are all taken by the reciting *guru*. The *upas karam* differs from other karam festivals in that it is performed only when a karam sprout has come out on the roof of a person's house. The usaual practice is that in this case the householder has to fast throughout the day when the sprout is taken down from the roof (hence the name *upas*); this is done in the evening and the tree is planted in the street just outside the house. Finally, the *mak more karam* is performed in respect of the *mak more* and is like the *manjhi karam*.

According to W.G.Archer (Archer, The Hill of Flutes: Life , Love and Poetry in Tribal India, A Portrait of the Santals, 1974, p. 256) the Jiwet' Karam('a Karam for the living') is a private ceremony and not an annual ceremony nor one that the village itself must regularly perform, but is rather an optional act sponsored by individuals in which the villagers assist. Like P.O.Bodding he is also of the opinion that the standard ceremony of Karam is performed on five further occasions: 'Manjhi Karam is done when a new headman first assumes office seeking to associate his term of service with fertility and welfare. Dangua Kram is done, once in five years, when village boys and girls are ripe for marriage and their early wedding is desired. Guru Karam celebrates the starting of an ojha's practice while Cela Karam marks the end of the pupil's class and celebrates their initiation. Mak' More Karam is done in continuation of a Mak' More festival as a thanksgiving for ending sickness and finally, Upas or Janam Karam celebrates the chance appearance of a Karam seedling on man's private plot'(p.256).

In W.G. Archer's view the standard ceremony or the main Jiwet' Karam festival is often held in the month of September and begins after dark with the villagers going to the man at whose instance the Karam is to be done. Having assembled at the location, they begin to sing:

**I**

Jogmanjhi
Jogmanjhi
O jogmanjhi
Get the light ready
Prepare prepare
I will touch the wick with flame
Make the lamp ready. (p. 256-57)

The required materials are then collected by women which include: a new winnowing fan, a battle-axe, vermilion, oil, dub grass, cotton, gur, milk, paddy and rice-beer. As the jogmanjhi sets out into the darknes after gathering everything up, the whole crowd goes singing with him:

**II**

Arise, headman
Come, O village five
Let us find and bring the Karam
Come with us, O five
And we will bring the Karam
Come with us
Ram, Lokhon
And we will cut
A Karam in the forest
Comc with us
Bhorot, Catur
And we will cut
A Karam in the thick, thick forest. (p. 257).

After reaching a karam tree, the villagers surround it where as the jogmanjhi washes his feet and sprinkles the tree with water. Now lighting a lamp, setting it by the trunk and choosing a fork with two small branches , the jogmanjhi winds the cotton round the two stems, dabbing oil on the fork and making three vermilion marks on each of the branches. During this period the crowd sings the following songs:

### III

O Karam
Why have you come?
Why have you arrived?
O Karam
I have come for you
For you I have arrived.
Jogmanjhi
Do not touch it
Leave it alone
First wash your feet
And sprinkle it with water
Jogmanjhi
Bring a skein of thread
And tie the Karam branch.(p.257-58)

### IV

Karmu
I shall not go
O Karmu, return
Go back
Karmu, for your love
I fasted
Ten years
For the sake of Karmu
I have eaten nothing
Twenty years
Do not weep, Karmu
Do not mourn
I will tke you
I will bring you
O Karmu
I will set you in my lap
I will put you on my hip
Karmu, Karmu
I will lift you in my arms
O Karmu
I will wash you in milk
I will wash your hair in curds
O Karmu
I will keep you ever at my waist. (p.258).

Thereafter, the jogmanjhi makes offering of rice-beer and either water or milk to Maran Buru and prays 'O Maran Buru, we are making you this offering. We are doing the Karam ceremony. Till today this tree was in the forest. Tonight we shall take it to the village. Let it stay green. Let everyone dance and sing. May there be no ache of belly or head. Give us your blessing.' Further, two unmarried boys are asked to hold each fork and the jogmanjhi unwinds the cotton and cuts the two stem with two quick strokes of the battle-axe. The crowd sings:

**IV**

Karam, Karam
The Karam has been cut
Karam is not cut
The ashes all are cut. (p.259)

Now the crowd of villagers dances around the tree after some time they move towards the house of the host with two boys going ahead. Reaching the house of the host, a girl welcomes the boys, the jogmanjhi and the guru by washing their feet. At this time the villagers sing:

**V**

O Amki Devi
Bring a plate of brass
A pot of water
I have brought a tree
From Brindaban
O mother wash my feet. (p. 259).

The following is an example of a song sung when the jogmanjhi takes a digging stick, making a small mound of earth:

**VI**

Jogmanjhi, bring
A digging stick of gold
A digging stick of silver
Dig deep a hole
And plant the Karam branches. (p. 259).

At the time of planting of the branches done by the two boys, the jogmanjhi winds the cotton round them and the plastering of the mound with water and cowdung is done by two girls from the host's family. The following song is sung at that time:

## VII

Jogmanjhi
Bring a skein of thread
Jogmanjhi
I have planted
Two Karam branches
Jogmanjhi
Tie the twin strands of branches
With your thin thread
Bring water of the sea
Amki Devi
And clean the dancing ground.
Jogmanjhi, I have brought
Sea water
I have brought
Cowdung
I have cleaned
The four corners. (p. 260).

Thereafter, women belonging to the host's family circle winnowing fans above the branches; a lamp is then lit and a cloth stained with turmeric is draped around the stems. The band of villagers sings the song:

## VIII

Mother, do the circling
Of the two Karam branches
The circling
Of the twin branches
Mother bring a length of cloth
And swathe the Karam branches. (p. 260).

W.G. Archer reports that the villagers then squat in a great circle round the tree and the guru faces east followed by a long recital of the Karam sermon. The sermon essentially includes the mythological story about how the genesis of the world took place; the morals about sex and incest and about the origin of Karam. Archer maintains that 'as the sermon draws to its close, tension relaxes, men and boys straighten up and soon there are separate groups dancing the rinja in the village street. A few go off to drum for the girls while others form a loosely strung out circle. The girls go edging round clapping their hands, while the men and boys perform some agile figures. They start by strutting round the circle, each dancer moving his arms with bold truculent jerks. Then the line faces inwards, they hold hands and the circle goes swinging round in a fast careering rush.when they have danced this through, they stand behind each other in a tightly fitting line. They grip each other's shoulders, lock the left foot in the calf of the man behind and the whole line goes stiffly hopping round. A little later, the spirit of joking daring quickens, they divide themselves in two, one line standing on the shoulders of the other and the line which is now two lines goes slowly marching round. Whenthey have covered the circle several times, they face inwards and the topmest line of dancers changes position. Each man now stands with his legsspread-eagled on the shoulders of the men below him. He holds the arms of his companions and a circle of inter-gripping limbs is thus imposed upon the lower ranks. When all is ready, the bnd starts to move and the towering edifice of forms goes tottering round the street. As the line revolves, the drummers, each on separate mounts, go quickly past it'.

According to W.G.Archer the villagers dance and sing throughout the night and the dances of this type go on. In between rice-beer is drunk and an air of riotous gaiety infects the village. As the morning approaches the dances gradually slow down and the dancers go to their home singing bhinsar or dawn songs:

**IX**

Rise, sun and moon
Rise on the Karam
In your light, O friend
I will do the bhinsar dance. (p. 267).

**X**

When the dogs bark
The day breaks
When the peacock calls
The dawn comes. (p.267)

**XI**

Rise, drunk brother
The horse is starting
The dogs bark
The night has turned to dawn. (p. 267)

**XII**

Get up, big bullock
And go and graze the grass
Above you, the golden vulture
Hovers in the sky. (p.268).

**XIII**

O vulture, eat the flesh
But leave the bones
The bones will go
To the deep deep sea. (p. 268).

W.G.Archer remarks that the last rites begin early morning before the sun gets high and to participate in the last ceremony the village again gathers at the branches and a circling ceremony is done once more. The jagmanjhi along with the two boys who assisted at the cutting, pulls the branches up and then the two girls who plastered the mound are presented some Karam leaves and they either exchange the leaves or put them in each other's hair. While this is going on a number of songs are sung , which depict the stream or pond, referring to bathing and washing and the cleaning of the hair. These songs describe the happy scenes of flirtation which streams witness and finally they summon the Karam branches for their last immersion. Some of those songs are mentioned below:

**XIV**

Whose is the pond, the pond
Whose is the tank
The tank with flowers?
The pond, the pond
It is the mother's pond
The tank, the tank
It is the father's tank with flowers. (p. 269).

**XV**

In the pond of mustard, mother
What is creeping?
In the flowering tank, father
What things are growing?
In the pond of mustard
The betel nut has crept

In the tank of flowers
The champa bloom has come. (p. 269).

**XVI**

Who are those two girls bathing?
I have smelt the oil of their hair
Who are those two girls cleaning their tresses?
I have smelt their scented oil. (p. 269).

**XVII**

The two girl friends were washing
And I smelt the oil of their hair
The two girl friends
Were cleaning their tresses
And I smelt their scented oil. (p. 269).

**XVIII**

My love plays his flute
By the river or the stream
My friend plays his flute
By the shore of the sea. (p. 270)

**XIX**

Rise, O Karam
Rise to your feet
Let us go, Karam
To wash and clean our hair. (p. 269-70).

**XX**

Where, O Karam
Will you wash your body?
Where, O Karam
Will you wash your hair?
At the last ghat , my Karmu
I will wash my body
At the meral ghat, my Karmu
I will clean my hair
At the last ghat, Karam
The water is like milk

At the meral ghat
The clay is soft as curds
At the last ghat, Karmu
You will wash in milk
At the meral ghat, Karmu
You will clean your hair in curds. (p. 270).

After the bestowal of the leaves, as they float away, all the dance groups gather and the following under-mentioned last songs are sung to bid adieu to Karam festival:

**XXI**

O Karam you are going
To the banks of the Ganges
O Karam
You are leaving me
On the dancing-floor
Stay, O Karam
Stay and come back
O Karam
Catch the reeds
In the river
Catch the bushes.
Dancer, do no weep
Do not mourn
In a year's time
I will return. (p. 270).

**XXII**

The water of the well is dry
The water of the pot remains
In the hand is the gold umbrella
On the head is the silken cloth
They are going from the dance-floor
The water of the well is dry
The water of the pot remains
In the hand is the gold umbrella
On the head is the silken cloth
The Karam branch
Is drifting to the sea

O brother with your goats
I saw the Karam
On the way
O brother, tending sheep
I saw the Karam
Going down

The dance, the dance is ending. (Archer, The Hill of Flutes: Life , Love and Poetry in Tribal India, A Portrait of the Santals, 1974, pp. 270-71).

Subhendu Sekhar Bhattacharya's study of the Santali Songs (Bhattacharya, Santal Songs: Different Types, 1979) shows that Karam festival is celebrated in the month of Bhadra and the whole village participates into it with gaity and enthusiasm. This festival is done with an intention to honour the 'Karam Gosain', the god who is supposed to have created the world with the mankind and animals into it. According to his view two branches of the Karam tree are planted at the centre of the dancing ground of the village. He asserts, 'circular dances go all through the night around the tree. Next morning the branch is puuled out, carried in a procession to the neighbouring stream or tank and thrown into it. The songs which are sung at the time of Karam festival are known as Karam songs'. Bhattacharya further argues that Karam is not the name of a tune but the tune of the song belongs to two different varieties: Rinja and Bhinsar.In his view, Rinja is the name of the songs sung at midnight and Bhinsar is the name of the songs sung at the small hours of night.

P.O.Bodding (Bodding, Studies in Santal Medicine and Connected Folklore, 1940, pp. 78-79) holds the view that having agreed to the *Guru*'s proposal of having the *Karam* festival, in the morning of the day appointed by the *guru,* the villagers bring all the beer to the *guru*'s house, and one pot is drunk at once; this is called *jan handi*, the beer of knowing, or intimation. In the evening people come together and after sunset some people start with drums to bring a branch of Karam tree( Adina cordifolia). Two unmarried young men cut the branch of the Karam tree and bring it and plant it in the village street just outside the entrance to the guru's house. Now the beer drinking and dancing begins with the village people firstly drinking in the ojha guru's house and going out to dance. P.O.Bodding informs us that the villagers dance some four *akhar*(rounds) and when they have done they call the people of some village or other whom they have seen being present. These people come in, get each two leaf-cups of beer and begin to dance. And when these people have done two akhar of dancing, thw people of another village are called and treated in the same manner until all villages present there have had their turn. Bodding tells us that according to the number of villages represented this dancing may continue until cock-crow or even longer. Upto this time they dance in the street round the planted *karam* branch a certain kind of dance known as *karam enec*. He says, 'There are songs sung to a special melody, the dancing drum is beaten to a special time. No one commences dancing before he is called with his village; but as soon as they have commenced, they may continue as much as they like'(p.79).

Thereafter, the dance is changed to what is called *bhinsar*, which has other dancing steps, other drumming and songs with other melodies.At the time of sunrise they have different practice: the two young men who brought and planted the *karam* branch go and pluck it up. The one who takes hold of it runs round with it a couple of times, keeping it high up. The girls present there jump up and try to pluck a leaf of the branch. If there are girls present there wishing to pledge themselves to special friendship, they put the leaf they have taken in each other's hair and from that time onwards these pairs are connected in special intimate friendship; they call each other *karam dar* (*karam* branch) and do not use their names. Thereupon, the two men run with the branch to a tank or other fairly deep water, enter the water until they are sufficiently in to be able to immerse themselves. The one having the branch lets it go while under water. Thereafter they take bath and return to their respective villages (Bodding, Studies in Santal Medicine and Connected Folklore, 1940, p. 79).

## (VIII) Dasae Seren

According to Joseph Troisi (Troisi J. , Tribal Religion: Religious Beliefs and Practices among the Santals, 1978, p. 215)*Dasae Parab* is the common name among the Santals for *Durga Puja* and it is celebrated in the month of *Asin* (September-October). For P.C.Hembram (Hembram P. , 1988, p. 45)*Dansae* is only a festival not accompanying any ritual puja. It begins with vermilion drops being offered at *akhara* in the name of twelve gurus, followed by dance performance. The dance is not confined to one single village, but the party moves from village to village. In Hembram's view this festival lasts for four days coinciding with Dussera or Durga puja of Hindus, giving us an indication that this festival might be having some relation with the Hindu festival. P.C.Hembram is of the opinion that as per a Santal lore Durga is not the original name of goddess Durga but as she killed Durga the tribal chief, she is called goddess Durga and this is evinced from the following Santali song:

**I**

'*Devire Durga dukin*
*Hudure hudure'*(Hembram P., 1988, p. 45).

In these lines it has been shown that Devi and Durga are in turmoil and the state of their quarrel is described as 'hudure hudure' and *hudure* is a thundering sound caused by turmoil and clash between two equal and opposite powers. Among the Santal children there is a popular saying:

**II**

'*Hadur Ja Durga Ja*
*Gurga Jam lebed pose : Ket'*(Hembram P. , 1988, p. 46).

(Oh thunder power! Oh Durga!
Your leg pressure broke the solid
Stone block)

Durga, their tribal leader, has been described here in the above-mentioned lines to be so strong and powerful that he could break even solid stone hammer into pieces with the pressure of his leg and it was a matter of disgrace for them that they lost their leader and were left with invoking other gurus such as: (i) Dharam guru, (ii) Gando Guru, (iii) Sid guru, (iv) Side guru, (v) Rahar guru, (vi) Bhuwang guru, (vii) Vendra guru, (viii) Chemong guru, (ix) Bhairam guru, (x) Veera guru, (xi) Lar guru, and xii) Kamru guru. Hembram's submission is that the above-mentioned gurus in the belief of the Santals possessed mysterious immense power and quality and were capable enough of guiding the Santals in a right direction. The santals made the following invocation prayer to the gurus:

**III**

*'Denting guru ho guru sunume sindur*
*Denting guru ho guru ainom kajal*
*Desh Lagit ho guru sunume sindur,*
*Disem ligit ho guru ainem kajal'*(Hembram P. , 1988, p. 46).

(Oh preceptor! Bless me with sunume sindur
Oh preceptor! Bless me with ainom kajal,
Sunume sindur is used to worship the country,
Ainom kajal is used to sharpening the eye-sight.)

According to P.O.Bodding (Bodding, Studies in Santal Medicine and Connected Folklore: Part I, II and III, 2001(Second Reprint), p. 83) *Dasãe seren* or also called *loboe seren* referes to a number of special songs sung by the Dasãe kora, the 'September boys' to special melodies that fit in with their dancing steps danced by them in the court-yards. The characteristic feature of the Dasãe songs is that these are all practically in Santali, with many poetical peculiarities as to the form of words and also as to the grammatical construction:

**IV**

*Bindire sutamteben tundan kan do,*
*Bindire toreteben gemen kan do;*
*Bindire Sin bir do lok kan do,*
*Bindire Man bir do hasa digiren.*

**Translation**

O spider, you two are moving along the thread(web),
O spider, you two are climbing slowly up the gossamer;
O spider, the Sin forest is burning,
O spider, the Man forest has become dust and ashes. (p. 83-84).

**V**

*Ot ma lolo Kamru guru, serma seton, Buan guru,*
*Yo haere, cela dolan lalaoketko.*
*Sui sutam gutukate senerre lan galankako,*
*Rear kanda, sita nala latarrelan dohokako.*

**Translation**

The earth is hot, o Kamru guru, the sky is fierce sunshine, o Buan guru;
Alas, alas, we we two have tantalized the disciples;
We two shall thread a needle and weave them on the rafter,
In a cool waterpot, below the sita valley we two shall put them. (p.84).

**VI**

*Tokoe guru nuralte pohoke doko nargolen?*
*Tokoe cela baherte pakareko tundan kan?*
*Kamru guru nuralte pohoko doko nargolen,*
*Kamru cela baherte do pakareko tundan kan.*

**Translation**

Through which guru's incitement did the locusts come down?
Through which disciples' calling out are the larvae moving about?
Through the incitement of Kamru guru the locusts came down.
Kamru's disciples calling them out the larvae are moving about. (p.85).

### VII

*Nare ma naigor hako biole boyole;*
*Hae hae! Gadare ma tayan biole boyole;*
*Hae hae! Nature ma nato kurikin bilit balan.*

**Translation**
In the big river the river fish are swimming about;
Alas, alas! in the big river the crocodile is swimming about;
Alas, alas, in the village the two village girls go glittering about. (p.85)

### VIII

*Horre hesak sakam hipire hipire,*
*Hoete hesak sakam hipir hipir;*
*Daharre bare sakam nohore nohore.*

**Translation**
On the road is the trembling pipol leaf,
Thw wind makes the pipol leaves tremble;
On the cart-track is the glossy banyan leaf. (p. 85).

### IX

*Horre kasmar kulai bir ma tilai lo,*
*Kulai pedel pedel, gate, kulai homor homor,*
*Marna lagae kulai do,*
*Kulai pedal pedal, gate, kulai homor homor.*

**Translation**
On the road a kasmar tree, a hare, in the forest the tilai bush is burnt,
The hare is jumping about, the hare is mourning, o companion,
The hare is going to die,
The hare is jumping about, o companion, thr hare is mourning. (p.85)

### X

*Cetane disom do, guru hoe dakketa ho, guru hoe dekketa ho;*
*Latare disom do, goru hoe jariketa ho, guru hoenjariketa ho.*
*Gan nai do, guru ho, perecena ho, guru ho, perecena ho,*
*Sora nai do, guru ho, coranenare, guru ho, coranenare.*
*Cekate, cekate, guru holan parom calak ho, guru lan parom calaka?*
*Mit sutam do, guru ho, cote lobere, hae hae!*
*Bar sutam do, guru ho, buane dandire, guru ho, buane dandier;*
*Mit janga do, guru ho, tore sutamre, guru ho, tore sutamre, hae hae!*
*Mit janga do, guru ho, buane dandier, guru ho, buane dandier.*

**Translation**

In the up-country, o guru, it rained, o guru it rained;
In the low-country, o guru, it poured, o guru, it poured.
The Ganges river, o guru, was filled, o guru, was filled,
The Sora river, o guru, ran overflowing, o guru, ran overflowing.
How, how, o guru, will we two get across, o guru, we two get across?
One thread, o guru, high above, o dear dear!
Two threads, o guru, in the buan stick, o guru, in the buan stick;
One foot, o guru, in the gossamer thread, o guru, in the gossamer thread
O dear, dear!
One foot, o guru,on the buan stick, o guru, on the buan stick. (p.86).

### XI

*Tokoe gururen cela doko nodonen dahades do, guru ho, dehades?*
*Tokoe gururen cela doko nodonen? Sarag dihan bharndo leka dhuriko notanei.*
*Kamru gururen cela doko nodonena, dehades do, guru ho, dehades do, hae, hae!*
*Kamru gururen cela doko nodonena, sarag dihan dhuriko notanet.*

**Translation**

Which guru's disciples have come out over the country, o guru, over the country?
Which guru's disciles have come out? Right upto heaven like a whirlwind they spread the dust.
Kamru guru's disciples have come out over the country, o guru, over the country; alas, alas!
Kamru guru's disciples have come out, right up to heaven they spread the dust. (p.86).

### XII

*Hako hako, guru ho, danda danda, hae!*
*Dhiri cetan, guru ho, hako bele, hae hae!*
*Caura cetan, guru ho, hakoe bubrum kan.*

**Translation**

Fish, fish, o guru, fins, fins, o dear, dear!
Upon the stone, o guru, the fish egg, o dear, dear!
Upon the rock, o guru, the fish is sitting on eggs! (p. 86).

### XIII

*Kurikin na toreteben tundan kana, hae hae!*
*Kurikin na toreteben gemen kana, hae hae!*
*Kurikin na naben nasul sangarte, nisi serman tetanena;*
*Nardo kurikin tohon nasulleben,*
*Nardo kurikin tohon sangarleben!*

**Translation**
You two girls, you are moving along the gossamer, o dear, dear,
You two girls, you are crawling along the gossamer, o dear, dear!
You two girls, supporting and taking about you two for twenty years I became utterly destitute;
Any more, you two girls, I shall certainly not support you two,
Any more, you two girls, I shall certainly not take you two about with me! (p. 87).

### XIV

*Tokoe gururen cela doko nodonena lale lal do , guru ho, lale lal do?*
*Tokoe gururen cela doko baherena, mat barahe, guru ho, carhi barahe?*
*Kamru gururen cela doko nodonena lale lal do, guru ho, lale lal do, hae hae!*
*Kamru gururen cela doko baherena, mat barahe, guru ho, carhi barahe!*

**Translation**
Which guru's disciples have come out so red, o guru, so red?
Which guru's disciples have come out in the country, with a rope of bamboo, o guru, with a three-stranded rope?
Kamru guru's disciples have come out so red, o guru, so red, o dear, dear!
Kamru guru's disciples have come out in the country, with a rope of bamboo, o guru, with a three-stranded rope! (p.87).

### XV

*Tokoe guru racare hesak belek kan, guru ho,*
*Hesak belek kan, hae hae?*
*Tokoe guru batere bare belek kan, guru ho,*
*Bare belek kan, hae hae?*
*Care kisnikin cero berok kan.*
*Mane huhar do gurukin kena kinik kan,*
*Gurukin kena kinik kan.*

**Translation**

In which guru's court-yard is the pipol ripening, o guru,
The pipol ripening, o dear, dear?
In which guru's property is the banyan ripening, o guru,
The banyan ripening, o dear, dear?
The two pied-starling are twittering,
The two fine green doves, o guru, are chattering,
O guru, the two are chattering. (p.87-88).

## XVI

*Tokoe guru racare divhe jolok kan, guru ho,*
*Hae hae, divhe bamberok?*
*Kamru guru racare divhe jolok kan, guru ho,*
*Hae hae, divhe bamberok.*

**Translation**

In which guru's court-yard is the lamp burning, o guru,
O dear, dear, the lamp shining?
In kamru guru's court-yard the lamp is burning, o guru,
O dear, dear, the lamp is shining. (p.88).

## XVII

*Tokoe guru ho, guru hoe akhraleta ho,*
*Guru hoe akhraleta ho, hae hae?*
*Kamru guru hoe akhraleta ho,*
*Guru hoe akhraleta ho, hae hae!*

**Translation**

Which guru, o guru, provided the place for performance,
O guru, provided the place for performance? O dear, dear!
Kamru guru provided the place for performance,
O guru, he provided the place for performance, o dear, dear!(p.88)

## XVIII

*Hae hae, Kamru cela do cela doe pindleta ho;*
*Cete lagit ho guru hoe akhraleta ho,*
*Guru hoe akhraleta ho?*
*Sunume sindur lagit guru hoe akhraleta;*
*Naenom kajar lagit cela hoe pindleta do.*

**Translation**

O dear, dear! Kamru's disciple, the disciple made an alter;

For what purpose did the guru provide a place for performance,
O guru, did he provide a place for performance?
To use oil and sindur, o guru, he provided a place for performance ,
To use eye-paint and lamp-black the disciple made an alter. (p.88)

### XIX

*Hae hae! Dur dese yaile, buhin, jhatkaite bidai de!*
*Haw hae! Jaite jaite badi dur jhatka, buhin, bidai de!*

**Translation**

O dear, dear! I have come to a country far away, o sister, be quick to send me off!
O dear, dear! Walking, walking I have come very far, be quick, o sister, and send me off! (p.89).

### XX

*Hae hae! Kisar near mec gando macire goe durup akan,*
*Hae hae! Dangua kuri satere goe racak kan.*
*Hae hae! Koce koceteye bengetadin,*
*Hae hae!kokombeye landawadin.*

**Translation**

O dear, dear! the master's wife is sitting on the chairs, planks and stools, o brother-in-law,
O dear, dear! the maiden is standing pulling the straw of the eaves, o brother-in-law.
O dear, dear! she looked at me sideways,
O dear, dear! she turned her head aslant and laughed to me.(p.89)

### XXI

*Hae hae! Sarag dihon patalreko enec kana,*
*Hae hae! guru do, guru doe nemok kan do suneme sindur,*
*Hae hae! cela do, cela doe nemok kan do naenom kajar.*

**Translation**

O dear, dear! right to heaven and in the netherworld they are dancing,
O dear, dear! the guru, the guru is giving oil and sindur,
O dear, dear! the disciple, the disciple is giving eye-paint and lamp-black. (p.89).

### XXII

*Hae hae! De go yayo bhik yayo,*
*Arwa cal, eka dali dar lagit,*

*Hae hae! Eka kodar mati lagit;*
*Yuhi dekho mora sangare bhai yayo.*

**Translation**
O dear, dear! do, o mother, o mother, give what I beg, o mother,
Sun-dried rice, one basket for the branches.
O dear, dear! one hoe for the earth;
See him, my dead brother-in-law, o mother. (p.89)

## XXIII

*Hae hae! Kuli kuli sunte jabo ghore ghore;*
*Hae hae! Khelte jab, hae hae! Na hami jabo, go,*
*Sebokero bari duare.*

**Translation**
O dear, dear! I shall go through the street to listen from house to house;
O dear, dear! I shall go to dance, o dear, dear! No, I am not going
To the door of the worshippers' house. (p.89-90).

## XXIV

*Hae hae! nape do, go nayo, norak duarre,*
*Hae hae! nale do, go nayo, serma setonre;*
*Hae hae!koe do, go nayo, nemalepe,*
*Hae hae! koe do, go nayo, bidakalepe!*

**Translation**
O dear, dear! you, o mother, o mother, are in your house and home,
O dear, dear! we, o mother, o mother, are in the heat of the sun in the sky,
O dear, dear! what we beg, o mother, o mother, give us,
O dear, dear! what we beg o mother, o mother, send us off with that! (Bodding, Studies in Santal Medicine and Connected Folklore, 1940, p. 90).

## XXV

*Hae hae! netom dangra do, guru ho, konerekade,*
*Hae hae! kone dangra do guru hoe etomrekade;*
*Hae hae! guru hoe burumrn do , guru hoe burumen do;*
*Kuya lekan kuri, guru hoe lai barae kan, guru hoe katha barae kan.*

**Translation**
O dear, dear! The right side bullock, o guru, he has put on the left side,

O dear, dear! The left side bullock he has, o guru, put on the right side.
O dear, dear! o guru, he lay down, o guru, he lay down;
A girl black like a wild dog, o guru, is telling it, o guru, she is spreading report of it. (Bodding, Studies in Santal Medicine and Connected Folklore, 1940).

### XXVI

*Hae hae! des lobe disom cayayen,*
*Hae hae! guru ho, delabon deste,*
*Hae hae! guru ho, delabon disomte;*
*Hae hae! des lobe disom baheren,*
*Hae hae! guru ho, delabon deeste,*
*Hae hae! guru ho, delabon deste,*
*Hae hae! guru ho, delabon disomte!*

**Translation**
O dear, dear! the desirable country, the land has become stinking,
O dear, dear! o guru, come let us go out into the country,
Odear, dear! o guru, come let us go out into the land;
O dear, dear! the desirable country has become defiled,
O dear, dear! o guru, come let us go out into the country,
O dear, dear! o guru, come let us go out into the land! (Bodding, Studies in Santal Medicine and Connected Folklore, 1940, p. 90).

### XXVII

*Hae hae! guru do, guru do, gel bar guru doko nacurenare;*
*Hae hae! cela do, cela do, gel bar cela doko baherana.*
*Hae hae! nodonako guru near basna dak do;*
*Hae hae! belako guru near pata gando do.*

**Translation**
O dear, dear! gurus, gurus, twelve gurus turned round;
O dear , dear! disciples, twelve disciples came out.
O dear, dear! the guru's wife will bring a cup of water,
O dear, dear! the guru's wife will place solid stools for them to sit on. (Bodding, Studies in Santal Medicine and Connected Folklore, 1940, p. 93).

### XXVIII

*Hae hae! toka disom darakeda, guru ho?*
*Hae hae! toka disom sangarkeda , guru ho?*

*Hae hae! bhand disom darakedan, cela ho,*
*Hae hae! Turuk disom, sangarkedan , cela ho.*
*Hae hae! bhand disom do, cela ho, bhondgea,*
*Hae hae! cela ho, Turuk disom do ban bogea.*

**Translation**

O dear, dear! which country di d you travel in , o guru?
O dear, dear! which country did you go about in, o guru?
O dear, dear! I travelled in the defiled country, o disciple;
O dear,dear! I went about in the Moghul country, o disciple.
O dear, dear!the defiled country, o disciple, is unclean?
O dear, dear! o disciple, the Moghul country is not good. (Bodding, Studies in Santal Medicine and Connected Folklore: Part I,II and III, 2001 (Second Reprint), p. 93).

According to W.G.Archer, (Archer, The Hill of Flutes: Life , Love and Poetry in Tribal India, A Portrait of the Santals, 1974, p. 72) Dasae dances are of pretty grace and are confined to girls and women. Boys, however, also indulge in pantomimic dancing for, towards the end of the rains, particularly those who have undertaken a course in tribal medicine under an ojha or medicine-man perform a series of 'plays'. Archer is of the view that these are part of the Dasae daran( 'september wanderings') and are mixture of dancing, pantomime and trance. He gives examples of some Dasae songs:

**XXIX**

Girls, how lovely you look
With your dress clinging
How lovely you look
With your cloth
Rucked in folds. (p. 74).

**XXX**

On the path the pipal fruit is ripe
And the pied mainas cry cero bero
The green pigeons twist their heads. (p.74)

**XXXI**

Parrot, do not cry
At the pain in your body
Do not mourn

In the bar tree by the road
Your father and mother
Are high up on the mountain
Dove, your father and brothers
Are out in the forest. (p.74-75)

**XXXII**

Two girls like sticks
With winding curves
O two girls
Stamp on the pounder
Clean the rice in a fan
O two girls
Listen to the bangles
Listen where the pounder calls
O two girls
Finish your rice
Finish making that curry. (p.75).

**XXXIII**

O you two girls
In a big house
With rounded thatch
Comb your tresses
Tie them in a knot
The Dasae boys are upon you
You must take their greetings. (p.75).

**XXXIV**

In the river, the alligator
Slashes with its tail
In the village the boys
Swagger up and down. (p.76)

**XXXV**

Mother give me my loin-cloth
Give me my fiddle
I am going, mother
To wander in the country

I am going, parrot
To rove about the land. (p.76)

**XXXVI**

At the village end is a bar tree
With a sound of bells
The two teachers met
The bells are jangling
The dust mixes
From the kicking feeet. (p.76).

**XXXVII**

Guru, for many days
You ruled your pupils
Now I will blind you like a dove
I will trap you like a quail.(p.76-77).

**XXXVIII**

Guru, your right foot
On a line of gossamer
Guru, your left foot
On a fiddle's bow. (p.77).

**XXXIX**

In a gold cloth
Is the Guru's wife
She is sitting in a chair
She is looking in a glass
And like a lotus leaf
She moves her head. (p.77).

For subhendu sekhar Bhattacharya (Bhattacharya, Santal Songs: Different Types, 1979, p. 28) the word 'Dasae' is a corruption of DASAMI implying the month of ASWIN in Santali. Battacharya observes that the Dasae festival is replica of the Durga Puja festival but that is the case owing to the ignorance of the santal mythology. Subhendu Bhattachrya feels that it is only by an accident that this festival of Dasae synchronises with that of Durga puja and lip service is offered to the Goddess in the song with which the dance begins: 'DASAERE JHALMALA DEBIRE DURGA'. In Bhattacharya's view the actual purpose of the songs is to bring back the mighty sorcerers of old. He asserts that these songs are not meaningful songs dealing with social and other topics but powerful incantations very often without meaning which revive the ancient magic. He maintains that the people have full faith in eight Gurus and believe that Kamru Guru and his associates(the names of the eight gurus are: Dhorom Guru, Kamru Guru, Maran Guru, Gando Guru, Rohra Guru, Sido Guru, Bhano Guru and Pobon Guru) will be pleased by the invocations and would exert their power and ward off the evil spirits from casting a malign influence. Dasae is a festival in which we are face to face with a ritual in which primitive magic and sorcery create an awe-inspiring situation bringing us to the core of the primitive religion.

Bhattacharya's research with respect to Dasae songs shows that they came across a word 'Loboe' and Mare Hapram was inclined to treat this as a separate tune in Dasae songs. Bhattacharya, however, argues that no separate songs designated as 'Loboe' are available in Santali tradition and only the dances performed during the festival are labelled as 'Loboe'. Loboe, therefore, as per the report of Bhattacharya, refers to a dance performed exclusively by males arranged in several lines and gaudily dressed with peacock feathers. In this dance the whole body moves forward with swift and vigorous steps falling in unison and suddenly swings a full right angle facing the opposite direction. Bhattacharya writes, 'the whole body again moves forward to the end when the retrograde movement starts again, clinging cymbals taking the principal part in the instrumental music, it is much alike a war-dance and bears strong contrast to the softer tone of Soharae and Baha dances.' It may be mentioned here that the Dasae dance is the only dance which is exclusively performed by men alone.

## (IX) Bir Seren

According to Rev. P.O.Bodding (Bodding, A Santal Dictionary: 7 Parts in Five Volumes, 1993(First published in India), p. 303) 'bir sereE ' implies forest song. He records that 'the bir seren are mostly obscene, and are not sung in the village and not when any of the other sex is present, but are sung also by women when they are away from people. There is a great number of these songs; some of them may be said to represent a kind of poetry; and the melodies or tunes are perhaps the most beautiful that the Santals have. Some of these songs give expression to the longing felt for their home by women who for the sake of a lover have had to leave home and friends.'

Charulal Mukherjea (Mukherjea, The Santals, 1962,Revised Edition, p. 427) remarks that love-adventures in jungles form the subject of a large number of folk-songs, called Bir Seren. In his view many of the subjects of

Bir Seren relate to escapades, first sex-experiences and their results. For Subhendu Sekhar Bhattacharya (Bhattacharya, Santal Songs: Different Types, 1979, p. 29) Bir Seren('Forest songs') are 'the vulgerest songs imaginable, couched in language of gross barbarity and accompanied by dances equally uncouth and ribald. As the name indicates the songs are not sung in the neibourhood of human habitation but in forests. The songs are sung particularly during the hunting festival where women have no access.'In Bhattacharya's view the demonstration of such songs and dance may be enjoyed once in a year at the Ajodhya Hunting.

Quoting Mare Hapram's observation on Bir Seren, Bhattacharya records that the forest songs mostly divorced women compose and they make girls their disciples, when they pluck vegetables and bring leaves. The young men learn from them. Also among the forest songs there are a few ones that are good. Otherwise they are only what is shameless; therefore they do not sing these in the villages or at home, and if they sing them here people scold them. Elderly married women do not sing forest songs but foppish half-elderly women sing such in the forest together with girls. Bir Seren is at present always accompanied by dance, namely, Duriger Dance.

Examples:

**I**

When her hair was short as an oriole's
And still there was no public hair
He took and took her (Archer, The Hill of Flutes: Life , Love and Poetry in Tribal India, A Portrait of the Santals, 1974, p. 55).

**II**

They are crackling the raher bushes
Where you went to have me
O Mirza boy, let me go
My bangles and anklets are tinkling
And all the traders will hear us (Archer, The Hill of Flutes: Life , Love and Poetry in Tribal India, A Portrait of the Santals, 1974, p. 88).

Among the Santals the conventions, sanctions and rules with respect to sex and privacy are to be observed by all Sntals in the very strictest sense. In the great majority of cases the rules have become so ingrained in their minds that obedience is automatic. From the early childhood their parents and other children have so impressed the rules on them that they have become, as it were, second nature to them. No rules, however, could survive without sanctions and it is probably because all breaches carry with them strict penalties that they are hardly ever broken. The rules are observed primarily because they constitute a valued code of Santal behavior, but if a rule is broken, Santals see to it that whoever breaks it is broken also.

In Dumarghati, W.G.Archer (Archer, The Hill of Flutes: Life , Love and Poetry in Tribal India, A Portrait of the Santals, 1974, p. 88) narrates, the daughter of Lodga Hembrom 'showed her thumb' to seven boys and defied them to take her. The seven accepted the challenge and one day they dragged her to the forest and attempted to have their way. The girl repulsed five but succumbed to the last two. The matter came to the village and all the eight were fined two rupees and eight anna each—the girl for inciting the boys to have her in public and the boys for accepting the challenge.

Archer further reports that in Basdume, Khare Murmu induced a girl of another village to go with him. The villagers caught them in each other's arms and themeeting punished Khara with a fine of fifteen rupees. In certain cases even though the boy and girl are merely anticipating marriage, they are liable to be punished if they are caught engaging publicaly (P.88).

In Siakhuri, Archer (Archer, The Hill of Flutes: Life , Love and Poetry in Tribal India, A Portrait of the Santals, 1974, p. 88) maintains that Nandhna Murmu was caught with his village girl inn actual intercourse. The villagers gave them a beating and although the boy's father paid a bride-price and the girl then and there accepted as a wife, the boy was fined five rupees and the girl two rupees and eight annas. The same principles apply to attempts and preparations. In Bodacapar, Chundka Murmu was caught with his village girl. They were about to start intercourse when the girl's brother reached the scene. Chundka was dragged to the headman and was fined five rupees. Even more important is the rule that intercourse must always be with the girl's consent. If a boy cannot win a girl by words or presents, he is not entitled to have his way by force. If, in spite of this, he takes her, the girl is entitled to five rupees as damages and the boy can also be fined. Finally, if after marriage a girl admits a lover, the adulterer must compensate the husband.

## III

O my friend
Find for us where the girls sleep
O my friend
I will search and look
The door is made of cotton wood

The bolt is of baru
O my friend, how will you break in? (Archer, The Hill of Flutes: Life, Love and Poetry in Tribal India, A Portrait of the Santals, 1974, pp. 104-05).

**IV**

O my love
The land is dark
Do not go out for water
Two handsome young coots
Are straying down. (p.106).

**V**

O you two boys on the mountain
Do not split faggots with your axes
O you two girls
Do not make bundles of leaves
On the lower hill
For the tears will fall
Will fall from the eyes. (p.107).

According to W.G.Archer (Archer, The Hill of Flutes: Life , Love and Poetry in Tribal India, A Portrait of the Santals, 1974, p. 110) , it is the the buxom girl who arouses a Santal's love and admiration. Besides having a robust and round figure, a girl should be full-bosomed and from this angle Santals employ a conventional classification. Potkel are breasts that are just appearing, kortal cunci when they are a little bigger 'like the raised portion of a pair of cymbals', sosor deren 'when the nipples get black', hapa mu 'when they are ripe for boys'. All these are in process of formation and are valued more for their promise than their actual shape. It is little later that they achieve their fullest charm:

**VI**

Darling
It was with you only
That I slept at the door
Like the budding horns of a calf
Were your little breasts
And they are round as bowls now (p.110)

The most lovely are sinjo towa, 'round and firm like the fruit of a bel' or tengo towa, 'breats that stand up firmly':

**VII**

O my love, your body is a mango
And your breats
Are the half-ripe fruits of a bel
O my love
Let me take them for the first time
And kiss them with my mouth. (p.110-11).

**VIII**

Boy, I am now a mother
And you are still untried
What is it roused your love?
Your thighs
Are mangoes
Your breasts
Are the half-ripe fruits of a bel
I saw them and they fired my love. (p.111).

In Archer's view the girl whose smart white cloth sets off to perfection the glossy brown of her skin, whose body shines with a clean freshness, whose skirt stresses the roundness of her figure, whose black hair is trimly set with a white flower- it is this type of girl who most inflames a Santal's love:

**IX**

O my love
Tie the cloth tightly round your thighs
And look to your body. (p.112)

**The Winning of a Lover**: W.G.Archer (Archer, The Hill of Flutes: Life , Love and Poetry in Tribal India, A Portrait of the Santals, 1974, p. 114) describes that once a boy has fallen in love, he has only one wish- to possess his girl as fully as possible, this desire is sometimes the result of a slowly deepening friendship, and a forest tale, which is sometimes related at annual hunts, describes how the change is finally accomplished: 'There was a girl who was my sister-in-law by village realtion. We used to graze the buffaloes together from the time that we were children. Then the girl grew bigger and whenever I saw her smooth uncovered thighs like a ripe mango, my sex reared like plantain stem. One day we were with the cattle and while we were sitting, her thighs became uncovered and I saw up to their end. I could check myself no longer and I pushed her down with my hand. The girl was a virgin and I had to hurt her. Her sex was very tight and I was full of joy. After that we grazed cattle together and I took her everyday' (Archer, The Hill of Flutes: Life , Love and Poetry in Tribal India, A Portrait of the Santals, 1974, p. 114) The same crisis in a youthful friendship is described in several forest songs. They show the girl protesting:

**X**

Phudan, my sex
Is a little bamboo shoot
And my waist
Is the bud of a plantain
Phudan, let me go
I am not yet ripe for love. (p.114).

**XI**

My breasts are mangoes, Sitaram
And my body is a young cucumber
Not this year, Sitaram
But next year
You may toss it up and down. (p.115).

**XII**

O my love,
Like a mango is your body
And like marrows your long breats.
All the body at the waist,
O my love,
I will give you
And you may do with it as you will
But my breasts
I will not let you have. (p.115).

**XIII**

We wandered into every jungle
Through a whole forest we went
But not a single shameful word you uttered
Now I am drawing water at the spring
Why are you tugging at my clothes?
No, no, I will not let you do it here. (p.115)

But the boy does not always listen and the girl must then suffer his first attack:

**XIV**

O my love
You are young
And I am still younger
Let me go.
O my young darling
You may cry and cry
But today, my love
I will not let you go. (p.115).

**XV**

Your body is full grown
And I am still too young
You will harm my young body
Do not catch at me
Do not force me, I shall weep.
With your young body
O my love
You may cry and cry
But I've seen your breasts
Poking from your dress
And I've caught them in my hands. (p.115-16)

W.G.Archer (Archer, The Hill of Flutes: Life , Love and Poetry in Tribal India, A Portrait of the Santals, 1974, p. 116) writes that while active love is sometimes the culmination of an early acquaintanceship, it may also result from a single sharp encounter. The boy and girl may not have known each other from before and love may suddenly flare from a chance meeting. When this happens, courtship is rapid and direct:

**XVI**

It was seeing you
That made me love
My love was not short
I cry when I think of you
I think of youand my eyes
Brim with tears. (p.116).

Sometimes the boy sees a girl from a distance, whistles to her and in this way 'overcomes her mind':

**XVIII**

Boy, from the mountain
You are whistling to me
If you want to take me, hurry down
If you want to keep me
Catch me by the hand. (p.117).

**XIX**

I am going
To a lower field
If your heart
Goes with me
Whistle on a finger
Wave your arm in a ring
And I will come to you
In a lower field. (p.117).

Or the girl herself may take the initiative:

**XX**

Below the garden plot
Your are going, boy
With a book under your arm
I asked you, boy, but you wept
I am going after you
You look so handsome. (p.117).

**XXI**

Below the headman's pond
Which is that boy
With a turban like a basket?
Shall I whistle to him
Or wave my hand?
O who is that boy
With a turban like a basket? (p.117-18)

Occasionally boys and girls meet on theirnway to market or when going to the forest and a dialogue then ensues. A boy says to another, 'some peacocks are passing. Let us go with them.' Sometimes they say to the girls, 'Where are you going?' 'To the market.' 'Come and buy some sweets with us.' Or a boy simply says, 'Girl, I am very thirsty.' In the late hot weather, when the mahua fruits are forming, a girl herself sometimes says, 'The mahua fruits are falling. I will eat some with you.' When she says this, a boy knows what she means and they fix a spot and meet.

But of all the aids to love, nothing is more compelling than the flute:

**XXII**

On the mountain of fiddles
A fiddle plays
On the hill of flutes
A flute is sounding
Listen, Sumi, Samia
Listen, you two girls
On the mountain of fiddles
A fiddle sounds
On the hill of flutes
A flute is playing. (Archer, The Hill of Flutes: Life , Love and Poetry in Tribal India, A Portrait of the Santals, 1974, p. 118).

Sometimes even after the marriage some couples are still unreconciled to their parents'choice:

**XXIII**

Friends, we have left going
To the rice field in the jungle
They have given you a wife
They have found for me a husband
O my friend, when we meet now
We must never flutter our eyebrows
Or show the teeth in our mouths. (Archer, The Hill of Flutes: Life , Love and Poetry in Tribal India, A Portrait of the Santals, 1974, p. 214).

But the mutual affection may prove to be too strong. If a girl has a boy in her village, she sometimes leaves her husband's house and goes rushing home. And if the boys say that 'even though you are married, I will never leave you', the girl cannot stay, she has to leave her husband.In these circumstances, one of two things may happen. Slowly and reluctantly the husband and wife may begin cohabitation and even if their thoughts are still on their former friends, they may gradually come to accept each other as permanent partners. The other alternative is the break-up of the marriage. If the boy and girl are quite determined , nothing that the parents or the other partner can do can prevent a final breach.

W. G. Archer (Archer, The Hill of Flutes: Life , Love and Poetry in Tribal India, A Portrait of the Santals, 1974, p. 222) argues that sexual intercourse is one of the chief ingredients in Santal happiness. In the years preceding marriage, it is the natural end of romantic love. Their attitudes are expressed in a host of love songs, sung either privately in the forest or openly in the village—at weddings, at the Sohrae festival and at social dances. In the case of forest songs, the references to sex are frank and unabashed:

**XXIV**

The hot earth
Scorches the feet
The hot sky
Is burning the body
O my love
Give me a gold umbrella
To cool my mango body. (p.222).

**XXV**

You took me from my home
You snatched me from my friends
To a stony lonely field you took me
And you made me ache for water. (p.223).

**XXVI**

Fumble at the door
Then for the legs of the cot
O my love
Grope your way in
To the legs of the inner door. (p.223).

**XXVII**

At the big river
The stony river
How I thirst for water

I am a grown girl
I am not a youngster
O my love
Do not shake my body. (p.223).

**XXVIII**

O my love
Have me, have me quickly
If you do not want it
Put back my clothes. (p.223)

**XXIX**

I am lying between two stones
And the babblers are calling
O eat my body
Eat and eat my vulva. (p.223).

**XXX**

My love
Like a ripe mango is your body
And like fruits are your breasts
O my love
Like a bees' comb is your hill.
Whose joint cracks on it? (p.226)

**XXXI**

In the rice field was her clitoris
And her mound was the breast of a dove
Like the horns of a young buffalo
She spread her thighs out to him. (p.227).

According to W.G. Archer (Archer, The Hill of Flutes: Life , Love and Poetry in Tribal India, A Portrait of the Santals, 1974, p. 228) the first act of sex is often distressing. 'when a girl has a boy for the first time, the tears come. The way has to be made. It is then it hurts. After that, she is happy:

**XXXII**

From who knows when, Rajaram
Have you been longing for me?

You are splitting me down
Like the new shoot of a kend
O Rjaram, you are fully grown
And I am still untried
Work your waist gently. (p.228)

In many cases the girl's hymen is still intact and its rupture causes her to bleed:

### XXXIII

In the morning you are drawing water, sister
But what is that blood upon your skirt?
Brother, you know the way a girl is born
A green kingfisher I caught up in my lime. (p.228)

In yet another song an encounter with vagina is described as a fight between a cow and a buffalo with the girl pretending that the blood on her cloth is the sap from a tree:

### XXXIV

Girl, on the cloth for your breasts
What blood is this?
Mother, it was you who told me
To take the buffaloes with the cows
There was a fight
Between a cow and buffalo
I lent against a munga
It is the blood of the munga, mother. (p.229)

### XXXV

Sister, the boys
All know too much
When they lift the thighs
It opens like a horn
And the fruit of the kend
Nods to and fro. (p.230)

### XXXVI

Broken are the strings of the cot
And it sags in the middle
O come to me if you are a man

If you are a bonga go away
I am opening my thighs
And closing them
About your waist. (p.230)

### XXXVII

On the ground
I lie above her
And it creaks and crfeaks.
Like the palm of my brother's hand
It pierces and goes on. (p.231).

### XXXVIII

Since there was no room on the floor
You had me on a rice bale
It was so cold you sat me on your knees
And from your lap you glued me to you. (p. 231).

### XXXIX

Boy, put your hands on my chest
And your legs in my thighs
And like a quail that flicks its tail
Slowly and gently sway your waist. (p. 232).

In the following song we come across a girl almost mad in her youthful ardour for love, offering herself into the arms of a young man:

### XL

Kuri: Dare umul ho achuren do,
Sakam binda hon rohoren do
Desc milua arakainme.
Kora: Alo mairem ror ase,
Alo mairem rak ase.
Kuri kora lan napam akan
Nanwan sagar pati leka lan
Thokao jalada.

**Translation**

Girl: The shade of the tree has moved away,
The sheaves of leaves have dried up.
Please leave me, leave me, O my lover!

Boy: O girl, don't say like that.
O girl, don't weep like that.
(We) a boy and girl. We have united(in love).
(As) a new cart-wheel mingles into a single block,

By hammering and hammering, we shall be one (in consummation). (Mukherjea, The Santals, 1962, Revised Edition, pp. 428-29).

The thrill of the girl after her coitus, is thus expressed:

### XLI

Kuri: Disom disom pirit babu ja
Pirit babu jain tahenkan do
Amleka do, babu ja banko dhankuc'.

Kora: Disom disom milua mairin tahenkan do.
Am leka do maire bako tanda.

**Translation**

Girl: In many places, I enjoyed coition, O my boy.
I cohabited in many places, O my boy.
Like you, O my boy, none could shake the loins (so well)

Boy: In many places, I enjoyed coition, O my girl,

Like you none could straddle so well. (Mukherjea, The Santals, 1962, Revised Edition, p. 429).

In the next song, a girl pleads that she was forcibly taken by a lad and she herself was innocent:

### XLII

Hatom hatomgoi ho ho kedo
Bane hatomgo anjom let do.
Ladeya bare latarte kubun kubungoi idikidindo,
Ladeya baru latarre picirrategoi derkidindo.

**Translation**

O my aunt! O my aunt! I shouted aloud!
You did not hear my call( at all).
He placed me on his arms, bent me double(dear),
Took me where the banyan (tree) bends,
There where the Kusu (tree) bends,

He made me straddle my legs and coition had. (Mukherjea, The Santals, 1962, Revised Edition, p. 431).

In the following song, a ravished girl is being scolded by her mother on seeing her condition:

### XLIII

A mayo dea dhuri nel tegem rak' utaret',
Saman senem nel lekhan cirerakap' cireangodo.
Bare bare biti mana ket' me niak' mana biti bam ajamlet',
Ni toda cet' in cekame.

**Translation**

Daughter: You have wept at the sight of the dust on my back
You have not (yet) seen the condition of my front, O mother!
It has been raptured both up nd down.

Mother: Times without number, I admonished you, O my daughter!
You did not care to listen to me, my dear,
What shall I do now? (Mukherjea, The Santals, 1962, Revised Edition, pp. 431-32).

In the following song a sister-in-law is explaining to her husband's younger brother, the posture how to effect coition:

### XLIV

A boy sings: Der der ko men hili ho
Cet' leka ko der koa ho.

Hili replies: Janga talarre dutup' kate,
Etom janga konnye bulure,
Konnye janga etom bulure,
Doho kate koram toare capokate
Bai baite danda babu ja hilaume.

**Translation**

Boy: "Coition, coition," men say, O sister-in-law!
How do they do it? How do they effect coition?

Reply: Sitting on the ground between the feet,
With right leg on the left thigh,
The left (leg) placed against the right(thigh),
Pressing the breasts on the chest,

Gently, gently shake thy waist. (Mukherjea, The Santals, 1962,Revised Edition, p. 435).

## References

Archer, W. (1974). *The Hill of Flutes: Life , Love and Poetry in Tribal India, A Portrait of the Santals.* London: George Allen & Unwin LTD.

Bhattacharya, S. S. (1979). Santal Songs: Different Types. In J. Troisi, *The Santals: Readings in Tribal Life, Vol.III: Myths and Folklore* (pp. 21-30). New Delhi: Indian Social Institute.

Biswas, P. (1956). *Santals of the Santal Parganas.* New Delhi: Bharatiya Adimjati Sewak Samaj, Kingsway Camp.

Bodding, P. (1940). Studies in Santal Medicine and Connected Folklore. *Memoirs of the Royal Asiatic Society of Bengal, VOL.X, No 3*, pp. 427-502.

Bodding, P. (1942(First Indian Reprint1994)). *Traditions and Institutions of the Santals.* New Delhi: Bahumukhi Prakashan.

Bodding, P. (1993(First published in India)). *A Santal Dictionary: 7 Parts in Five Volumes.* New Delhi: Gyan Publishing House.

Bodding, P. (2001(Second Reprint)). *Studies in Santal Medicine and Connected Folklore: Part I,II and III.* Kolkata: The Asiatic Society.

Culshaw, W. (1949). *Tribal Heritage: A Study of the Santals.* London: Lutherworth Press.

Culshaw, W. (2004(Published in India)). *Tribal Heritage: A Study of the Santals.* New Delhi: Gyan Publishing House.

Gautam, M. K. (1977). *In Search of an Identity:A case of the Santal of Northern India.* Leiden.

Hembram, P. (1988). *Sari-Sarna( Santhal Religion).* Delhi: Mittal Publications.

Hembrom, T. (1996). *The Santals: Anthrropological-Theological Reflections on Santali & Biblical Creation Traditions.* Calcutta: Punthi Pustak.

Hunter, W. (1979). Ten Santal Festivals. In J. Troisi, *The Santals: Readings in Tribal Life, Volume1: Religion and Magic* (pp. 274-75). New Delhi: Indian Social Institute.

Majumdar, N. (1956). *The Santal: Memoir 2.* Deptt of Anthropology, Govt. of India, pp. 49& 103.

Man, E. (1983(First Indian Edition)). *Sonthalia and the Sonthals.* Delhi: Mittal Publications.

Mukherjea, C. (1962,Revised Edition). *The Santals.* Calcutta: A. Mukherjee & Co. Private Ltd.

Orans, M. (1965). *The Santal: A Tribe in Search of a Great Tradition.* Detroit: Wayne State University Press.

Raha, M. K. (1979). Santal Folksong. In J.Troisi, *The Santals: Readings in Tribal Life, Vol III: Myths and Folklore* (pp. 255-63). New Delhi: Indian Social Institute.

Raj, V. (1990). *A Santal Theology of Liberation.* New Delhi: Uppal Publishing House.

Sarkar, H. B. (1964). A Study on the Agricultural activities and ritualistic performances among the Santals of Belpahari. *Bulletin*, Vol III, No 1, pp. 52-61.

Troisi, J. (1978). *Tribal Religion: Religious Beliefs and Practices among the Santals.* New Delhi: Manohar Publications.

# Chapter Five

# Postmodern/Modern Impact on Santali Dance-songs

> Solidarity which comes from likeness is at its maximum when the collective conscience completely envelops our whole conscience and coincides in all points with it. But, at that moment, our individuality is nil. It can be born only if the community takes smaller toll of us. There are, here, two contrary forces, one centripetal, the other centrifugal, which cannot flourish at the same time. We cannot, at one and the same time, develop ourselves in two opposite senses.—if our ideal is to present a singular and personal appearance, we do not want to resemble everybody else. (Durkheim, 1933, p. 130).

Every society has its unique characteristics, value systems, traditional mores, life-attitudes, social hierarchies and conceptions relating to status and authority. Besides, it has its own approach to disease and sickness, life and death, individual and community, religion and tradition, and above all, a sense of its identity and this sense of identity or cultural self-image has always a positive and negative face; it defines the traits of solidarity and uniqueness of the group, and also seelk to set it apart from other groups in the larger society around. There is no denying the fact that the tradition has a very important role to play in defining the sense of identity and the Santals as a tribe are extremely proud of their tradition, and they believe in the idea of a Great Tradition to which they are heirs. But this sense of Great Tradition is largely an elitist preoccupation among them. Its infiltration into the popular imagination has been slow and halting. Owing to its exposure to forces of rapid modernization significant cultural, political and economic transformations are taking place in the Santal communities of Jharkhand. New technology in agriculture, greater irrigation facilities, family planning and health measures and the Panchayati Raj system of political participation have come into these areas. The Santals are facing the new world of industry, monetized market, sophisticated goods and the more intelligent and crafty outsiders whom they prefer to call as *dikus*.

Esprit de Corps, that is, 'the solidity' of a traditional society such as the Santal society depends upon two factors: an internal and an external factor. As is evident from the passage above that according to Durkheim the internal solidarity of traditional Santal society has always depended importantly on what Durkheim has referred to as the principle of "likeness", that is, those shared cultural characteristics which serve to bind together as a society. Those shared characteristics consists in those shared symbols and symbolic acts which represent and give recognition to existing social units; and what is of significant importance are the 'shared understandings' and countless such similar behavior patterns and similar material manifestations of behavior which function as 'the cultural bonds' of a society or community. 'A myth of creation' is for the Santals an official symbol of unity and a constitution as traditional Santal society has attained promoting the 'cultural bonds'. The 'Santali language' is another entity which binds the santal people together and whose strength can hardly be overestimated. The Santal themselves are deeply cognizant of language as a basis for intimacy. Moreover, there are numerous ceremonies, rituals, ritual paraphernalia, deities, and religious concepts which the Santal hold in common. Apart from those important deities that belong exclusively to the various social units(house, local lineage, village, and the multi-village Pargana), there are a series of closely associated deities that belong to all the Santal. These deities have a special abode known as the "Sacred Grove" (Jaher), a clump of trees, lying just beyond each village. .The Sacred Grove is particularly the residence of Maran Buru, a kind of 'national spirir of the Santal' also regarded as a kind of chief deity.

The research scholars suggest that 'the Santal Pleasure' is equally important for the Santals in terms of a shared understanding serving the solidarity of the Santal. 'Pleasure' as per the understanding of the Santal is a pre-eminently a social phenomenon which obtains essentially during festivals, which are community events; it derives from a festive atmosphere, which only the assembled community can create; and it reaches its community-centered peak as throngs of men and women form a large dancing circle, men and women alternating so that each one has a member of opposite sex on each side, hands joined together. It is important to state here that such performances are a potent source as well as a reflection of community solidarity. During and just after such dancing there is generally great camaraderie, and everyone exchanges rice-beer while moving about from one house to another. Therefore, 'Pleasure' for the Santal, is a shared understanding which creates immediate bonds with co-tribals wherever they may be from. In fact, W.J.Culshaw(Culshaw, 2004(Published in India), p. 39) beginning his chapter on "Dancing, Music, and Poetry" comments that the word "raska meaning 'pleasure' is often on the lips of the Santal, and it is dear to their hearts". Here 'pleasure' implies dancing and singing, playing and listening to music, eating festively, drinking rice-beer, and implicitly sexual activity and in practice these are the activities characteristic of a Santal festival.

Given the transition taking place in the Santal community, it can be stated that the Santal community is caught up between two worlds of existence: the world of supernatural and the world of the matter-of-fact rational, that is to say, on the one hand they have their mythological past of glorious traditions and on the other hand they have the present modern/ postmodern world dominant with cybernetic and hypertextual world of entities. The world of rituals depends upon an intuitive perception of reality by a mind attuned to such perception, and an implicit faith in the efficacy of the activities associated with the ritual for the solution of life-crises and the foundation of such belief is an unquestioning faith that accepts things either because they are sanctified by tradition, or because non-observance of them is taboo. The world of rationalism, on the other hand, impinges on this kind of unquestioning faith; it is not satisfied by the explanations readily offered, and would like to go beyond simple answers. Technology is the product and expression of a temper based on such a logical frame of mind and is thus, in a way, directly inimical to primitive ritual. In fact, the confrontation between these two frames of mind is evident in several fields of economic activities and societal relations such as agricultural operations, attitude towards sickness, disease and death, divination and the supernatural, approach to medicine, political and social leadership and, above all, in attitudes towards life and death (Mahapatra, 1986, p. 109).

According to Mahapatra (Mahapatra, 1986) this kind of confrontation between two worlds of meaning in Santal society has a social significance whose importance cannot be underestimated and such confrontation is universal in cultures undergoing rapid transformation, when tradition comes face to face with the modern temper and the new approaches to reality. Such confrontation has a relevance for modernization and development and sometimes an entire village is face to face with such opposing forces. Jackson (Jackson, 1956, p. 30) remarks that 'when a village is faced with a suggestion of change, there exists a balance of forces. On the one side of the scales are those forces which are against change—conservation, apathy, fear and the like; on the other side are the forces for change—dissatisfaction with existing conditions, village pride and so on. Successful community development consists largely of choosing those projects where the balance is almost even, and then trying to lighten the forces against change or to increase the factors making for the change'.

Thereupon the tensions generated as a result of such confrontation between tradition and modernity, technology and ritual can be looked upon according to Mahapatra both as psychological and sociological phenomena. At one level it leads to the development of an ambivalent personality-structure with one face looking to the Great Tradition, fortified in the belief that the present is only a passing phase of decadence to be suffered, and what needs to be done is to resuscitate and revive the glorious tradition. The other face looking all the time to the pragmatic benefits of modernization, the flow of economic benefits, the access to and the advantages of political power which it offers, in short, towards what Martin Orans called the 'political rank-path'.

Mahapatra (Mahapatra, 1986) suggests that the Santal society , like most underdeveloped societies, shows a typical inability to maintain an organization. The capacity of a culture to maintain an organization depends on its related capacity of synthesizing a large number of social values to the level of community-acceptnce and participative action. The contradictions within a culture which impede corporate objectives and actions are also those that impede modernization. The confrontation between technology and ritual is not a simplistic one. It is true that a technological system also tends to develop its own rituals. But ritual in the traditional sense implies a host of symbolic functions which are kept outside the realm of logic and rationalism. The technological world, on the other hand, calls less for intuition and more for reason and the ability to analyse and coordinate details rather than to take an intuitive world-view. However, the paradox is that the same technology which creates this numbness in us, also creates a new sensitivity to what is happening. Especially among young people, the erosion of old concepts of authority, open the way to 'acute awareness of this new bondage'. The new political system and the new technology in the field of agriculture, medicine, education and economic development, therefore bring in value-systems and attitudes which are in direct conflict with the ritual based approach to life and reality. It would not be unwise to say that the technology also is secular in its impact, like political democracy or the Panchayati Raj.

The Santals believe that the Hindus are trying to have better standard of life hitherto denied to the hill and jungle-folk. Development plans of the government, community projects, programmes of tribal uplift are gradually throwing open to them roads, transportation facilities, schools, colleges and fineries and other modern techniques. With all the glare of modernism in their eyes so long living idyllic lives of in the backwoods of songs and dances are ceetainly likely to be puzzled at the threshold of a new world of existence. Old sets of value now seem to be disturbed. However, the Santals are trying their best to cope up with the new world of modernism and one could well notice new house-types with windows and furnitures and other amenities which they lacked in the past. The Santals can be now found chewing betels, drinking less and taking to milk and tea and cigarettes. Many have given up beef like the Hindus, even buffalo meat and pork have gone off their menu. According to Charulal Mukherjea (Mukherjea, 1962, pp. 382-83) the old Santal would not grow potato due to their conservative instincts even when Ponter asked them, now they grow it along with tomato. The women now wear mill-made saris and in the urban areas of Santal Parganas, they seem indistinguishable from their Hindu sisters, because they generally dress alike in fairs and rallies.

Charullal Mukherjea (Mukherjea, 1962, p. 385) says that one of the paradoxes of modern times is that civilization , as we understand the term, has been considered by some social thinkers, as a questionable blessing to the Santals. Others, have advised a very cautious approach in the programme of their uplift and reforms. That there is a good deal of truth behind this opinion cannot be doubted and what is best for the Santal must be left to time, their choice and to the natural laws of absorption. The capacity, however, of taking kindly to factors of civilization varies greatly with different situations. But the Santal have one distinctive feature in them and that is that they have learnt to adjust themselves to the influences of civilization.

Very relevant here is an extract from the opinion of H.C.Chakladar (Chakladar) quoted by Charulal Mukherjea (Mukherjea, 1962, pp. 387-88) on the effect of civilization on aboriginals: "There are forces, however, that withstand an unlimited diffusion of culture elements. The mental activity or psychological character of the people to whom a new culture trait is presented, plays a great role in its dissemination. They must be psychologically adapted to receive it; otherwise it is likely to be rejected. And if culture is forcibly introduced among a people not so adapted, it leads to disastrous consequences. The intrusion of Euro-American culture everywhere, in America, Australia, Africa, is being followed by the quick extinction of the native population while the slow and silent absorption of the Hindu culture...by tribes at a comparatively low stage of cultural development, like the Santal… and others…has not only kept them alive, but has been producing lasting benefits to…the communities concerned. This process of natural diffusion by unobtrusive filtration, without any organized effort of the parties concerned, that has been going on for hundred years ever since civilization dawned on the banks of the lower Ganges, and is yet far from complete, has led to a distinct uplift of the primitive peoples, and has been making highly desirable additions to the culture of the civilized community".

In a situation of such confrontation between tradition and modernization, between riual and technology, a degree of uncertainty and instability in social hierarchy and social values are perhaps inescapable. Various kinds of tensions are generated in the context of such a confrontation, and it is interesting to watch the modalities through which the tribal society like the Santal seeks to assimilate and reconcile these tensions and conflicts and find a new refurbished image of cultural identity for itself.

There is no denying the fact that the phenomenon of urbanization is taking its stronghold everywhere and growing at unusually rapid pace in developing countries. The emergence of new nation states after the World War II actually opened a new era of population movements towards the cities from the countryside in search of better life. Strategically, the cities are now becoming the central places for government, commerce, education, arts, crafts, and intellectual life. City centers emerged as nodal points for all kinds of activities and there is a universal expectation that moving from rural to urban areas will lead one to success. In reality, however, success rates vary. Once in the city, the rural peasant or ethnic groups have to adapt to the city environment and various problems associated with adaptation must be faced. On a general level, adaptation refers to changes and modification of cultural manifestations that people undergo in order to fit themselves into a new environmental setting.

From a different theoretical consideration, however, we may note that urbanization involves not only moving to the city and the concomitant reorganization from agricultural to other pursuits, but also a shift in patterns of behavior and beliefs. The transitional period can be characterized as a situation in which a person must learn to function in terms of several cultural systems simultaneously. At one extreme level of adaptation to the city, the migrants may assimilate to the host society and totally absorb the way of life of the city people and eventually become a part of the host community.

There are two situations that occur at the time of migration that the migrants have to face : on the one hand, the ecological determinants of a city would have certain social consequences, notably anonymity, dependence on impersonal relations and sanctions, sophistication, and tolerance of change. Adjustment to a new socio-cultural context and the acquiring of control over an unfamiliar environment frequently require the abandonment of traditional customs and values . On the other hand, there are circumstances that may not permit complete assimilation of the migrants into the city. the total process of adaptation, and whether traditional or rural culture can continue to function in the city setting without major breakdown, depending upon the prevailing historic, economic, social, and cultural conditions In the case of folk migrants like the Santal, who have little information and knowledge about city life, this process is beset with numerous obstacles and difficulties. There is always uncertainty associated with moving into the city because the Santal usually do not have adequate information about employment and settlement opportunities. Generally the Santal enter the city via their kin, a friend's network They concentrate into clusters where the same ethnic groups settled earlier, thus limiting the process of assimilation and acculturation into the host (urban) complex groups. The slow rates of acculturation, in turn, help to account for the survival of indigenous culture patterns.

It has been observed that the close proximity with their own clan ethnic villagers in a very intimate residential arrangement helps the Santal migrants to retain certain traditional elements of their culture. While the core social and cultural elements have not been disorganized or destabilized, under the pressure of complex urban influence a minor transformation is apparent. Some changes have occurred in the Santal beliefs, rituals, practices, symbols, and behavior, and some rural and folk forms have been slightly shifted and transformed or lost due to the different environment. Some symbols are retranslated or manipulated by the migrants to cope with the new setting.

Loking at the ritual ceremonies and practices, it seems that as we have seen in the earlier chapters a series of rituals and ceremonies that strictly regulates folk customs and beliefs is associated with the life cycle of the Santal. They have to perform these rituals and ceremonies from infancy to death. Although few forms of some ceremonial activities have changed after urban migration, they have not been totally forsaken. These rituals and ceremonies serve to restore folk identity and constrain total assimilation with other urban groups. Songs and dances are categorized depending on the nature of the festival being celebrated as we have seen before and still. different forms of songs and dances are observed depending upon the occasion of the ceremony.

Onkar Prasad (Prasad o. , 1985) has observed that there are a substantial number of Santali songs such as the songs of 'awakening the cattle' and 'mock-play' with the bullocks' sung during the *sohrae*, are the versions of the songs associated with the cattle worship of the Bengali Hindu peasants, which they call 'ahira gan'. According to Onkar Prasad the Santals seem to have emulated these songs in the process of adopting rice-cultivation and the rituals associated with after they settled in their neighbourhood. There is another issue which Onkar is trying to address which is concerning the authorship/copy right of the Santali Songs. He is of the opinion that from the collection of the Santal songs of the area it has been observed that they neither bear the names of authors nor can be claimed by any individual as the property of his own. Giving an example of Debu Murmu, he remarks that when Debu Murmu a Santal from Sarpukurdanga, who composes songs, was asked whether he could claim his authorship on the compositions he made, he gave the following answer: "Once I compose a song and render it before community members it becomes the property of the community because once it is spread it is very very difficult to have a personal claim over it". Hence the Santal songs have to be branded 'anonymous'. In the Santal society like other ideal folk societies, composers do not come forward and hence are not recognized. In fact, the composers or subjects do not isolate themselves from the common membership of the society and there exists only a common subject which is the people, and really the people in the poet or composers (Prasad o. , 1985, p. 118)

In view of Onkar Prasad (Prasad o. , 1985) the Santals consider some of the musical instruments, specially the drums such as the *tamak*' and the *tumdak*', as bestowal from supernatural forces. The Santals also consider their musical instruments as a means to establish communication with their non-living entities. Besides, they consider some of the musical instruments specially the *banam(s*) and the *tirio(s)* as manifestation of their physical-self. Thus establishing an organic relationship with the latter, also looking upon *banam(s)* as a living human being as apparent from the analogy of different parts of the musical instrumrnts with bodily parts of human being such as the *bohok'*(head), *lutur*(ear), *hotok*(neck), (stomach) etc. Here the basis of the analogy seems to be the morphology of the instruments on the one hand and the 'human like-sound' emitted on the other.

Discussing the essential features of the music of the Santals, Onkar Prasad (Prasad o. , 1985, p. 119)writes that the social norms of performance of music have been to great extent responsible in the development of melodies. He goes on to say that a melody in the Santl society is rendered by an "interlocked" style of singing where each individual sings independently but within the group. In this situation the singers are not differentiated from one another in contrast to stratified societies where even if the singing is done in group it is marked by a differentiated role for one who leads and for those who either follow or answer. It has been argued that the singer in a folk society is bound to sing what moves the hearts of all the people.

In his scholarly research book, Martin Orans (Orans, 1965) looks at the task of examining processes by which the Santal tribe of Jharkhand, India, are creating a "great tradition" for them- selves. The author's careful presentation and analysis not only sheds light on acculturation among the Santals but also provides a theory of sociocultural change applicable to encysted societies such as the Santal society. Martin Orans is of the view that Urbanized Santals, having migrated to the urban cities, have received more education than their country brethern, resulting in greater upliftment in terms of social prestige and acculturation. Using 'beef-eating' as a factor to bring distinction between urban brethren and country brethren, Martin's submission is that this is a factor which is creating a lacuna in this Santal community and this "cul- tural gap" among the Santals weakens tribal solidarity on the one hand. On the other hand, considerations of power and communal sentiment create pressures in favor of solidarity. This situation results in a paradox: non-Hindu social practices serve as boundary markers for Santal society and contribute to social solidarity; these practices, however, are simultaneously the attributes of low status in the prevailing system of caste ranking resulting into a condition of ambivalence which creates, according to Martin Orans, an "emulation-solidarity conflict."

One section of the book talks about "the new solidarity," which paradoxically emerges out of life in the industrial setting where the Jharkand movement flourishes. This movement primarily attempts to raise the status of the Santal, as a group, by means of political agency. One of its most important tasks is the stimulation of cultural creativity. Martin remarks that the Santal, having accepted much from their Hindu neighbors, but "desirous of maintaining their identity, decided to create a 'great tradition' of their consisting of a curious mixture of Hindu and non-Hindu elements, regarded by the Santals as symbols of their unity and distinctiveness. In another section of the book, talking about the "rank concession syndrome," he argues that it consists of processes "which may be applicable to all encysted societies which have conceded rank to a dominant society." He explains that the encysted society typically emulates the dominant one, resulting in a borrowing that is destructive of solidarity. According to him, the necessity of preserving solidarity is the countervailing force, and the success of attempts at maintaining solidarity depends to a great extent on the particular avenues of mobility, or what he terms as "rank paths," that are chosen by members of the encysted society.

## The Santal Rebellion

Ever since the Santal rebellion of 1855-57 Hindu-Santal contact in the region has been long and intense and the Santals themselves have undergone considerable Hindu acculturation and some fission and Hindu assimilation. Needless to say that all the tribes in this area have been heavily influenced by Hindu culture, some have been partially and others totally absorbed in the Hindu social order. It can be argued that perhaps the single most important event in the history of Santal-Hindu relations was the Santal rebellion of 1855-57 and this is the major event which drew the serious attention of India's English rulers to the Santal and revealed at once the nature of Santal-Hindu relations and the strengths and limitations of Santal solidarity. Commemorated in Santal songs and discussions, it has become part of the Santal living cultural heritage and hence of continuing influence. Researchers have held the view that by legal and extra-legal means the Santal were systematically being stripped of their ownership rights over theor land and becoming tenants and even slaves of Hindus who knew how to manipulate the law and were accustomed to gaining their ends in the context of the market.

There is no denying the fact that the emphasis in their culture on "redistribution" and other leveling mechanisms plus their heavy commitment to 'pleasure' made the Santal easy prey of the merchant and moneylender. The british observers and the Hindus found the Santal to be "improvident" which ultimately led the Santal to raise a violent revolt against them. This is conveyed by such an enduring songs as the following:

Sido, why are you bathed in blood?
Kanhu, why do you cry hul hul?
For our people we have bathed in blood
For the merchant thieves have robbed us of our land.
Saheb rule is trouble full;
Shall we go or shall we stay?
Eating, drinking, clothing,
For everything we are troubled.
Shall we go or shall we stay?

It should be borne in the mind that the profound changes in the Santal society just during and after the Santal Rebellion were visible at the structural level as those who led the rebellion, foresaw in victory not only economic relief but also increased political power and an opportunity to improve the rank of the Santal. These changes were noticeable in the form of a number of ritual practices emulative of Hindu customs which accompanied the rebellion, such as putting on the sacred thread, ritual use of sun-dried rice and oil and vermilion, and purification with cow dung (Culshaw W. a., 1945). It has been observed that wishing to triumph over the oppressive Hindus, the Santal thought of cashing in on the victory with traditional Hindu symbols of rank.

It seems that the defeat of the Santal rebellion of 1855-57 appears to have led to increased Hinduization, perhaps in part because the path to higher rank through military force seemed closed and soon after the rebellion the Kherwar movement developed among the northern Santal. What is important to note here is the fact that those who joined this Hinduized sect adopted a number of critical Hindu symbols of rank, such as wearing the sacred thread. They were said to 'regard themselves as socially superior to those who do not wear sacred thread. Datta-Majumdar (Majumdar, 1956, p. 62) remarks that the "*janeo dhari* Santal (those who wore the sacred thread) were reluctant to intermarry or have social intercourse with the non-*janeo dhari* Santal.

Apart from this there were several Hindu festivals which were embraced by the Santal and were celebrated by them. The Karam festival is one of them and the other Hindu ceremonies were also practiced by the Santal such as Sakrat( Hindi: Sankranti), and Dasae (Hindi: Dasserah). Thus it can be seen that the pattern of Santal-Hindu relations is thus one of Hindu domination and exploitation combined with considerable cultural influence. There is no denying the fact that the advent of the market, population pressure, and increasing wealth differences among the Santal which developed during the latter part of the nineteenth century significantly affected the processes of acculturation and assimilation resulting into the disintegration and gradual decay of the Santal traditional practices which included folklores and traditional dance-songs as well.

History shows that the infiltration of civilization in early times generally pushed the tribe into backwoods where they could live well their primitive care-free life. Charulal Mukherjea (Mukherjea, 1962, p. 391) shows how the Santal Guru Kolean informed Rev. Skrefsrud that, since the very beginning of things, the Santals were ever migrating "like caterpillars, advancing, grazing and eating". We come across a folk-song of the Santals that throws some light on the inner urge to perpetual movement towards the newer beauties that the earth can offer to them , as an ever-present instinct in the heart and soul of the tribe:

> We eat and drink and make us merry,
> We live our lives in joy divine;
> This earthly body gasps for breath,
> What's the joy in the sleep of death?
> There's joy in a wander-lust,
> Joy in treks from land to land.
> Like morning dew sparkling, fading,
> Like dancing drops on glistening leaves,
> Our lives in balance tremble here. (Mukherjea, 1962, p. 389)

The poem reveals the virgin nature thus claiming to be "both law and impulse" to the Santals and this throws light on the frank, straightforward and essentially truthful nature of the tribes.

The source of the Santal's joy lies embedded in the lines in the middle of the song celebrating the Santal's wander-lust, his joy in "treks from land to land", in the lure of the virgin soil, newer flowers and leaves.

So far, judged by modern civilized standards, it may at best appear to be the survey of primitive order of life, but little can the average reader understand how forces and ideas of the modern/postmodern world have penetrated into the aboriginal tribal fabric. It can be observed now that mass awakening/sensitization regarding the developed world, knowledge and idea of civilization is getting instilled in the minds of the educated Santals who are educating their brethren about it and this could not have been possible had they been entirely living in the dream-world of community feasts, drinks, songs and dances. Thanks to positive impact of modernism and postmodernism coming in the form of 'Education', 'Mass awareness', 'Mass Sensitization' because of which at present no longer does the average Santal want to retire into the backwoods with the advance of modernism and postmodernism, as knowledge and ideas of civilization have entered into the tribe both consciously and unconsciously. Presently, we find the Santals of the Jharkhand state under the special protection of the state and there are ministries of tribal welfare specially devoted to their interests. Literacy is increasing (thanks to the opening of tribal schools) and education is spreading and progressing fast.

The transformation, development and progress among the Santals due to the impact of modernism/postmodernism should not be studied unilaterally or in vacuum but in the background of deeper moorings in the heart of the Santals as a result of centuries of culture-contact with the rest of the population, that is, mostly Hindus. Study reveals that these tribals have mostly lived not in watertight compartments, but with the rest of the more civilized people of India, therefore, though slowly and imperceptibly, acculturation has been going on.and when carefully traversing through the Santal myths and tradition one comes to the inevitable conclusion that for ages and ages they have tried to form a part of the Hindu society. For instance, use of vermilion during marriage, wearing of *alta* marks on the feet of women, characterisig the Supreme deity as Thakur Jiu, observance of festivals like Charak(Pata-the hook swinging festival), the strange resemblance of some Santal dances with the *Rasa* dance as described in the Vishnu Purana, singing of essentially Vaishnava songs during the *Sohrae*, the shouting of *Haribol* during marriage, funeral and other ceremonies, the worship of Durga in Santal Pargana, the special puja to Kali in Dumka and most importantly, the assemblage *en masse* of the Santals to sing and dance during Hindu festivals, have very deep implications that these are broadly based on a synthesis peculiar to Indian Hindu culture.

Charulal Mukherjea (Mukherjea, 1962, p. 383) remarks that 'with ideas of reform in the atmosphere, some acting as disintegrating forces, others operating on a constructive basis, it was no surprise to us to come across a manifesto signed by some prominent educated Santals of Bengal and some parts of Bihar calling upon their brethren …to engage in social reforms of the maintenance of their tribal honour'. It stated that the Santals had firmly resolved that:

I. No Santal, man or woman, should drink *Pochoi* (rice-beer) in shops as the tribe hd been ruined by drink while the grog-shop owners had *mahajans* were becoming rich. Temperance would help the Santals financially.

II. Carrion should not be eaten. The signatories refer to this custom with feelings of shame.

III. Santals should not dance or sing anywhere except in their houses or villages. The manifesto reminds the tribe that the Europeans, Hindusthanis, the eastern hill-tribes sing and dance, but they avoid the hill-sides and public places. The ancient Santals had no public dancing.

IV. Force should not be resorted to without reason as it slackens the marriage tie and gives rise to various vices.

V. Santals should wear coarse cloth and their women should give up wearing glass-bangles. (Mukherjea, 1962, pp. 383-84)

One can find the air thick with these ideas, especially among the educated Santals and there is noticeable tendency to give up dancing and singing in public. It is becoming clear that the Santal sets of value and philosophy of life are undergoing a perceptible change. Times are gone when the tribes joined with the rest of the population in their pujas and festivals as in the past. The infiltration of political ideas and realization of their rather poor economic life, has cast a pall of gloom even on the denizens of forests, hill-tops and the habitat of the hitherto happy and care-free children of nature.

## The advent of the Market

According to Martin Orans (Orans, 1965, p. 39) the spread of the market, British Indian law and British protection, however, led to a greater influx of Hindus into the Santal living areas and the Hindu influx as well as the general growth of population , both Hindu and tribal, rapidly reduced the amount of unexploited land. In Martin's view the Santal record is full of examples of hiving off and forming new villages, new local lineages and new sub-clans. This resulted into the increase of wealth differences. It has been observed that a major impact of increased wealth differences has been the strain placed on internal solidarity by "envy" and even more by fear of "envy". This term implies the malicious intent based upon desire for what another possesses. Although the Santal society has long been plagued with accusations of witchcraft, the notion that its practice is almost invariably deliberate and that it arises from envy is of modern origin.

It seems that it is difficult to square the basic reciprocity of relations in a kin society like that of the Santal with the impersonal and contractual relations of the market. Though the Santal struggle over land with as much ferocity as any peasants, they find it hard to insist on strictly market relations with other commodities. It has been observed that a few Santal enterpreneurs have gained notoriety by their greed, but more have failed in business from having granted credit and finding it difficult to collect the debt. Traditional Santal are poor at haggling even with non-Santal, though they understand the basic principle of market and may even be conversant with a variety of devices used to swindle the unsuspecting bargainer.

The historical evidence indicates that contact with Hindu society has been long and intensive and that portion of Santal culture shared by all Santal is so marked with Hindu traits that it would be a monumental task to indicate all of them although we can enlist a few of them. All Santal call on neighboring Hindus of low caste to deliver babies. Although the Santal used to do some weaving and pottery-making, they have traditionally obtained almost everything except foodstuffs and a few forest products from neighboring tribal or Hindu peoples. What is interesting is the fact that even the drums and the flutes which are so integrated in the "pleasure" complex are invariably purchased from Hindu specialists. However, emulation of Hindus did not always go unnoticed and it will be recalled that there is evidence of resistance to such Hinduization.

Martin Orans (Orans, 1965, p. 47) rightly remarks that 'the advent of the market and the failure of the Santal rebellions to achieve significant political power led to a decrease in Santal solidarity and thereby contributed to an increase in acculturation and assimilation. This effect, however, was limited to so long as there was no major industrial development. But with the rise of Jamshedpur and its associated industry and educational establishments Santal solidarity seriously declined. A critical factor in this process has been the severance of the Santal from the web of the traditional social relationships resulting from migration to industrial development.

At the threshold of the horizon of modernity the Santals started abhorring their traditional music and dances in the process of emulating higher social values of neighbouring Hindus, for they, as the Santals realized, were the attributes of low-status in the prevailing system of caste hierarchy. During the era of postmodernity, however, they have stated taking pride in them with the purpose of enveloping the scism in the framework of a new Santal identity, aiming for the common Santal cultural heritage and binding them together.

## Postmodernity and Globalization

According to Maidul Islam (Islam, 2006) in the contemporary world the international finance capital is seemingly becoming the most dominant regulatory mechanism to exert the power reflecting the impact of postmodernity and globalisation and he aptly asserts that 'the contemporary world has been witnessing the phenomena of globalization under the aegis of international finance capital with the aspiration of recolonising the third world. This monological globalization is perpetrated by the present day theses of the market economists of the overdeveloped west and lapped up by quite a few countries in the developing and underdeveloped world, may be under coercive compulsions imposed by the Bretton Woods institutions like World Bank, IMF and recently WTO'. Conceptualizing globalization is difficult as no single universally agreed or uncontested definition exists. Globalization as a concept refers both to the compression of the world and the intensification of consciousness of the world as a whole: both concrete global interdependence and consciousness of the global whole. It refers to an increasing level of interdependence between national systems by way of trade, military alliance and domination and 'cultural imperialism'. As Ahmad (Ahmad, 2002) says that 'at the ideological and cultural level, globalization has been observed as a symptom of' late imperial culture' and the 'most recent and highest stage of imperialism'.

The Santali culture has, throughout the past many decades, been the victim of the adverse impact of modernism, now post-modernism and globalization which have been instrumental elements and factors in the gradual degeneration of the Santali culture, customs, traditions and practices including folk dances. Robertson (Robertson, 1992) remarks that 'the post-1970s incidents are very simplistically put under the banner of globalization e.g. growth of information technology, speculative investments in financial or stock markets, petro-dollar regime, free cross-border mobility of international finance capital, popularizing Disney (cartoon) culture, growth of mass-media, global warming, declining power of nation-states, post-modernity, all of these are generally included under the category of globalization'.

What is of prime importance here to notice is the fact that like globalization, the concept of culture is also diffused. Most discussions on culture, as they take place in academic circles and in the dominant media, tend to confuse 'culture' with 'civilization' and 'civilization' with 'religion' and we are forced to embrace a materialist conception that looks at culture not as a spiritual or religious heritage but as a set of material practices through which people live and produce the meanings of their lives. It can be observed significantly that the thematic point for discussion and such an analysis is not the heritage of the past but the actual realities of the present, and one of the things that most crucially matter, is the degree of access to cultural goods that different classes and social groups have in real life. Looking at culture in this way, we immediately recognize that social conflicts of various kinds, along lines of class, caste, gender, ethnicity etc. actually leave very little room for all the people or even majority of the people, to have roughly equal access to cultural practices and traditions leaving behind the legacy of cultural practices under the carpet (Islam, 2006).

Fanonian discourse (Fanon, 1967) too talks about Culture as a site for struggle and contestation. For Fanon cultural objects are either treated like museum pieces, to be locked behind glasses or like trophies from 'a banal search for exoticism'. It seems to me that what Fanon argues further very aptly applies with the Santali culture which is moving toward destruction in a very systematic fashion and his argument is this 'that this cultural obliteration is made possible by the negation of national reality, by new legal relations introduced by the occupying power, by the banishment of the natives and their customs to outlying districts by colonial society, by expropriation, and by the systematic enslaving of men and women The colonial situation calls a halt to national culture in almost every field. A national culture under colonial domination is a contested culture whose destruction is sought in systematic fashion. It very quickly becomes a culture condemned to secrecy. This idea of clandestine culture is immediately seen in the reactions of the occupying power. This persistence in following the forms of culture which are already condemned to extinction is already a demonstration of nationality; but it is a demonstration which is a throw-back to the laws of inertia'. (Fanon, 1967)

Given the anthropological and historical research done in this field, it can be argued that there is and had always been an autonomous space for folk culture which is nothing but an amalgamation of folklore, oral tradition, folk life, folk practices etc. which is currently under threat from the neo-colonial neo-liberal globalization in the garb of postmodern cultural globalization just like the colonial cultural production thwarted the growth and development of indigenous cultural forms of the Santal heritage.

I believe that folklife is a body of customs, legends, beliefs and superstitions passed on by oral traditions and behavioural example. It may include folk dances, folk songs, folk medicine and folk tales (myths, rhymes and proverbs). Folk customs, legends and beliefs may be taken in sum as the imaginative expression by a people of its desires, attitudes and cultural values. It must be borne in mind that the study of folklore, as already discussed in the theoretical chapter, emerged significantly in the nineteenth century partly out of the rise of European Romanticism, with its interest in the past, the particular and the human, and partly out of Nationalism, with its stress on the indigenous. If a folk tradition belongs to a people, then it is a culture in itself, and not subservient to some overarching culture. Such a culture is often sustained by nation-states and its dominant alliance of ruling classes in their effort to manufacture an integrated fabric of'national culture' While a theoretical exposition may serve to rearrange our mental house-hold it should not be forgotten that the state-sponsored culture is always present there—it is a quotidian political reality—and it does a lot of violence to autochthonous folk cultures in carrying out its agenda of national integration.and it can be believed that one day the folk culture of the Santal might one day exhaust in the dialogic interaction with the state culture. The crust will crack and the indigenous would spill out of the bowels of the state cultural digest in the Bhakhtinian celebrations of the marginalized (Islam, 2006).

It is evidently visible that the Santal are becoming victim of cultural globalization and cultural imperialism.The critical discourse on culture, folk life and globalization often ponders us to critically engage with the discourse of postmodernism and postmodernity. Before we discuss the impact of postmodernized cultural globalization let us take a quick look at the theoretical scene of postmodernism and postmodernity. Barry Smart has written about the "post-modern flip" inflicted upon the modern paradigm. 'The postmodern flip' is simply an inversion of the old "man-culture" relation. The modern paradigm makes 'Man', 'Society', the 'Individual', etc into creators of culture/subjects. The postmodern paradigm(s) reverse the privilege by interpreting 'Man', 'Society', the 'Individual', etc as 'mere' signifiers, elements in discourses and texts, discursive operators and subject positions. Postmodernity is the triumph of culture over life as the 'central idea', to express it. Postmodernity is the age of cultural hegemony, and the 'culture' that we are talking about here has become almost or fully objectified, a 'web' of objects ('contents') and operations ('forms') with no central unit of internal control. The flip: we (very inclusively meant) once thought that culture served us, but now we know better that actually, we are culture's servants, even though we know that culture exists only through our 'praxis' (Islam, 2006).

Maidul Islam (Islam, 2006) argues that Postmodernism can be described as the philosophical-ideological discourse or framework which poses 'incredulity towards metanarratives' by following Jean Francois Lyotard (Lyotard, 1984). According to Turner (Turner, 1994) postmodernism can be regarded as a methodology that virulently criticizes the grand metanarratives and offers a simultaneous condemnation of exploitative capitalism and bureaucratic socialism which have imposed a barren sameness on the modern social world. Postmodernism along its important allies like feminism and anti-colonialism condemns the uniform, patriarchal, rationalist and hierarchical structures of Western modernism. Postmodernists argue that it actually offers a new vision of justice which gives primacy to difference, to heterogeneity, to paradox, contradiction and to local knowledge. Now much of the postmodern debate has been concerned to assert the importance of difference and otherness. So there is a connection between a postmodern critique of universalistic categories and the process of indigenization. Thus, both indigenization and postmodernism have a fascination for the textuality of knowledge; it's local, embedded, contextual quality and highlights the problems of universalization or generalization.

Postmodern methodologies are sensitive to the richness and complexity of local meanings of folk practices and beliefs and particularly sensitive to ironic meaning and intention.

On the other hand, Turner (Turner, 1994) is of the view that postmodernity in the simplest sense can be seen as a feature of advanced consumerism, the reorganization of cities in the late twentieth century, the impact of new forms of technology and information on social life, the consequences of global tourism and the increasingly risky nature of the social environment. Simmel G. (Simmel, 1991) argues that postmodernity refers to the extension of the processes of commodification of everyday life and the impact of mass consumer cultures on cultural systems, blurring the distinction between high and low culture. Postmodernism on the other hand means the use of simulation in cultural production, and in stylistic terms it involves self parody and irony.

Maidul Islam (Islam, 2006) remarks that there are 'becomings', according to Gilles Deleuze (Deleuze, 1987), such as actions, perceptions, variations and so on; and from this flux of becomings we perceive and/or organize beings. Organizing the 'being' out of becomings invariably involves an arbitrary history of conscious choice: that is, accepting what the subject is willing to accept; rejecting what it finds redundant or deleterious to self-interest. In this regard, the 'everyday' as an object of critical thought is difficult to discover. It is difficult because at each moment of its becoming, it escapes our attempt to comprehend it. It goes on, around the clock, over the year in the lives of the people. It repeats itself in the same monotony of routine. Yet it is the everydayness of peoples' lives which constitutes their being, forms their existence and in a way shaping the local and the folk. By virtue of its untranslatability into verbal or visual media, the folk culture resists appearance. Yet, at the depths of life it continues anonymously. It moves on in the same rhythm of continuities and make up the material civilization of the rural spaces and its inhabitants. The food the village people eat, the clothes they wear, the slang they use, the beds on which they lie, the anxieties they share, the pets they have, the fears they hide, the spices they use? all form their quotidian existence. Why didn't we look into them instead of consciously searching for the effects of globalization and consumerism in rural India? Are we trying to draw a hierarchy between the happening and the non-happening, the active and the dormant, the occasional and the everyday by placing the 'everyday' in a disprivileged location? To begin with, all these can be appropriate questions or in a methodological sense, the problems of research for a serious study on the marginalization of folk cultures in India.

The western cultural imperialism produces a 'global consumer culture'for which such value-laden terms as 'Americanization', 'Cocacolonization', and 'McDonaldization' are often employed and not without good reason. These terms imply that the consumer culture that was developed in United States in the mid-twentieth century has been mass mediated to all parts of the world. The consumer culture means more than the simple consumption. In a consumer culture the items consumed take on a symbolic and not merely a material value (Baudrillard, 1995). It arises in societies where powerful groups, usually those seeking to accumulate capital, in caricature, encourage consumers to 'want' more than they 'need' (Jameson, 1985). Not surprising enough, the Pepsi advertisement in India gives the message? "Yeh Dil Maange More" (This Heart Wants More). Under a consumer culture, consumption becomes the main form of self-expression and the chief source of identity. It implies that both material and non-material items, including kinship, affection, art and intellect becomes commodified, that is their value is assessed by the context of their exchange rather than the context of their production or use (Bourdieu, 1995). An advanced or post-modernized consumer culture experiences hyper-commodification in which minute differences between products or minute improvements in them can determine variations in demand. In this context of hyper-consumerism, consumption is differentiated on the basis of the signifiers known as 'brand names' (Wernick, 1991) for which the craze for 'spending' in glossy shopping malls is often noticed. Paradoxically, as consumption becomes universalized through globally available brands, production can become localized according to cost advantages. So, for example, Levi jeans are available globally but are produced in the low labour costly environment of the Philippines and many of the 'Big Macs' sold in Europe contain Australian shredded lettuce, air-freighted overnight. Thus, the current Mantra of global capital is not "Think Global, Act Local" as Theodor Levit observed but "Sell Global, Pack Local". Under the dominance of global brand market, the local cottage and household industry that is an inherent part and parcel of a particular form of folk culture is withering away very fast. There is a profound sense of globalism brought about by tourism, by world sport, world news, McDonaldization, Cocacolonization, AIDS (both biological and economic), human rights and so on. Globalization and localization go together according to Partha Chatterjee (Chatterjee, 2003) He is of the view that wherever there is an emergence of global consciousness, there will be a reaction which promotes an anti-global movement. Here Chatterjee argues that this current hostility towards globalization is in response to a result of comparisons made with an ebb situation in the middle decades of the twentieth century when international financial exchanges were restored and some order was maintained to control it (Islam, 2006).

In the postmodern world, Maidul Islam (Islam, 2006) contends, that the figure of the author/painter/artist as the inspired genius is sufficiently desacralized , while greater interpretative agency is bestowed in the reader/ viewer. According to Foucault the author is dead after he produces the work. This phenomenon can be noticed in a cybernetic world where the global popular culture is produced, controlled and marketed. Foucault argues that the author kills himself in the hypertextual world. One can no more define the author by what is seen in the cyberspace. There is no clear distinction in the cyberspace that this is the work of an author and that is the work of another's. A description may be enough to describe an author, but in the hypertextual world.

A comprehensive change in the Santali dance-songs , the community and their social practices can be attributed to the growing Sanskritization of some Indian communities and their cultures. There are also external contacts and inflences which are also responsible for the changes in the Santal culture. The Santals have become exceedingly aware of other societies like the Christian and the Hindu over the last few centuries. The ideas and ideologies of these dominant religions have been intercepted in the Santal worldview bringing about enormous changes in their culture. Young Santalis have strived to assimilate into these cultures while at the same time trying to hold on to their traditions and values. There is no denying the fact that the Sanskritization process can be witnessed in the Santal dance-songs as well. The fact of the matter is that the young generations in particular are not being enchanted by the beauty of the traditional dance-songs and it is very unfortunate that an appreciation of the latent qualities and social significance of these dance-songs is going unnoticed because of an overpowering impact of globalization, which has already started showing its impct on such cultures. The existence of some festivals known by Hindu names is already mentioned earlier but now the social practices have also been altered by these religions. We have seen earlier that the Santals utilize their festivals, fairs and social occasions to display their artistic instincts and talents but with growing homogeneity, the nature of these festivals has undergone a tremendous change .

The Santals now hardly enjoy the secluded, isolated or self-contained existence. They are now exposed to the supposedly superior cultures and with it has developed an aspiration in them to be identified with the dominant or superior cultures. The attempts to imitate or to get assilmilated in dominant cultural folds by adopting some socio-cultural practices are clearly visible in their ways. Moreover, technology has also played its role in encouraging the process of obsoletion of these dance-songs. Stereos, CDs, mobile phones have brought in new waves of music from the outer world to the Santals which are easily available, thereby reducing the aura and charm of the Santali dance-songs. However, it is not that the Santals have stopped performing or loving their music and dance but the decreasing interest of the youth in the traditional forms of music and dance is something to be worried about.

Due to the impact of new forms of technology and information on social life significant socio-economic changes are taking place in the world of the Santal. The introduction of new technologies in different spheres of their lives, the concept of decentralization and people's participation are affecting the social order. The Santal can no onger remain geographically or socially exclusive. It can be observed that the older generation is anxious to maintain the old social and moral order by invoking the great tradition emanating from the belief in the 'Santali Raj' but the existing tradition of education, agriculture and health practices which is anchored in the old value system is facing new onslaughts. Consequently, the Santal is face-to-face with two worlds which are rooted in very different premises and this fact generates an attitude of ambivalence to its tradition and processes of modernization. Faced with challengesof the time, sometimes the propitiation of the supernatural order which determines the moral order also becomes intense and intimate. A new technological system tends to develop its own rituals but these call for less of intuition and more of reason. There has been a desperate attempt by the tribal elite to reinforce ethnic identity by devising an elaborate , historical, literary and mythological account of tribal ancestry with a golden shared past. There is no doubt that there is stress on cultural exclusiveness and cultural revivalism and there is new emphasis on cultural forms, myths, symbols, scripts, oral literature, religious beliefs and traditional values (Sachchidananda, 2001, pp. 172-73).

It is pertinent to mention here that a new script known as O1 Chiki was invented by Raghunath Murmu so that the Santals from different states of the country could use a common script and the literature created by Raghunath Murmu is a reinterpretation of Santali myth and tradition. Moreover, through his creative writing, plays and compilations, he has sought to socialize and culturalize the entire concept of Santali identity and solidarity. He has used myths, histories in his own idea to project a great tradition and has called upon his Santali brethren to live up to it trying to forge a sense of identity and create awareness. In this way, the Santals have tried to create, maintain and fight for the identity as well as their worldview in diverse ways. And to a great extent they have been able to retain the essential features of their social and moral order without denying themselves the benefits of new development efforts. It can , thus be observed that the worldview of the Santal is characterized by both continuity and change which is evinced from their resilience manifested in their values, attitudes and behavior (Sachchidananda, 2001, p. 173).

A.B.Chaudhury (Chaudhuri, 1993, p. 173) is of the view that the imperceptible stream of social consciousness has led the Santal tribe to find out other avenues of self assertion and it has adopted insurgency as a method to attain self-assertion seeking a land and trying to reach new ideas to the tribal society. Besides, the traditional leadership has been guarding its prerogative with intense zeal resulting into a conflict between the two sets of elites-old and new- raging in the rural areas, leading to loss of life at times. Furthermore, the weakening traditional leadership has been giving way to political power-groups, and new elements are developing in the rural areas who work as intermediaries between such power-groups and the village society. The Santal tribe has already been initiated in the politics of number, and made conscious of its privileges as a Scheduled Tribe. Unfortunately, most of the privileges are beyond the reach of ordinary tribals living in the rural areas. It is very unfortunate that no viable alternative has so far reached the Santals even through the industrial diversification. The traditional leadership has been failing perceptibly and poverty, lack of governmental patronage, increasing pressure from non-tribal neighbours, and such impediments have been gnawing at the root of his strength. With the approach of the new elites, the traditional leadership has tended to become apprehensive of social disintegration.

In the opinion of A.B.Chaudhury (Chaudhuri, 1993, p. 174) the internal solidarity of the Santal tribe has been adversely affected thereby and the apprehended social disintegration cannot be stopped. The need of the hour is to devise a programme in which the Santal tribe can participate as a whole. The Santals will have to accept the responsibility of much of their actions and maladies, and re-model their pattern of thinking accordingly. Spread of education will definitely help them to appreciate their real difficulties standing on the way of attaining power. A fusion of the traditional and the new elites would greatly facilitate their uphill task. The fact of the matter is that the Santal tribe can no longer ignore the sea of changes around it, and a positive approach to adjust itself to the changed politico-economic circumstances prevailing around is imperative. Chaudhury further asserts that a very significant development has already taken place in the life of the tribe. Instead of ushering the 'personality', it has stood behind the organization-an entity beyond the society, the traditional leadership having no control over it. In times to come the Santal society as a whole, will take part in the movement seeking self-assertion which is, according to Sachchidanand (Sachchidananda, 2001, p. 172), tied up with systems of access to or control and the management of land and land-based resources but it is unfortunate that with the increasing loss of control over resources the notion of self-management is only confined to the socio-religious sphere.

## References

Ahmad, A. (2002). 'Globalization and Culture'. In A. Ahmad, *On Communalism and Globalization: Offensives of the far right.* New Delhi: Three Essay Collective.

Baudrillard, J. (1995). 'On Consumer Society'. In J. Faubian(ed.), *Rethinking the subject:An Anthology of Contemporary European Social Thought.* Boulder Colorado: Westview Press.

Bourdieu, P. (1995). *Free exchange.* Cambridge: Polity Press.

Chakladar, H. (n.d.). *Man in India*, Vol. XXI, no. 4, p. 216.

Chatterjee, P. (2003). 'The world after the Great Peace'. In *The Politics of the Governed: Reflections on Popular Politics in most of the World.* New Delhi: Permanent Black.

Chaudhuri, A. (1993). *State Formation among Tribals: A Quest for Santal Identity.* New Delhi: Gyan Publishing House.

Culshaw, W. (2004(Published in India)). *Tribal Heritage: A Study of the Santals.* New Delhi: Gyan Publishing House.

Culshaw, W. a. (1945). "The Santal Rebellion". *Man in India*, Vol. XXV.

Deleuze, G. &. (1987). *A Thousand Plateaus:Capitalism and Scizophrenia.* trans.by B. Massumi, Minneapolis: University of Minnesota Press.

Dirks, N. (1992). *Colonialism and Culture.* Ann Arbor: University of Michigan Press.

Durkheim, E. (1933). *On the Division of Labor in Society.* Translated by George Simpson.New York: The Mcmillan Company.

Fanon, F. (1967). *The Wretched of the Earth.* London: Penguin Books.

Islam, M. (2006). Postmodernized Cultural Globalisation: Threatening Folk Culture(s) in India. *Social Scientist*, Vol. 34, No. 9/10 (Sep. - Oct., 2006), pp. 48-71. JSTOR.Web. 02 Jan.2018.

Jackson, I. (1956). *Advance in Africa: A Study of Community Development in Eastern Nigeria.* London: Oxford University Press.

Jameson, F. (1985). 'Postmodernism and consumer society'. In H.Foster(ed.), *Postmodern Culture.* London & Sidney: Pluto Press.

Lyotard, J. (1984). *The Postmodern Condition.* Minneapolis: University of Minnesota Press.

Mahapatra, S. (1986). *Modernization and Ritual: Identity and Change in Santal Society.* Calcutta: Oxford University Press.

Majumdar, N. (1956). *The Santal: Memoir 2.* Deptt of Anthropology, Govt. of India, pp. 49& 103.

Mathur, N. (2001). *Santhal Worldview.* New Delhi: Concept Publishing Company.

Mukherjea, C. (1962). *The Santals.* Calcutta: A.Mukherjee &CO. Pr. Ltd.

Orans, M. (1965). *The Santal: A Tribe in search of a Great Tradition.* Detroit: Wayne State University Press.

Prasad, o. (1985). *Santal Music: A Study in Pattern and Process of Cultural Persistence.* New Delhi: Inter-India Publications.

Robertson, R. (1992). *Globalization: Social Theory and Global Culture.* London and Newbury Park ,CA: Sage.

Sachchidananda. (2001). Chage and Continuity in Santhal Worldview. In N. Mathur, *Santhal Worldview* (pp. 162-173). New Delhi: Concept Publishing Company.

Simmel, G. (1991). 'Money in Modern Culture'. *Theory, Culture and Society*, 8(3): 17-31.

Turner, B. (1994). *Orientalism,Postmodernism and Globalism.* London & New York: Routledge.

Wernick, A. (1991). *Promotional Culture.* London: Sage.

# Conclusion

Once upon a time, there were a tiger and a hunter in a forest. One day when the hunter saw the tiger, started talking to each other; and while interacting they started liking each other. After a few days, the hunter invited the tiger for lunch. Tiger responded positively, and according to the schedule tiger reached hunter's hut. After entering the tiger saw a painting hanging in the wall of the hut. The painting depicted that a dead tiger was lying under the feet of an armed hunter. After seeing the picture, the tiger became curious and asked the hunter about the person portrayed in that image. The hunter proudly said that, it was his grandpa who was a great hunter, and claimed that, the picture was a proof of his achievement. Tiger then asked, 'who is the painter?' The hunter replied, 'my father, who was not only a successful hunter, but also a good painter'. Tiger then smiled and commented, 'instead of a human, if a tiger painted it, then the picture would be a different one'.

(From a Santhal folk-tale- 'A picture on wall'; (Majumdar, 2006)).

In the present era of globalization, when the life is more polarized and bifurcated, this research examines the cultural practices such as the Santali dance-songs of Jharkhand, which have, so far, been either neglected or misrepresented by the dominant discourses, which has resulted in an incomplete understanding of culture; simultaneously this work looks at cultural nuances, conditions and lives of the Santal community, their folk culture, folklores, folk dances, especially Santali Dance-songs to understand, legitimate and create awareness about how dominant forces/ structures/ knowledge are enjoying privileges and how they are constantly marginalizing 'other' in hegemonic-centric neoliberal landscape. In contrast, the Santal worldview fundamentally situates co-operation, mutual care and love as the foundation of their epistemology.

There is no denying the fact that since the beginning of the civilization powerful hegemonic forces always tried to propagate/ establish an image of their superiority and authenticity to serve their purposes and interests. In this process they invariably de-legitimated, marginalized, degraded the 'others' and their existence. For example, according to Chattopadhyay (Chattopadhyaya, 1999) about 2400 years ago, in a *shloka* of *Maitri Upanishad* furnished the names of communities that were the polluters of dominant 'sacred' *Vedic* knowledge. Some of them were folk performers, indigenous subalterns (*shudras*), etc. From that depiction two things are evident: firstly, in that ancient period folk-culture and anti-hegemonic subaltern voices were present in society and secondly, the practice of marginalization and erasing other ways of knowing was a part of dominant representations/ discourses. That articulation essentially portrayed a system of social stratification. Hence, before the colonial rule, it was the upper-class or *Brahminical* epistemology that discarded the voices and narratives of subalterns from the discursive spaces.

Using several epistemological pursuits and methodological tools, much of the research work done in the past with respect to cultural practices, cultural resistance and cultural development has engaged with issues related to micro and macro-level interplays of power, control and domination and in exploring these elements, much of this research has taken for granted the 'dominant constructed knowledge' or 'hegemonic-centric locales' as the powerful regulatory mechanism within which resistance has been articulated. Furthermore, such dominant narratives have often taken resistance beyond the realm of culture and culturally situated politics to theorize about universalities in resistive politics as if resistance exists in a-cultural vacuum.

In this project, we seek to understand the organizing processes of cultural practices, cultural resistance, and thereby cultural changes taking place in the Santal community seen through the lens of Culture-centered approach by looking at various Santali Dance-songs as they challenge the master narratives of development articulated in the modernist framework. This project engages with possibilities for dialoguing with alternative narratives resulting from numerous dance-songs in the form of Santali subaltern narratives with respect to cultural practices and development that challenge meta-narratives produced by powerful hegemonic forces. It is pertinent to mention that the culture-centered approach concerns itself with the voices of marginalized groups and explores the interaction between culture and structure that create conditions of marginality. The commitment of the approach is to writing theory from below, and to defining praxis through the engagement with subaltern classes who have traditionally been marginalized and absent in dominant theories and models.

The present research shows that, the Santal community has remained very close to nature and consequently, they recognize nature as one of the foundations of their worldview. Their life conditions, struggles, philosophies are reflected in their narratives/ folklores. And, their dance-songs have become an important means to share and convey knowledge and messages. Oftentimes, these knowledges were intentionally hidden and esoteric in nature. Essentially, these tactics strategically help them to convey secret and anti-hegemonic messages. The dance-songs are not a mere traditional medium of entertainment; but they also play crucial role in communicating and raising consciousness about solidarity, resistive acts and emancipation. The research work shows how through folk dance-songs the Santals communicate an alternate philosophy of life. As a part of this communicative act, the Santal community on one hand conveys their epistemology of love and care, and on the other hand it articulates anti-dominant discourses; thereby the folk dance-songs generate a possibility of social transformation.

The Santali folk dance-songs represent multifaceted, multilayered philosophies and worldview of indigenous people. Thereby these articulations become an important aspect/ function of the Santal community. Through the practice of dance-songs they not only talk about their traditions, histories, spirituality, religion, belief systems and everyday practices; but they also legitimate their collective and individual struggle for survivals, resistive acts, issues of human rights, development, empowerment, identity, solidarity, and essence of their knowledge and philosophies. Furthermore, these folk dance-songs play an important role in communicating and creating awareness about ¯their ancestors; creation of the Santal world; seasonal rites and festivals related to their agriculture; rites and ceremonies relating to their life-cycle such as birth, initiation, marriage, and death; the creativity, the beauty, the abundance of ideas, the depth of soul, the extended mental capacity, and all-encompassing spirituality and richness which are embedded in their culture.

It is pertinent to mention here that dancing and singing hold a very important role in almost all the festive occasions for the Santals and it would not be wrong to assert that a social feature of Santal dancing and singing is their social character. From the time a girl can toddle, she joins the line of dancers, while little boys ape the antics of the drummers (Troisi, 1978, p. 124). The Santals have a large number of different dances according to the special seasons and festivals. According to Mukherjea, 'these dances…are a part and parcel of the tribal religious life' (Mukherjea, 1962, p. 365). Bodding (Bodding, 1993(First published in India)) mentions thirty-one types of dances, most of which are performed by men and women together though some are reserved for either of the sexes. For example, 'the *lagre* is the most common of the Santal dances and may be danced at any time, though preferably during moonlight. *Don* is usually danced during marriage festivals. *Jatur* is performed during the *Sohrae* and the *Baha* festivals. *Danta* is also danced during the *Sohrae*. Women generally do not join in this dance. On the other hand, only women dance the *Baha* dance which, as the name implies, is performed during the *Baha* festival. During the *Karam* festival, the Annual Hunt and *Bitlaha*, the menfolk perform special dances' (Troisi, 1978, p. 124).

J.Troisi comments that drumming plays a very important part during dancing since the rhythm and style of the latter depends much on the way in which the drums are played. The Santals essentially use two types of drums during their dancing—the tamak or kettle drum which is made of iron and is shaped like a big bowl nd covered with buffalo or bullock hide, and the tumdak or dancing drum made of burnt clay and conical in shape, the narrow end being covered with goat's skin and the broad end with bullock, buffalo or goat's hide. The tumdak which is played with the hands sets the rhythm while the tamak, played with small sticks, echoes and adds to the rhythm (Troisi, 1978, p. 124) Dancing is often connected with singing. Raha (Raha, 1967) rightly observes, 'when any new event is marked by the Santals they at once give it a poetic expression and sing spontaneously on their way to or during any festival'. As the Santals have different dances for different festive occasions, so also they have elaborate song cycles for various festivals. According to Bhattacharya (Bhattacharya, 1962) the Santals have more than twenty different tunes though most of the songs are ancestral. It is also part of the vitality of Santals to compose songs on the spur of the moment and undoubtedly these songs reflect certain feelings, emotions and sentiments of the Santals (Troisi, 1978, p. 125).

From the previous discussion it can be observed that *Santali dance-songs* have been found to be of various types and some of them are accompanied by music and dance. The songs which are accompanied by dance are: Lagre, Dou, Guluari, Dahar, Daha, Rinja, Vinsar, Jhika, Humti, Gunjar, Soharae, Loboe, Dunger, Durumjak, Tundum,Thabur and Jatur. The Songs which are not accompanied by dance are: Horo, Rohoe, Bapla, Binti and Morna. Your attention is drawn to the fact that the composers of the songs are not known and some of the songs are very old and at times the songs are either highly philosophical or vulgar. Some of the songs are spontaneous overflow of powerful feelings and full of deep thoughts, emotions and sentiments.

Since my research work was confined to Santali dance- songs, I desired to focus on Santali songs accompanied by dance. It has been observed that most Santali songs are accompanied by dance and I proposed to deal with them as they form the overwhelming majority among Santali songs. For my research work I opted for nine principle varieties of Santali songs with dance: (i) *lagre seren*, (ii) *pata seren*, (iii) *dong seren*, (iv) *sohrae seren*, (v) *dahar seren*, (vi) *baha seren*, (vii) *karam seren*, (viii) *dasae seren*, and (ix) *bir seren*.

It has been observed that Santali dance-songs are highly spontaneous and impromptu and we do realize that as in every culture there are elements that are prone to change and/or evolution, likewise in Santali culture also we encounter elements that have evolved or metamorphosed over the time. It is very difficult to codify the different shapes, pyramid formations and feet movement used in Santali dance-songs because the movements are subject to improvisation and innovation. So it can be inferred from this that the Santali dance-songs are in a creative flux and the individual as well as community's intervention in culture is persistent and this interface offers culture reality dynamism unique to itself. It is a fact that the Santals cherish their subjectivity and agency in their performance. All the participants are equally free to introduce a new move to the already established and repetitive structure of dance. Interestingly, even the audience, especially the old people, encourage the performers to do something surprisingly refreshing and prod to break the monotony or the set pattern of performance. This is perhaps rare in a Baudrillardian hyperreal world which is bombarded with 'simulcra or simulations' controlled from above that leaves a postmodern subject stripped off agency and subjectivity.

## Nature/culture binary

The Santali dance-songs show the community's close proximity with the nature and have always remained as close to nature as possible. And animals and birds have been integral part of Santali life and culture. The Santals have a very elevated attitude towards animals and birds. They are worshipped as gods and their existence is held as high as the human beings. Thus this shows their intimacy with nature and culture devoid of nature is beyond their understanding. Moreover, the Santal community's connection to nature and forest /jungle is more intimate and mysterious than any other community. At times it can be observed that they have flourished in seclusion and have faced devastation when confronted by the outsiders. Their attachment to the jungle is a constituent of their lives and is inseparable from their culture. Their spiritual or transcendental bonding has developed due to their lives in the forest in isolation from the other human societies. This seclusion, however, should not be read as an act of hiding themselves.

This existential reality has shaped their dependence and reverence for nature and their distancing and suspicion for other societal groups. They have been very much aware of the external world and its ways which fails to connect with nature in the manner in which they do.

The performance space used by the Santals for their dance-songs also requires our attention to resolve the issue of nature/culture binary. Unlike a very formal space carved out for performance nowadays, the Santal's selection of performance space is influenced by their closeness to nature. The non-existence of permanent auditorium or theatre house in such a community obsessed with dance performances can bewilder an outsider. The fact of the matter is that a theatre space has never been a necessity for them because firstly, they don't have the resources to build a permanent space and secondly, they have been nature friendly so creation of permanent performance structures have never occurred to them and most importantly, the beauty and essence of their dance-songs will be lost if it is not performed in the village courtyards. The Santals use their village, ponds, fields, rivers and entire jungle as performance arena. Given the subject matter of these songs, the natural surroundings contribute to the aesthetic experience. Any performance detached from the milieu would be incomplete. That is why the zeal, enthusiasm, and the spirit is missing in the standardized and managed dance performances that the Santal cultural groups perform for the outsiders. They often lack spontaneity and fervor in their performances. Thus, a divide between the Santali dance-songs and their natural surroundings is impossible from an aesthetic point of view.

It has been observed that in the Santali dance-songs there is absolute blurring of the nature/culture dichotomy. It does not mean that binaries don't exist in Santal community but as far as our current discussion is concerned, the nature/culture binary seems irrelevant. Instead of a binary what is apparent in Santali dance-songs is a harmonious confluence of nature and culture. Dance-songs of the Santals must be viewed as an extension of nature itself because Santali culture constitutes a celebration of nature. Their dance-songs are about hunting, fishing, changing season,etc and are essentially basic narratives of their daily lives and their communion with nature. The dance-songs are a means of socialization used to spread material and spiritual values in the Santal community. Thus, the nature/culture binary also emerges as metanarrative which excludes such societies from its discourse.

I strongly hold the view that the Santal dance-songs prove to be contrary to the nature/culture binary, which seem totally inappropriate to explain their cultural systems and beliefs. What we learn from the Santali dance-songs and their culture is the fact that nature and culture are intertwined and a gap between these two is hardly visible. From the performance space to the content of these dance-songs, the Santals prefer to maintain proximity with nature. Their faith in nature is not just material for this community but it is marked by a spiritual bond. And this bond is reflected in their culture through their dance-songs. Thus, the nature/culture binary has to be circumvented to comprehend the Santali culture. I believe that the Santali culture is resplendent with natural elements; reverence for nature is deep-rooted and this belief is culturally transmitted to the future generations. And most importantly, the culture of the Santal community seen through the lens of culture-centered approach reveals no artificial barriers between nature and culture; instead shows close intimate proximity and complementarity between nature and the Santali culture.

## Rural/urban binary

There is no denying the fact that the distinction between 'rural' and 'urban' culture has badly affected the domain of culture studies in India as most of the Indian scholars and thinkers, triggered by the western ideas on culture, are focusing on urban industrial societies, thus undermining and ignoring the 'rural'culture despite the fact that the vast majority of the Santals resides in the vilages and that it is the village which is the fertile ground for the existence fo myriad of art forms be it music, painting, theatre, dances, puppetry, sculpture, etc. We should not forget that India is still not transformed into a fully urban society like the west. It is , rather, a strange juncture, where an amalgamation of many facets can be witnessed simultaneously and recognition of one culture over the other is a fatal mistake in such a scenario. The Santals and their culture are also going through a tumultuous socio-cultural phase and the marginalization, invisibilisation, or exclusion of such cultures existing at the periphery would be a huge loss to our rich cultural extinction. The problem of obsession with urban folk is that it leads to negligence of other cultural forms thereby endangering their existence. It seems to me that the urban/rural divide in culture studies must be done away with to widen the scope of culture studies in India.

## Folk/culture binary

It seems to me that the academic distinction between the folk and the classical creates an obstacle for a free research to be carried out across disciplines and topics. It reduces folk to a matter of antiquity or remoteness simultaneously reducing the scope of any research in 'folk culture'. The western folklore studies or folkloristics came into existence because of a desire to constitute national history and a tendency to see folk not as something still prevalent and thriving, creating a hierarchy in culture studies departments where folk is brushed aside on the pretext that it has limited or marginal scope. It is very unfortunate to see the way folk is transformed and regarded as classical when a particular folk form finds support from the dominant sections of the society.

It is needless to say that the aesthetic parameters are constructed and institutionalized by the dominant sections of the society which are then applied to different cultural forms such as music, dance, theatre, painting, literature, etc. to classify art forms and codify the dominant view in art as 'fine taste', thereby producing an elite form of the 'classical' for the masses.

It can then be argued that the folk/classical divide aptly plays the function of hierarchising the different art forms and such institutionalization of some art forms in the name of classical is taking place here in India as well and it is unfortunate that the tribal art forms like the Santali dance-forms are easily becoming the easy prey for them. Therefore, the boundaries between these two types have to be blurred if culture like the Santali dance-songs are to be given their due place. And the classification of folk and classical fails to appreciate the Santali dance-songs consequently we need to go beyond this binary to understand the potency, content and cultural discourses of the Santal community.

## The Santal Aesthetics: binary of art for art's sake or art for society's sake

Given the aesthetic standpoint, it is essential to have a look at the binary of art for art's sake/art for society's sake from the Santal point of view. The Santals always try to solve every mystery through their lived experience driven by a need to survive in adverse circumstances. Therefore, the primary concern of the Santals is not an abstract theorization of a lived experience unlike the 'advanced' and the 'civilised' human beings elsewhere, but that of survival. These people are occupied with the riddles of survival so much so that for them a desire to solve it becomes secondary. Their life is like a river full of torrents, beautiful forms outside but violent within; violent not because the Santals are violent, but beacause life is violent to them in all its wilderness and hardships.

For the Santals, dance-songs exist not for any 'aesthetic' or comprehensible beauty but as a requirement to face the wilderness in its totality. These people are as close, physically as well as emotionally to nature as possible though it is very unfortunate that the claws of 'civilization' have destroyed their way of life to a great extent but they have still managed to survive into their tribal heritage.It is pertinent to mention here that the Santals with their unique tribal heritage may or may not adhere to the principle of art as an end in itself. The Santals can be identified as a society which utilizes art for proper social functioning while embellishing it with attributes worthy to be perceived as beautiful. There is no doubt that the Santals are aware of the importance of beauty in a performance, but the functional aspect remains dominant in their dance-songs. Most importantly, it is this reconciliation of the external appearance and the functionality of their discursive songs which seeks our attention to comprehend the attitude of such a primitive society towards art and aesthetics. Consider an example. While talking about a tree the Santals would not be as much interested in the beauty, name and appearance of the tree as in the utility of the tree. This approach dismantles the desire of knowledge for the sake of it which is dominant in many societies. This does not imply that the Santals don't seek to acquire knowledge but their inquisitiveness is shaped by their needs. Looking at their circumstances, we must keep this in mind that they hardly have the time and energy to engage themselves in debate and discourses irrelevant to explain the world around them.

The Santali dance-songs manifest an aura of enchanted beauty. Their appearance, decoration and properties used in the dance-songs depict them as enchanted with the idea of beauty so much so that a separation of their notion of beauty from its social utility is unimaginable. The Santal dance-songs, in fact epitomize the ancient concept of *aucitya*(utility) as the defining characteristic of their idea of beauty. It is fascinating to note that their social occasions, festivals and lyrics are profound with indications that beauty is functional in its essence. The Santali dance-songs are an important medium of socialization but at the same time it is impregnate with emotions. They beautify themselves for a purpose and their art forms whether performed for others/self-have utility of expressing their emotions(when sung on weary journeys or during rigorous labour in the forests) or of socializing and binding the society together (when performed on social occasions or fairs and festivals). It is difficult to discern whether the Santali dance-songs are art forms for their own sake —as their performance is not guided by any eternal forces say the market it is performed naturally by them and for themselves—or for the society as their performances have social function and significance.

## Oral mode of transmission of knowledge

It has been observed that the Santali dance-songs are one of the oral modes of knowledge transmission passed on from one generation to another generation. This mode of knowledge impartation is not unique to the Santals but it is found in many other civilizations as well. Ancient Indian knowledge traditions use the same method which is called *Sruti*. The subject matter of these dance-songs encompasses their life, birth, death, hunting, love, marriage, intercourse, pre/extra marital affairs, etc. Nothing that happens in a Santal's life escapes these songs. It weaves a tapestry of shared experience rich in emotions.

The Santali dance-songs are a tool of socialization for the Santal community. Its discursive subject matter is in a constant negotiation with the situations that occur in their daily lives. These songs transmit a particular message to serve in conceptualizing how the Santals should lead their lives. Entertainment and beauty are undoubtedly valued in the Santal community but according to them, it must not be devoid of message and teaching. And because of this reason the Santali dance-songs are not an individual urge but a communitarian quest for socialization. During a performance, the Santals are part of a performance but it is a process where subjectivity merges into a communitarian cause. The individual improvisation and contribution is valued but it should also add to the welfare of the society. And in this case the individual will is not completely subject to general will, rather, the individual modifies it every time s/he contributes to the discourse generated by these dance-songs.

The Santali dance-songs work as oral manuals for the young Santalis who are exposed to harsh conditions. They have Santali dance-songs on almost every aspect of their lives like, birth, adolescence, induction ceremony(the Caco Chatiar ceremony), different festivals, sex, hunting, fishing, etc. What we have here, therefore, is an amazing informal education system which uses social occasions and music as a medium to disseminate traditional values and wisdom. The orality of these songs is what makes them unique because they are easy to remember nad comprehend. Unlike the vedic tradition, these dance-songs are not strictly remembered as *Sruti* but the cultural impression left by them serves as guiding light for the newer generation. It should be borne in the mind that this educational tool is not controlled, maneuvered or manipulated by a class or a section of the society. These Santali dance-songs are a communicative genre which also operates as a cognitive system explaining the existential realities of the Santals.

## Postmodernity, Globalization, Cybernetic world/Hyper-textual world

The postmodernist Western cultural imperialism through such value-laden terms as 'Americanization', 'Cocacolonization', and 'McDonaldization' has produced a 'global consumer culture' based on the philosophy of the Pepsi advertisement in India giving the message: "Yeh Dil Maange More" (This Heart Wants More) thus adversely affecting the traditional Santali culture of Jharkhand, India. It implies that both material and non-material items, including kinship, affection, art and intellect become commodified, that is their value is assessed by the context of their exchange rather than the context of their production or use. An advanced or post-modernized consumer culture experiences hyper-commodification in which minute differences between products or minute improvements in them can determine variations in demand. In this context of hyper-consumerism, consumption is differentiated on the basis of the signifiers known as 'brand names' for which the craze for 'spending' in glossy shopping malls is often noticed. Paradoxically, as consumption becomes universalized through globally available brands, production can become localized according to cost advantages.

Thus, the current Mantra of global capital is not "Think Global, Act Local" as Theodor Levit observed but "Sell Global, Pack Local". Under the dominance of global brand market, the local cottage and household industry that is an inherent part and parcel of a particular form of folk culture is withering away very fast. This phenomenon can be noticed in a cybernetic world where the global popular culture is produced, controlled and marketed. The young Santals are now getting exposed to the supposedly superior cultures and with it has developed an aspiration in them to be identified with the dominant or superior cultures. The attempts to imitate or to get assilmilated in dominant cultural folds by adopting some socio-cultural practices are clearly visible in their ways. Most importantly, the technology has also played its role in encouraging the process of obsoletion of these dance-songs. Stereos, CDs, mobile phones have brought in new waves of music from the outer world to the Santals which are easily available, thereby reducing the aura and charm of the Santali dance-songs in the young new generation of the Santal community.

## Method

A substantial number of research shows that dominant ideas of resistance hinges on the grand narratives of class conflict and revolutionary struggle, drawing upon universals, and treating the subaltern sectors as devoid of agency and/or consciousness. Whenever indigenous resistance is indeed acknowledged, it is constructed as a natural response in a stimulus-response sense, devoid of consciousness. Such an understanding has its theoretical limitations as it suggests a simplistic relation between the subordinated and the dominant.

The culture-centered approach concerns itself with the voices of marginalized groups and explores the interaction between culture and structure that create conditions of marginality. The commitment of the approach is to writing theory from below, and to defining praxis through the engagement with subaltern classes who have traditionally been marginalized and absent in dominant theories and models. The dominant theories construct the postcolonial spaces as traditional and underdeveloped to legitimize the neo-liberal logic of development and modernity. In doing so, they silence the voices of the subaltern by rendering them passive and agency-less. The culture-centered approach engages with the silences and absences and generates meanings by a participatory framework that creates entry points for engaging with subaltern voices.

Considering basic issues of human rights that are connected to the subaltern resistance, the culture-centered approach locates the focus of research in the people, rather than mainstream organizations. In other words, through its discursive engagement with subaltern communities that have hitherto been erased, the culture-centered framework resists the dominant discourse of management function by introducing alternative discourses and meaning structures. By bringing forth alternative possibilities that have otherwise been obscured, it creates opportunities for transformative and emancipatory politics.

With this understanding of the culture-centered approach against the backdrop of dominant managerial emphasis of organizational practice and scholarship, our goal to explore the communicative processes manifested through several dance-songs embodying resistance in a subaltern context has the potential to offer new ways of thinking about organizational communication and public relations. By questioning such taken-for-granted assumptions, the culture-centered approach to communication demonstrates the logic of the dominant theories built upon universal applicability of modernist rationality (Dutta, 2008). In other words, by engaging with the voices of communities that are typically marginalized through mainstream communicative practices, the culture-centered approach demonstrates its emancipatory commitment by including them in the dominant discursive space. Such an understanding of subaltern activism poses an epistemic rupture to dominant assumptions of neo-liberal logic that operates through the universal rhetoric of progress and development globally and locally. The subaltern resistance brings forth a contradiction to the universal logic opening up avenues for alternative meanings and change in the local, national and global policies. Hence, understanding subaltern resistance through the culture-centered lens suggests understanding the discourses that emerge in relation to structures informed by the subaltern context.

Folk-expressions and folktales are essentially symbolic forms of expression of indigenous subalterns and these communicative articulations are grounded in the reality of their everyday experience. These symbolic communications often contain the essence of creativity and aesthetics. This artistic means of sharing experience through their narratives enables/ empowers subalterns to legitimate/ represent their silenced and marginalized existence in a symbolic way.

In this journey, narratives and stories not only just flow from one generation to the next generation, but they also travel from one place to other and from one culture to another. For example, as per a traditional Indian folktale, a carpenter‘s had one old knife. One day a philosopher asked him ‘how old is this knife‘? In reply carpenter stated, ‘we are using this knife for many generations. Many a time the handle got replaced, many times the steel was changed, but it is the very same knife we are using for generation’. This construction was a metaphoric representation of the tradition of folk-tales. Therefore scholars conceptualized folk-narratives as a living traditional culture.

As this form is fundamentally dynamic and essentially responds to contemporary socio-cultural situation/condition; the contents and expressions of narrative undergo a process of continuous modification in order to become fit/ relevant to ever-changing dynamic socio-political circumstances. In the present era of globalization, when the life is more polarized and bifurcated, we need to re-examine the conditions and lives of the subaltern communities their folktales to understand, legitimate and create awareness about how dominant forces/ structures/ knowledge are enjoying privileges and how they are constantly marginalizing ‘other’ in west-centric neoliberal landscape. In contrast, indigenous worldview fundamentally situates co-operation, mutual care and love as the foundation of their epistemology.

Folklores and folktales are self-contained communication medium through which communities express its voices, values, creativities, experiences and commentaries of social reality opined that folktales are also an important source/ treasure of historical information/ materials which can be useful for further research activities for scholars. Moreover it is a dynamic and pragmatic form of representation of reality, and is primarily based on, and situate in everyday contexts, survival and cultures of subalterns; therefore it is not a static/ inert form or a variety of cultural fossil .

Like their stories, indigenous people themselves are marginalized and silenced in the mainstream discursive spaces. Scholars showed that, folk environments and expressions are created, developed and nurtured by rural, indigenous, peasant communities who oftentimes reside in isolated geographical regions and thereby are able to maintain a continued tradition and heritage. Folktales are not only the means to articulate their dreams, wishes, cultural identities but they are also expressions to convey the reality of their everyday existence, experiences and struggles. Folk-representations are illustrations of their long relentless battle for sheer survival against grinding poverty, appalling exploitation, unmitigated oppressions, spiraling prices, lurking fear and chronic shortage of daily needs

Indian tradition recognizes interactions between nature and culture as the foundation of its philosophy. According to one of these theories, the material and living world is made of the elements of nature. And after death/ destruction everything ultimately dissolves/ transforms/ disintegrates as elements. This theory recognizes nine elements: five *bhutas*- earth, water, fire, air and sky, and four *dravyas*- time, direction, mind and soul as the fundamental elements. According to indigenous worldview, these elements are fundamentally related to their lives and cultures and also connected to the processes of meaning making and knowledge production.

Indigenous philosophy considers all the phases of life from birth to death are full of pain, agony and pleasure. For example, indigenous *Santhal* community recognizes both pain and pleasure as parts of their lives. For them pleasure is temporal/ short and pain is more acute/ more permanent in reality. Socio-religious principles of many indigenous communities are different from (if not more human than) many dominant constructions and societal rules/realities that prevails in mainstream societies of India. Considering again the example of *Santhal* community, one may notice that (i) *Santhals* do not approve caste hierarchy in society, (ii). by birth no person/ group can be considered as superior or inferior, (iii). there is no provision of idol/ image worship or prayer-place in their society (as they consider that God is present everywhere in every manifestation of the elements.

## References

Bhattacharya, S. S. (1962). 'Santal Songs: Different Types'. *Bulletin of the Cultural Research Institute*, Calcutta, 1 (2), pp. 54-61.

Bodding, P. (1993(First published in India)). *A Santal Dictionary: 7 Parts in Five Volumes.* New Delhi: Gyan Publishing House.

Chattopadhyaya, D. (1999). Lokosanskriti o Lokayata Darshan. In M. Bhattacharya, *Lokoshruti Prabandha Sankalan (in Bengali)* (pp. 3-6). Kolkata, India: West Bengal Folk and Tribal Research Centre.

Culshaw, W. (2004(Published in India)). *Tribal Heritage: A Study of the Santals.* New Delhi: Gyan Publishing House.

Dutta, M. (2008). *Communicating health: A culture-centred approach.* UK: Polity.

Majumdar, D. (2006). *Paschimbanger Adibasi Lokokatha( in Bengali).* Kolkata: West Bengal Folk and Tribal Research Centre.

Mukherjea, C. (1962). *The Santals.* Calcutta: A.Mukherjee &CO. Pr. Ltd.

Raha, M. K. (1967). 'Folk Songs of the Tribals of West Bengal- An Analytical Study of Continuity and Change'. In H. Biswas, *Folk Music and Folk-lore, An Anthology* (pp. 57-81). Vol. 1, Calcutta: Folk Music and Folkl-lore Research Institute.

Troisi, J. (1978). *Tribal Religion: Religious Beliefs and Practices among the Santals.* New Delhi: Manohar Publications.

Wernick, A. (1991). *Promotional Culture.* London: Sage.

# Select Bibliography


A.L. Kroeber and C. Kluckholn. (1952). *Culture:A Critical Review of Concepts and Definitions.* New York: Vantage Books.

Adaire, C. (1992). *Women and Dance:Sylphs and Sirens.* New York: New York University Press.

Adshead, J. (1988). *Dance Analysis: Theory and Practice.* London: Dance Books.

Alexandra Carter and Janet O'Shea. (2010). *The Dance Studies Reader.* New York: Routledge.

Allison, L. (1996). 'Power'. In I. McLean(ed.), *The Concise Oxford Dictionary of Politics* (pp. 396-9). Oxford: Oxford University Press.

Anand, S. (2014). *Annihilation of Caste: The Annotated Critical Edition.* New Delhi: Navayana Publishing Pvt Ltd.

Apperley, A. (1996). 'Foucault Michel'. In I. McLean(ed.), *The Concise Oxford Dictionary of Politics* (p. 187). Oxford: Oxford University Press.

Archer, M. S. (1988). *Culture and Agency: The place of Culture in Social Theory.* Cambridge: Cambridge University Prcss.

Archer, W. (1943). 'Santal Poetry'. *Man in India*, XXIII, 147-53.

Archer, W. (1944). 'Festival Songs'. *Man in India*, XXIV, 70-74.

Archer, W. (1944). 'More Santal Songs'. *Man in India*, XXIV,141-44.

Archer, W. (1945). 'Santal Rebellion Songs'. *Man in India*, XXV, 207.

Archer, W. (1946). 'Santal Transplantation Songs'. *Man in India*, XXVI, 6-7.

Austin, J. L. (1962). *How to Do Things with Words.* Oxford: Oxford University Press.

Averill, G. (1997). *A Day for the Hunter, Aday for the Prey: Popular Music and Power in Haiti.* Chicago,IL: Chicago University Press.

'Aadivaasi', B. M. (n.d.). *Jhaali.* Dumka: Santali Sahitya Prasarak Sewa Mandal.

'Adivaasi', B. M. (1999). *Disaam Bhokta(Santali Kahani).* Dumka: Santali Sahitya Prasarak Sevamandal.

Archer, W. (1944 , Sept). 'More Santal Songs',. *Man in India*, Ranchi, 24.(3) pp.9-13.

Archer, W. (June 1943). 'Santal Poetry'. *Man in India*, Ranchi, 23 (2), pp. 98-105.

Archer, W. (March 1946). 'Santal Transplantation Songs'. *Man in India*, Ranchi, 26 (1), pp. 6-7.

Archer, W.G., and Soren Gopal Gamaliel. (1943). *Hor Seren.* (Santal Songs), Benageria: The Mission Press.

Archer, W.G.,and Soren, Gopal Gamaliel. (1943). *Don Soren.Hor Seren Reak Dosar Hatin.* (Don Songs. The Second part of Santal Songs), Benageria: The Mission Press, pp. 435.

'Armaan', B. k. (2009). *Pe Pawa Chaawle.* Dumka: Santali Sahitya Prasarak Sewa Mandal.

Archer, W. (1974). *The Hill of Flutes: Life , Love and Poetry in Tribal India, A Portrait of the Santals.* London: George Allen & Unwin LTD.

Archer, W. (1979). Santal Poetry. In J. Troisi, *The Santals: Readings in Tribal Life, Volume III: Myths and Folklore* (pp. 9-13). New Delhi: Indian Social Institute.

Archer, W. (1979). Santal Transplantation songs. In J. Troisi, *The Santals: Readings in Tribal Life, Volume III: Myths and Folklore* (pp. 19-20). New Delhi: Indian Social Institute.

Archer, W. (1979). The Santal Sohrae. In J. Troisi, *The Santals: Readings in Tribal Life* (pp. 1-3). New Delhi: Indian Social Institute.

Bag, D. (1987). *In the Midst of Santals.* Calcutta: Subarnarekha.

Banerji, P. (1959). *The Folk-Dance of India.* Allahabad: Kitabistan.

Besra, B. (1977). *More Soros Kahni.* Kolkata: The Santali Literary & Cultural Society.

Besra, V. (2010). *Vidrao.* Ranchi: Santali Literature Publication Pvt.Ltd.

Bhattacharya, S. S. (1962). 'Santal Songs: Different Types'. *Bulletin of the Cultural Research Institute*, Calcutta, 1 (2), pp. 54-61.

Bhattacharya, S. S. (1964). 'Woodland Verses'. *Bulletin of the Cultural Research Institute*, Calcutta, 3 (3-4), pp. 49-64.

Bodding, P. (1942). *Traditions and Institutions of the Santals(Horkoren Mare Hapramko Reak Katha).* New Delhi: Bahumukhi Prakashan.

Bodding, P. (1942(First Indian Reprint1994)). *Traditions and Institutions of the Santals.* New Delhi: Bahumukhi Prakashan.

Bodding, P. (1993(First published in India)). *A Santal Dictionary: 7 Parts in Five Volumes.* New Delhi: Gyan Publishing House.

Bodding, P. (2001(Second Reprint)). *Studies in Santal Medicine and Connected Folklore: Part I,II and III.* Kolkata: The Asiatic Society.

Bag, D. (1987). *In the Midst of Santals.* Calcutta: Subarnarekha.

Banerji, P. (1959). *The Folk-Dance of India.* Allahabad: Kitabistan.

Besra, B. (1977). *More Soros Kahni.* Kolkata: The Santali Literary & Cultural Society.

Besra, V. (2010). *Vidrao.* Ranchi: Santali Literature Publication Pvt.Ltd.

Bhattacharya, S. S. (1962). 'Santal Songs: Different Types'. *Bulletin of the Cultural Research Institute*, Calcutta, 1 (2), pp. 54-61.

Bhattacharya, S. S. (1964). 'Woodland Verses'. *Bulletin of the Cultural Research Institute*, Calcutta, 3 (3-4), pp. 49-64.

Bodding, P. (1942). *Traditions and Institutions of the Santals(Horkoren Mare Hapramko Reak Katha).* New Delhi: Bahumukhi Prakashan.

Bodding, P. (1942(First Indian Reprint1994)). *Traditions and Institutions of the Santals.* New Delhi: Bahumukhi Prakashan.

Bodding, P. (1993(First published in India)). *A Santal Dictionary: 7 Parts in Five Volumes.* New Delhi: Gyan Publishing House.

Bodding, P. (2001(Second Reprint)). *Studies in Santal Medicine and Connected Folklore: Part I,II and III.* Kolkata: The Asiatic Society.

Bhattacharya, S. S. (1962). 'Santal Songs: Different Types'. *Bulletin of the Cultural Research Institute*, Calcutta, 1 (2), pp. 54-61.

Bodding, P. (1993(First published in India)). *A Santal Dictionary: 7 Parts in Five Volumes.* New Delhi: Gyan Publishing House.

B.Agger. (1992). *Cultural Studies as Critical Theory.* London: Falmer.

Banes, S. (1998). *Dancing Women:Female Bodies on Stage.* London: Routledge.

Barthes, R. (1970 (1975)). *S/Z.* trans. Richard Millar,Oxford: Blackwell.

Barthes, R. (1972(1957)). *Mythologies.* London: Trans. Annette Lavers, Cape.

Barthes, R. (1972(1964)). *Critical Essays.* Evanston,ILL: Northwestern University Press.

Barthes, R. (1977). "The Death of the Author". In t. Heath, *Image-Music-Text* (pp. 142-48). New York: Hill and Wang.

Barthes, R. (1977). The death of the author. In R. Barthes, *Image-Music-Text.* Ed.Stephen Heath,London: Collins.

Baudrillard, J. (1988). *Selected Writings. Ed.Mark Poster.* Stanford, Calif.: Stanford University Press.

Bauman, Richard and Charles L. Briggs. (1990). Poetics and Performance as Critical Perspectives on Language and Social Life. *Annual Reviews of Anthropology 19*, 59-88.

Bhabha, H. K. (1994). *The Location of Culture.* London: Routledge.

Bhattacharya, S. (1968). *Ethnomusicology and India.* Calcutta: Indian Publications.

Bhowmick, A. C. (1999). Santal Dance. In R. D. Tribhuwan, *Tribal Dances of India* (pp. 303-305). New Delhi: Discovery Publishing House.

Bodding, P. (1916). *The Traditions and Institutions of the Santals.* Second Edition of HORKOREAN MARE HAPRAMKO REAK' KATHA with a foreword by P.O.Bodding.Benagaria: Santal Mission Press.

Bohlman, P. (2007). *The Silence of Music.* British Library/Royal Holloway Lectures in Musicology 2006/7, February/March 2007.

Bompas, C. (1909). *Folklore of the Santal Parganas.* London.

Bourdieu, P. (1993). *The Field of Cultural Production: Essays on Art and Literature.* Trans. Richard Nice. Cambridge: Polity.

Bowman, P. (2003). *Interrogating cultural studies: theory, politics, and practice.* London: Pluto Press.

Brandel, R. (1961). *The Music of Central Africa.* Natherlands: The Hague Martinus Nijhoff.

Browning, B. (1995). *Samba: Resistance inMotion.* Bloomington, IN: Indiana University Press.

Bruckner, Heidrun.et al. (2007). *The Power of Performance: Actors,, Audiences and Observers of Cultural Performances in India.* New Delhi: Manohar Publications.

Burke, P. (1996). *Popular Culture in Early Modern Europe, revised reprint.* Aldershot: Scolar Press.

Burridge, Stephanies, and Wang Yunyu. (2012). *Identity and Diversity: Celebrating Dance in Taiwan.* New Delhi: Routledge.

Burt, R. (1995). *The Male Dancer: Bodies, Spectacle, Sexualities.* London: Routledge.

*Chotrae Deshmanjhi Reak Katha.* (1986). The Literature Committee of the Northern Evangelical Lutheran Church.

Campbell, A. (1894). 'Traditional Migration of the Santal Tribes'. *Indian Antiquary*, pp.103-4.

Campbell, A. (June 1916). 'Santal Legends'. *Journal of the Bihar and Orissa Research Society*, Patna, 2 (2), pp. 191-200.

Campbell, A. (March 1916). 'The Traditions of the Santals'. *Journal of the Bihar and Orissa Research Society*, Patna, 2 (1), pp. 15-29.

Canney, M. (1928). 'The Santals and their Folklore'. *Folklore*, London, 39, pp. 329-43.

'Chaasa', B. H. (2003). *Baha Seren.* Dumka: Santali Sahitya Prasarak Sewa Mandal.

Chaudhury, P. (1965). *Bihar District Gazetteers: Santal Parganas.* Patna: Th Superintendent Secretariat Press, Bihar.

Culshaw, W. (1949). *Tribal Heritage: A Study of the Santals.* London: Lutherworth Press.

Culshaw, W. (March 1946). 'Notes and Queries. Santal Songs'. *Man in India*, Ranchi, 26 (1), pp. 66-67.

Carver, T. (1982). *Marx's Social Theory.* oxford: Oxford University Press.

Cashmore, E. a. (1999). *Dictionary of Cultural Theorists.* London: Arnold.

Castaldi, F. (2006). *Choreographies of African Identities: Negritude, Dance, and the National Ballet of Senegal.* Champaign, IL: University of Illinois Press.

Clifford, J. (1988). *The Predicament of Culture: Twentieth-Century Ethnography, Literature, and Art.* Cambridge, M.A.: Harward University Press.

Clifford, J. (1988). *The predicament of culture:Twentieth-century ethnography, literature, and art.* Cambridge,MA: Harvard University Press.

Coles, A. (2000). *Site Specificity: The Ethnographic Turn.* London: Black Dog Publishing.

Culshaw, W. (1949). *Tribal Heritage: A Study of the Santals.* London: Lutterworth Press.

Culshaw, W. (2004(Indian Edition)). *Tribal Heritage: A Study of the Santals.* New Delhi: Gyan Publishing House.

Daly, A. (1987). 'The Balanchine Woman:of hummingbirds and channel swimmers'. In *The Drama Review(TDR)31* (pp. 3-12).

David, L. a. (1996). *Encyclopedia of Cultural anthropology, Vol.1.* New York: Henry Holt Books.

DasGupta, S. (May 1963). 'A Short Introduction to the Variety of Folk Dances in India'. *Folklore*, Calcutta, 4 (5), pp. 163-91.

Deshmanjhi, C. (1938). *Chotrae Deshmanjhi reak Katha.* Benagaria.

During, S. (1993). *The Cultural Studies Reader.* London and New York: Routledge.

During, S. (1999). *The Cultural Studies Reader.* New York: Routledge.

Foster, G. M. (1953). What Is Folk Culture? *American Anthropologist*, New Series, Vol. 55, No. 2, Part 1 (Apr. - Jun., 1953),pp. 159-173.

Foster, S. (1986). *Reading Dancing: Bodies and Subjects in Contemporary American Dance.* Berkeley,CA: University of California Press.

Foster, S. (1986). *Reading Dancing: Bodies and Subjects in Contemporary American Dance.* Berkeley,CA: University of California Press.

Foucault, M. (1977). *Discipline and Punish: The Birth of the Prison.* Harmondsworth: Penguin.

Franco, M. (1995). *Dancing Modernism/Performing Oilitics.* Bloomington,IN: Indiana University Press.

Gates, H. L. (1988). *The Signifying Monkey.* Oxford: Oxford University Press.

Gausdal, J. (1960). *The Santal Khuts.* Oslo: H. Aschehoug & Co.

'Godet', J. S. (2015). *Sirjonpuri Ar Udgau Aran.* Kolkata: Diamond Art Press.

Geertz, C. (1972). Deep Play: Notes on the Balinese Cockfight. *Daedalus 101*, 159-69.

Geertz, C. (1973). *The Interpretation of Cultures.* New York: Basic Books.

Geertz, C. (1973b). 'Ideology as a Cultural System'. In C. Geertz, *The Interpretation of Cultures* (pp. 193-233). New York: Basic Books.

Genette, G. (1982). *Palimpsestes: la litterature au second degre.* Paris: Seuil.

Goodenough, W. H. (1963). *Cooperation in Change.* New York: Russell Sage Foundation.

Goodenough, W. H. (1965). "Rethinking 'Status' and 'Role': Toward a General Model of the Cultural Organization of Social Relationships". In B. Michael, *The Relevance of Models for Social Anthropology.* London: Tavistock.

Goodenough, W. H. (1981). *Culture, Language, and Society.* Calif: Benjamin-Cummings.

Gramsci, A. (1971). *Selections from the Prison Notebooks.Selected and tr. by Quentin Hoare et.al.* London: Lawrence and Wishart.

Greenblatt, S. (1982). *The Forms of Power and the Power of Forms in the Renaissance.* Norman: University of Oklahoma Press and Pilgrim Books.

Habermas, J. (1971). *Knowledge and Human Interests.* Boston: Beacon.

Habermas, J. (1975). *Legitimation Crisis.* Boston: Beacon.

Habermas, J. (1979). *Communication and the Evolution of Society.* Boston: Beacon.

Habermas, J. (1985(1987)). *The Philosophical Discourse of Modernity.* trans. Frederick Lawrence, Cambridge: Polity Press.

Hall, S. (1992). 'Cultural Studies and its Theoretical Legacies'. In L. e. Grossberg, *Cultural Studies.* London: Routledge.

Hall, S. (1997a). 'The Spectacle of the"other"'. In S. Hall(ed.), *Representation: Cultural Representations and Signifying Practices* (pp. 223-79). London: Sage/ Open University.

Hall, S. (1997b). 'The Work of Representation'. In S. Hall, *Representation: Cultural Representations and Signifying Practices.* London: Sage/Open University.

Hansdak, '. B. (1994). *Tiriya Baadoli.* Dumka: Santali Sahitya Prasarak Sewa Mandal.

Hembram, N. (1982). *Austric Civilization of India:Prevedic Kherwal-Santal civilization.* Calcutta: Hari Pada Sahoo Books& News.

Hembram, P. (1988). *Sari-Sarna( Santhal Religion).* Delhi: Mittal Publications.

Hembrom, T. (1996). *The Santals: Anthrropological-Theological Reflections on Santali & Biblical Creation Traditions.* Calcutta: Punthi Pustak.

Herzfeld, M. (1991). 'Silence, Submission, and Subversion:Towards a Poetics of Womanhood'. In P. L. Papataxiarchis(eds), *Contested Identities: Gender and Kinship in Modern Greece* (pp. 79-97). Princeton, NJ: Princeton University Press.

Hirschkop,Ken and shepherd, David. (1989). *Bakhtin and cultural theory.* Manchester and New York: Manchester University Press.

Jenks, C. (1993). *Culture.* London: Routledge.

Joseph, S. (1998). *Interrogating Culture: Critical Perspectives on Contemporary Social Theory.* New Delhi: Sage Publications.

Kisku, D. (2000). *The Santals And Their Ancestors: History.* Dumka: Hihiri Pipiri Dudhani-Kurua.

Kisku, D. (2001). *Karam Thakur Samanre.* Dumka: Hihiri Pipiri.

Kisku, D. B. (2001). *Maran Thakur Samanre: Religious Literature.* Dumka: Hihiri Pipiri.

Kristeva, J. (1986). 'Word, dialogue and novel'. In T. Moi, *The Kristeva Reader.* Oxford: Blackwell.

Kunst, J. (1955). *Ethno-Musicology.* Natherlands: The Hague Martinus Nijhoff.

Kurath, G. (1964). *Iroquois Music and Dance.* Washington: Smithsonian Institution Bureau of American Anthology.

L.O.Skrefsrud and Kolean, Haram. (1928(7th edition1968)). *Horkoren Mare Hapramko reak' Katha.* Benagaria: Santal Mission Press.

Leppert, Richard and McClary Susan. (1987). *Music and society: The Politics of Composition, Performance and Reception.* New York: Cambridge University Press.

Lipsitz, G. (1994). *Dangerous Crossroads: Popular Music, , Postmodernism and the Poetics of Place.* London: Verso.

Lomax, A. (1968). *Folk Song Style and Culture.* Washington: American Association for the Advancement of Science.

Lovejoy, M. (1997). *Postmodern Currents: Art and Artists in the Age of Electronic Media.2nd Ed.* Upper Saddle River, NJ: Prentice Hall.

Man, E. (1867). *Sonthalia and the Santhals.* Calcutta: Geo Wyman & Co.

Martin Clayton, Byron Dueck, and Laura Leante. (2013). *Experience and Meaning in Music Performance.* New York: Oxford University Press.

Martin, M. (2003). The Projection of Cultural Studies. In P. Bowman, *Interrogating Cultural Studies: Theory, Politics and Practice* (pp. 41-55). London: Pluto Press.

Majumdar, S. (1925). Some Santal Songs. *The Visva-Bharati Quarterly III*, pp. 67-9.

Man, E. (1983(First Indian Edition)). *Sonthalia and the Sonthals.* Delhi: Mittal Publications.

Manjhi, C. P. (2001). Santhal Language and Culture . In N. Mathur, *Santhal Worlview* (pp. 89-99). New Delhi: Concept Publishing Company.

Marandi, C. (n.d.). *Hor Hopon.* (Songs of Men), Dumka: Alka Printing Press, pp. 20.

Mitchell, J. (Nov. 1875). 'Santal Songs with Translation'. *The Indian Antiquary*, Bombay, 4, pp. 342-44.

Mitra, A. (1953). *Census 1951. West Bengal. The Tribes and Castes of West Bengal.* Calcutta: Superintendent, West Bengal Government Press, pp. 414.

Mitra, S. C. (1926). 'Santali life in a Santali Folksong'. *Journal of the Anthropological Society of Bombay*, Bombay, 13 (1), pp. 47-51.

Mitra, S. C. (Sept. 1929). 'The "Magical Conflict" in Santali, Bengali and Ao Naga Folklore'. *Man in India*, Ranchi, 9 (3), pp. 173-80.

Mukherjea, C. (1962). *The Santals.* Calcutta: A.Mukherjee &CO. Pr. Ltd.

Mukherjea, C. (1962,Revised Edition). *The Santals.* Calcutta: A. Mukherjee & Co. Private Ltd.

Mukherjea, C. (July-Dec 1936). 'Santal Folk Poetry'. *The New Review*, Calcutta, 4, pp. 220-26.

Murmu, B. C. (2011). *Sabarnakha.* Ranchi: Novelty Art Press.

Murmu, K. (2012). *Lantiti.* Kolkata: Kranti Press.

Murmu, L. (2010). *Golden Passport to Jeret Jivha.* New Delhi: Santali Literature Publication Pvt. Ltd. Ranchi.

Murmu, S. H. (1961). *Hor Bapla Puthi: Pahil Hatin (A Santal Marriage Book).* Benagaria: Benagaria Mission Press.Reprint in 2015.Kranti Press, Kolkata.

Murmu, T. (2010). *Towa Baahaa Maalaa.* Dumka: Santali Sahitya Prasarak Sewa Mandal.

McMains, J. (2006). *Glamour Addiction: Inside the American Ballroom Dance Industry.* Middletown,CT: Wesleyan University Press.

Meduri, A. (n.d.).

Meduri, A. (1988). 'Bharat Natyam:What are you? In *Asian Theatre Journal, 5,1(Spring)* (pp. 1-22).

Merriam, A. (1967). *Ethnomusicology of Flathead Indians.* New York: Wenner-Gren Foundation for Anthropological Research.

Morris, G. (1996). 'Introduction'. In G. Morris, *Moving Words: Re-writing Dance.* London: Routledge.

Nayar, P. K. (2006). *Reading Culture: theory, praxis, politics.* New Delhi: Sage Publications.

Ness, S. (1992). *Body, Movement and Culture: Kinesthetic and Visual Symbolism in a Philippine Community.* Philadelphia, P.A.: University of Pennsylvania Press.

Nettle, B. (1956). *Music in Primitive Culture.* Cambridge: Harvard University Press.

Nooshin, L. (2009). *Music and the Play of power in the Middle East, North Africa and Cenal Asia.* England: Ashgat ePublishing Ltd.

Novack, C. (1990). *Sharing the Dance: Contact Improvisation and American Culture.* PhD dissertation: Columbia University.

O' Malley, L. (1938). *District Gazetteer of Santal Parganas.* pp.108-119.

O'Shea, J. (2010). Roots/Routes of Dance Studies. In A. C. O'Shea, *The Dance Studies Reader* (pp. 1-15). New York: Routledge.

Parry, H. (1899). "Inaugural Address". *Jounal of the Folk Song Society*, 1:1, 1-3.

Pasayat, C. (1998). *Tribe, Caste and Folk Culture.* New Delhi: Rawat Publications.

Payne, M. (1996). *A Dictionary of Cultural and Critical Theory.* Oxford: Blackwell.

Peter, B. (1999). *Cultural theory: a glossary.* London: Arnold Publishers.

Prasad, O. (1987). *Folk Music and Folk Dances of Banaras.* Calcutta: Anthropological Survey of India.

Qureshi, R. B. (2002). *Music and Marx: Ideas, Practice,Politics.* New York: Routledge.

Raglan, L. (1947, Jun). The Origin of Folk-Culture,Vol. 58, No. 2. *Folklore*, pp. 250-260.

Ray, S. (1973). *Music of Eastern India.* Calcutta: Firma K.L.Mukhopadhhaya.

Redfield, R. (1934). Culture Changes in Yucatan. *American Anthropologist, New Series, Vol. 36, No. 1 (Jan. - Mar., 1934),*, 57-69.

Redfield, R. (1940). The Folk Society and Culture. *American Journal of Sociology*, Vol. 45, No. 5 (Mar., 1940), pp 731-742.

Redfield, R. (1947). The Folk Society. *American Journal of Sociology*, Vol. 52, No. 4 (Jan., 1947), pp. 293-308.

Ricoeur, P. (1986). *Lectures on Ideology and Utopia.* ed. Geogre H.Taylor. New York: Columbia University Press.

Riffaterre, M. (1979 (1983)). *Text Production.* trans. Terese Lyons, New York: Columbia University Press.

Sachchidananda. (1965). *Profiles of Tribal Culture in Bihar.* Calcutta: Firma K. L. Mukhopadhyay.

'Santali', S. A. (2009). *Goso Baahaa.* Ranchi: Santali Litearature Publication Pvt.Ltd.

Satyarthi, D. (1951). *Meet My People. Indian Folk Poetry.* Hyderabad: Chetna Prakashan Ltd., pp. 304.

Sinha, S. K. (June 1946). 'Santal Folk Songs'. *Journal of the Bihar and Orissa Research Society*, Patna, 32 (2), pp. 184-88.

'Sonali', M. S. (1995). *Jiyon Jhaarnaa.* Dumka: Santali Sahitya Parishad.

'Sonali', M. S. (2008). *Bir Baajaal Onol Puthi.* Dumka: Santali Sahitya Parishad.

Soren, '. M. (1987). *Tiriya Baadoli.* Dumka: Dharam Printing Press.

Soren, J. J. (2002). *Sogoe Pajher.* Dumka.

Soren, J. J. (n.d.). *Kubi Gaona.*

Soren, N. (1999). *Haarhaam Baabaavaak Gaam Kaahni.* Dumka: Santali Sahitya Prasaarak Sevamandal.

Soren, N. (1999). *Jeevet Karam Seren.* Dumka: Santali Sahitya Prasarak Sewa Mandal.

Soren, N. (n.d.). *Aasadh Binti.* Dumka: Santali Sahitya Prasarak Sewa Mandal.

Soren, N. (n.d.). *Jawae Dhuti Seren.* (Betrothal Songs), Dumka: Alka Printing Works, pp. 17.

Soren, N. (n.d.). *Maran Din Seren.* (Christmas Songs), Dumka: Alka Printing Works, pp. 16.

Soren, N. (n.d.). *Sohrae Porob ar Sohrae Seren.* (The Harvest Feast and Harvest Songs), Dumka: Alka Printing Works, pp. 16.

Soren, V. (2006). *Mitten Kukmu.* Dumka: Minerva Press.

Soren, V. (2010). *Taaraal Baasaal.* Dumka: Minarva Press.

Sachs, C. (1937). *World History of the Dance, trans. Bessie Schonberg.* New York: W.W. Norton.

Said, E. (1979). *The Question of Palestine.* New York: Random House.

Said, E. (1993). *Culture and Imperialism.* New York: Alfred A. Knopf.

Savigliano, M. (1995). *Tango and the Political Economy of Passion.* Boulder,C.O.: Westview Press.

Schechner, R. (1985). *Between Theatre and Anthropology.* Philadelphia: University of Pennsylvania.

Scott, J. C. (1990). *Domination and the Arts of Resistance: Hidden Transcripts.* New Haven,CT: Yale University Press.

Sedgwick, A. E. (1999). *Key Concepts in Cultural Theory.* London: Routledge.

Sharp, C. J. (1907). *English Folk-Song: Some conclusions.* London: Novello.

Shelemay, K. K. (2001). *Soundscapes: Exploring Music ina Changing World.* New York: Norton.

Shiach, M. (1989). *Discourse on Popular Culture.* Cambridge: Polity Press.

Singer, M. (1972). *When a Great Tradition Modernizes: An Anthropological Approach to Indian Civilization.* London: Pall Mall Press.

Sinha, P. (1970). *An Approach to the Study of Indian Music.* Calcutta: Indian Publications.

Slobin, M. (1976). *Music in the Culture of Northern Afghanistan.* Vikingfund Publications in Anthropology No.54.

Sparks, C. (1996). 'The Evolution of Cultural Studies...'. In J. Storey, *What is Cultural Studies?: A Reader* (pp. 14-30). London: Arnold.

Storey, J. (1994). *Cultural Theory and Popular Culture: A Reader.* Hemel Hempstead: Harvester Wheatsheaf.

Storey, J. (1996). *Cultural Studies and the Study of Popular Culture: Theories and Methods.* Edinburgh: Edinburgh University Press.

Storey, J. (1996). *What is Cultural Studies? : A Reader.* London: Arnold.

Storey, J. (2003). *Inventing Popular Culture: From Folklore to Globalization.* UK: Blackwell Publishing.

O' Malley, L. (1938). *District Gazetteer of Santal Parganas.* pp.108-119.

Prasad, O. (1985). *Santal Music: A Study in Pattern and Process of Cultural Persistence.* New Delhi: Inter-India Publications.

Raha, M. K. (1967). 'Folk Songs of the Tribals of West Bengal- An Analytical Study of Continuity and Change'. In H. Biswas, *Folk Music and Folk-lore, An Anthology* (pp. 57-81). Vol. 1, Calcutta: Folk Music and Folkl-lore Research Institute.

'Santali', S. A. (2009). *Goso Baahaa.* Ranchi: Santali Litearature Publication Pvt.Ltd.

Satyarthi, D. (1951). *Meet My People. Indian Folk Poetry.* Hyderabad: Chetna Prakashan Ltd., pp. 304.

Sinha, S. K. (June 1946). 'Santal Folk Songs'. *Journal of the Bihar and Orissa Research Society*, Patna, 32 (2), pp. 184-88.

'Sonali', M. S. (1995). *Jiyon Jhaarnaa.* Dumka: Santali Sahitya Parishad.

'Sonali', M. S. (2008). *Bir Baajaal Onol Puthi.* Dumka: Santali Sahitya Parishad.

Soren, '. M. (1987). *Tiriya Baadoli.* Dumka: Dharam Printing Press.

Soren, J. J. (2002). *Sogoe Pajher.* Dumka.

Soren, J. J. (n.d.). *Kubi Gaona.*

Soren, N. (1999). *Haarhaam Baabaavaak Gaam Kaahni.* Dumka: Santali Sahitya Prasaarak Sevamandal.

Soren, N. (1999). *Jeevet Karam Seren.* Dumka: Santali Sahitya Prasarak Sewa Mandal.

Soren, N. (n.d.). *Aasadh Binti.* Dumka: Santali Sahitya Prasarak Sewa Mandal.

Soren, N. (n.d.). *Jawae Dhuti Seren.* (Betrothal Songs), Dumka: Alka Printing Works, pp. 17.

Soren, N. (n.d.). *Maran Din Seren.* (Christmas Songs), Dumka: Alka Printing Works, pp. 16.

Soren, N. (n.d.). *Sohrae Porob ar Sohrae Seren.* (The Harvest Feast and Harvest Songs), Dumka: Alka Printing Works, pp. 16.

Soren, V. (2006). *Mitten Kukmu.* Dumka: Minerva Press.

Soren, V. (2010). *Taaraal Baasaal.* Dumka: Minarva Press.

'Thakur', B. M. (2010). *Dong Seren.* Ranchi: Santali Literature Publication Pvt. Ltd.

Troisi, J. (1976). *The Santals: A Classified and annotated Bibliography.* New Delhi: Manohar Book House.

Troisi, J. (1978). *Tribal Religion: Religious Beliefs and Practices among the Santals.* New Delhi: Manohar Publications.

Tuddu, K. (1984). *Santali Padya Sangrah(Saantarhi Gaathni Gaadel).* Ranchi: Santali Sahitya Parisad.

Tuddu, S. C. (2002). *Taaraas.* Jamshedpur: Sangeeta Printers.

Thomas Carmichael and Alison Lee. (2000). *Postmodern Times.* Dekalb: Northern Illinos University Press.

Thompson, E. (1961). 'Review of The Long Revolution'. *New Left Review,9*, 24-33.

Tony Bennett, L. G. (2005). *New Keywords: A Revised Vocabulary of Culture and Society.* UK: Blackwell.

Tribhuwan, Robin D. and Preeti R. Tribhuwan. (1999). *Tribal Dances of India.* New Delhi: Discovery Publishing House.

Troisi, J. (1979). *The Santals: Readings in Santal Life; Volume 1: Religion and Magic.* New Delhi: Indian Social Institute.

Turino, T. (1983). 'The Charango and the Sirena: Music, Magic, and the Power of Love'. *Latin American Music Review*, 4(1),81-119.

Turino, T. (1984). 'The Urban-Mestizo Charango Tradition in Southern Peru: A Statement of Shifting Identity'. *Ethnomusicology*, 28(2), 253-70.

Turner, V. (1982). *From Ritual to Theatre: The Human Seriousness of Play.* New York: Performing Arts Journal Publications.

Vatsyayan, K. (1976). *Traditions of Indian Folk Dance.* New Delhi: Clarion Books.

Wallerstein, I. (2000). Culture as the Ideological Battleground of the Modern Worl-system. In D. V. Brydon, *Postcolonialism: Critical concepts in literary and cultural studies* (pp. 1824-45). New York: Routledge.

Waterman, C. A. (1990). *Juju: A Social History and Ethnography of an African Popular Music.* Chicago,IL: University of Chicago.

Williams, R. (1976). *Keywords: A Vocabulary of Culture and Society.* London: Fontana.

Williams, R. (1979). *Politics and Letters.* London: Verso.

Williams, R. (1981). *Culture.* London: Collins.

Wilson, J. (1858). *India Three Thousand Years Ago.* Bombay: Smith,Taylor and co.

Wuthnow, R. J. (1984). *Cultural Analysis: the work of Peter L.Berger, Mary Douglas, Michel Foucault, and Jurgen Habermas.* London: Routledge & Kegan Paul.

# Index